HARE & HARE, LANDSCAPE ARCHITECTS AND CITY PLANNERS

LALH
Library of American Landscape History

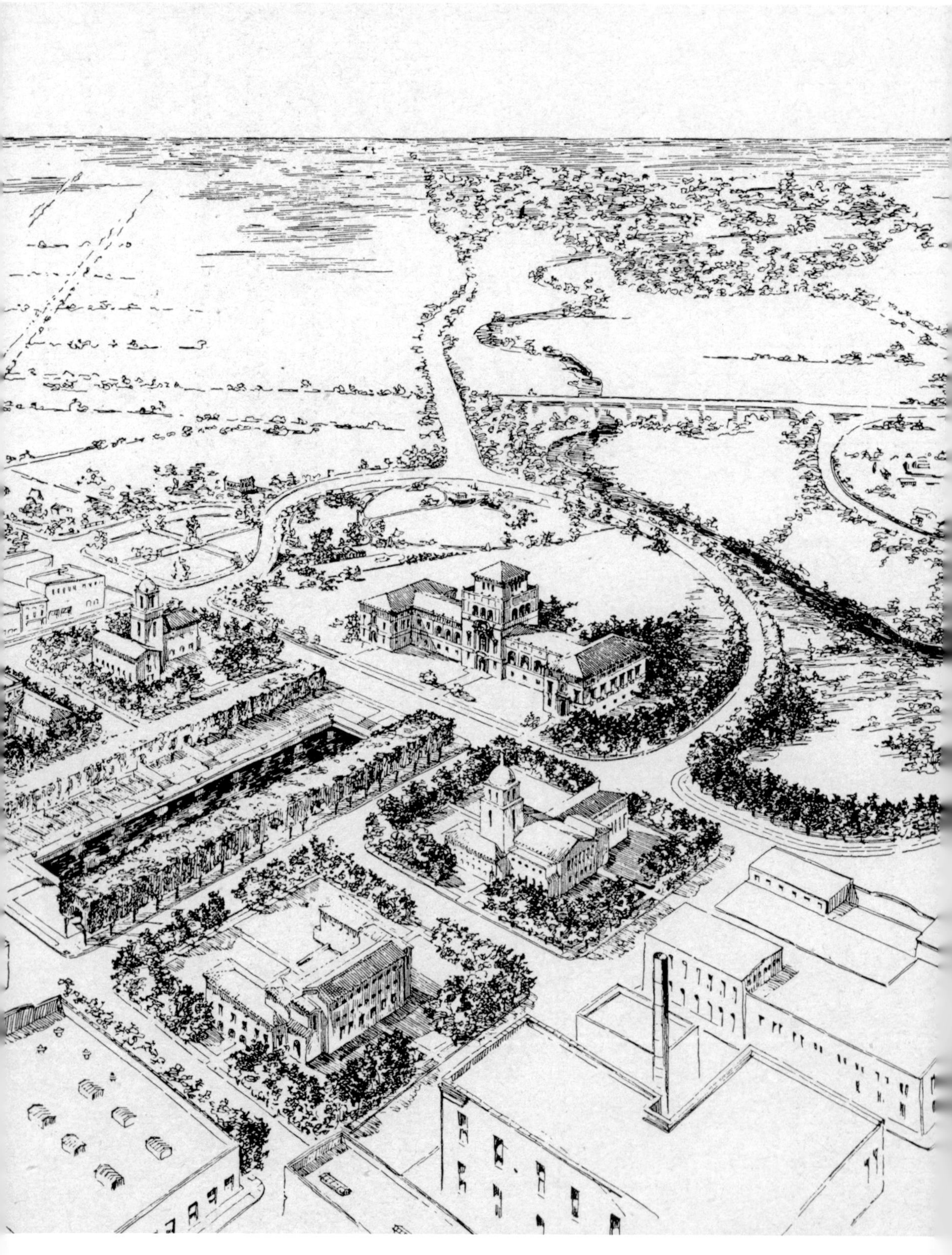

HARE & HARE, LANDSCAPE ARCHITECTS AND CITY PLANNERS

CAROL GROVE AND

CYDNEY MILLSTEIN

LIBRARY OF AMERICAN LANDSCAPE HISTORY

AMHERST, MASSACHUSETTS

THE UNIVERSITY OF GEORGIA PRESS

ATHENS

Published by the University of Georgia Press
Athens, Georgia 30602
www.ugapress.org
in association with
Library of American Landscape History
www.lalh.org

Designed by Jonathan D. Lippincott
Set in New Caledonia
Printed and bound by Thomson-Shore

The paper in this book meets the guidelines for permanence and durability of the Committee on Production Guidelines for Book Longevity of the Council on Library Resources.

Printed in the United States of America
19 20 21 22 23 C 5 4 3 2 1

Library of Congress Control Number: 2018961619
ISBN: 9780820354811 (hardcover : alk. paper)

Frontispiece: Hare & Hare's proposed Houston Civic Center (detail), 1929.
State Historical Society of Missouri Research Center–Kansas City.

Contents

Preface

Sidney J. Hare (1860–1938) was fifty years old when he invited his son, S. Herbert (1888–1960), to join him as a partner in his Kansas City landscape design practice. At the time, Sid had completed more than seventy projects—residential subdivisions, institutional grounds, parks, and cemeteries, his specialty. Two years earlier Herbert had begun the new master's degree program at Harvard, where his studies were introducing him to the international history of landscape design and the new profession of city planning. Over the ensuing five decades, the firm of Hare & Hare flourished, a consequence of the talents of father and son, their business acumen, and the complementary nature of their skills and temperaments.

A socially retiring lover of nature, Sid achieved considerable mastery in civil engineering and horticulture, areas of expertise that served him well as the practice moved from a nineteenth-century nature-based approach to large, programmatically complex projects. Affable, well-traveled Herbert, who was also an accomplished draftsman, maintained his lifelong interest in art and the history of landscape design even as the firm took on the planning commissions that Herbert referred to as more "scientific" in nature.

Their collaboration resulted in an innovative and beautifully detailed body of work. By the time of Herbert's death in 1960, Hare & Hare listed more than four thousand projects in over thirty states, Canada, and Costa Rica. The scope, quality, and geographic range of these commissions stagger the imagination, especially in comparison with other firms of the era. Despite the relatively small size of Hare & Hare, which never had more than thirteen employees, Sid and Herbert outpaced both Olmsted Brothers and the peripatetic Warren H. Manning.

For their study of this remarkable design partnership, authors Carol Grove and Cydney Millstein selected several of the most important of the Hares' commissions and weave discussions of them into a compelling father-son biography. Their story begins with the eleven-day steamboat journey Sid Hare's parents took from Louisville, Kentucky, just after the Civil War ended, to Kansas City, then a rocky, rough-hewn town literally blasted out of the bluffs. It ends with Herbert's death in 1960 and his burial at Forest Hill Cemetery. Hare & Hare's practice of hiring and training younger practitioners in a "stair-step of ages approach" ensured the continuance of the firm, even up to the present day.

The Hares left a considerable imprint on the American landscape. Their work can be seen at Point Defiance Park in Tacoma, Washington, for example, where their 1911 plan protected wildness while accommodating active sports and a zoo. The Olmstedian lessons Herbert learned at Harvard provided the firm with a flexible design approach that would guide similar parks and park systems in the Pacific Northwest and throughout the Midwest and Texas, where their work can still be seen in Dallas and especially Forth Worth and Houston.

Hare & Hare was a leading force in the envisioning of Missouri's state parks, an initiative that began in 1933 with the creation of 55,000-acre Lake of the Ozarks. They teamed up with the planner Harland Bartholomew for this effort and with him wrote a series of influential reports that eventually led to the protection of several free-flowing streams, the first such river initiative in the country. The authors also cover the creation of North Oaks Farms, a model village outside St. Paul, Minnesota, where the firm was involved for more than two decades, and Hodges Gardens, a 1950s reclamation project in central Louisiana that resulted in a garden structured by curves reflective of the modernist era into which the firm had gracefully entered.

We are pleased to publish this important book, which covers so much formerly uncharted territory in the history of American landscape design. I am grateful to Carol Grove for bringing the project to LALH as a follow-up to her influential book on Henry Shaw (LALH, 2005). I thank both authors for their diligent work on the manuscript and the team of editors who collaborated with them at various stages: Joel Ray, Sarah Allaback, Carol Betsch, and Mary Bellino, who also created the index.

The book's elegant design is the work of LALH design manager and assistant director Jonathan D. Lippincott.

Generous funding for *Hare & Hare* was provided by the William T. Kemper Foundation; Ann Douglass and Clayton Wilhite, Ann Arbor Area Community Foundation; Hubbard Educational Foundation; and the Foundation for Landscape Studies.

Robin Karson
Executive Director
LALH

Acknowledgments

The beginnings of this project go back thirty years to when Ralph Ochsner, then principal of the Kansas City landscape architecture firm Ochsner, Hare & Hare invited Cydney Millstein to look over the Hare & Hare files that were stored in his basement and his office. Access to these documents and drawings resulted in a series of articles on Hare & Hare and numerous National Register of Historic Places nominations. Other early writings included Bettina Van Dyke's 1972 master's thesis for Kansas State University, "The Evolution of Nineteenth- and Twentieth-Century Landscape Types as Exemplified by Hare & Hare's Cemetery Designs," and articles by Ralph Ochsner (1997) and William S. Worley (2001) in *Kawsmouth: A Journal of Regional History* and *Kansas History*, respectively. Despite these publications, knowledge of the firm did not extend very far beyond the Midwest. Realizing that the firm and its work deserved to be known by a wider audience and acknowledged in the canon of American landscape history, we committed ourselves to making Hare & Hare our next joint effort.

In 1987 and 1994, Ralph Ochsner donated his Hare & Hare collection to the State Historical Society of Missouri–Kansas City (SHSMO-KC)—more than 650 linear feet of documents and drawings. It took us considerable time over many visits to assess the archive, questioning, reconsidering, and confirming our observations. In the beginning, this involved a lot of piecing together of evidence to form a clear picture, and more than once we recalled the remark made by David Boutros, former director of what was then the Western Historical Manuscript Collection, that "sometimes evidence is what is unsaid." We have researched Hare & Hare for more than a decade now, sifting both the said and the unsaid, and we feel confident that the history that follows does justice to Sid and Herbert Hare and the firm they established.

The Hare & Hare Company Records Collection at the SHSMO-KC forms the basis of our research. Aside from job folders that contain correspondence, notes on planning, and financial records, the collection includes one thousand rolls of plans and drawings. The collection also has pages from what had been the "company scrapbook," which contained images of representative commissions and office personnel employed over four decades. In addition, there are hundreds of black-and-white photographs, most of which were taken by Herbert Hare. Many of these record his travels in Europe in summer 1924 and served as references for his work. He photographed sweeping landscapes and details. At Italy's Villa Lante, for example, he documented staircases, urns, and balustrades. That one can, nearly ninety-five years later, stand in precisely the same spot and see as Herbert did is nothing less than inspirational.

We are grateful for the assistance we received from the staff at the SHSMO in Kansas City and Columbia. Early guidance came from David L. Boutros, director when the collection was donated, and from Nancy Piepenbring, former manuscript specialist, who knew its contents better than anyone. More recently we were aided by Lucinda Adams, associate director, and Kansas City staff, in particular Rachel Forester, Mimi Loren, and Michael Sweeney. The Columbia staff always worked as a team and never grumbled when they were asked to deliver countless boxes of drawings and files to the research center's reading room at our request. Special thanks are due to Peter McCarthy, Laura Jolley, and Anne Cox and to Kim Harper for her enthusiasm for the project. Joan Stack, curator, and Grieg Thompson, manager of art collections, contributed to *The Landscape Architecture of Hare & Hare*, an exhibition held in Columbia in summer–fall 2016; in September 2017, we were invited to present "From Garden Design to Master Planning" as a part of the Kimball Lecture Series at SHSMO's Center for Missouri Studies at Kansas City. We are grateful to Gary Kremer, director of SHSMO, for his support on both projects and of our research in general.

Another important institution with holdings on Hare & Hare is the Kansas City Public Library and its Missouri Valley Special Collections. Our thanks go to Eli Paul, Jeremy Drouin, Michael Wells, Joanna Marsh,

Kara Evans, Kate Hill, David Cox, and staff there. We are grateful as well to the reference and interlibrary loan staff of the University of Missouri's Ellis Library in Columbia and the gracious InterLibrary Services at Michigan State University, which was happy to loan the most obscure publications for our use.

The number of archivists and curators from numerous institutions who contributed to our research reflects the scope of Hare & Hare's work. Primary among these are Caitlin Eckard of the Jackson County (Missouri) Historical Society; Thomas E. Young, librarian and archivist at the Philbrook Art Museum; Kim Kelly, former site manager of Hodges Gardens State Park; and Samantha Bruer, architectural archivist at the Houston Metropolitan Research Center of the Houston Public Library. We also appreciate the help of Michael R. Davis at the Mary Baker Eddy Library and Melissa McGinnis of Metro Parks, Tacoma. In addition, individuals who fielded questions about Hare & Hare include Booker Rucker, former director of the Cultural and Natural Resource Management Program, Missouri Department of Natural Resources; Mike Robertson, city manager of North Oaks, Minnesota; Andrew Engel, Hagley Library; Lynn McBee, Bellaire Historical Society; Mark Jarvis, City of Billings, Montana; and Dennis Northcott, Missouri Historical Society Library and Research Center, St. Louis.

Observations from readers of early drafts helped shape and refine the text. We thank Joel Ray, Susan Klaus, and Judith Tankard for their input and Texans Stephen Fox and Susan Allen Kline for their comments. Early meetings with Ralph Ochsner and Kim Sorensen of Ochsner, Hare & Hare helped us guide our thinking, as did insight from Kansas City historian William S. Worley and his research on J. C. Nichols and the Country Club Plaza. Silvia Mooney, current resident of Sidney J. Hare's home, Harecliff, who shared "the box" of photos and clippings that came with house when she purchased it; Patsy Teas of Bellaire, Texas; and Mari Harpur of North Oaks, Minnesota, all provided their insight and firsthand knowledge of those places.

Most of the images in the book come from the Hare & Hare Company Records at SHSMO-KC, but many others were contributed by institutions across the country. For these we are grateful to Sarah Biggerstaff, Nelson-Atkins Museum of Art, Kansas City; Denise Morrison, Kansas City Museum; Ann McFerrin, Kansas City Parks and Recreation; and the staff at Forest Hill Cemetery, Kansas City. Assistance also came from Kim Dillion, cultural resource management section chief, and staff at Missouri State Parks; reference staff at the Columbiana County Archives in Lisbon,

Ohio; Leslie Simpson, Post Memorial Reference Library in Joplin; Michele Hansford, Powers Museum, Carthage, Missouri; Chris Skaugset and staff, Longview (Washington) Public Library; Debbie Smith and intern Derek Linn, National Center for Preservation Technology and Training, Natchitoches, Louisiana; Charlene Bonnette, State Library of Louisiana; Cathy Spitzenberger, University of Texas–Arlington; Gerald Moorhead, AIA, of Houston; Rebecca Russell, Woodson Research Center, Rice University; Jennifer Sessa and Tim Ronk, Houston Metropolitan Research Center; Nancy Klein, Philmont Scott Ranch, Cimarron, New Mexico; Melissa McGinnis and Claire Keller-Scholz, Metro Parks, Tacoma, Washington; Robyne Platzer and Kim Pogue, North Oaks, Minnesota. Our thanks also go to Richard Welnowski for contemporary photographs of Hare & Hare neighborhoods in Missouri and Kansas.

We are indebted to Jonathan Kemper and Samuel Bennett at the William T. Kemper Foundation for their support. Jonathan has long been an admirer, and promoter, of Hare & Hare, and his backing was fundamental. We are also grateful to Elizabeth Barlow Rogers and the Foundation for Landscape Studies for awarding the project their David R. Coffin Publication Grant, and to Richard Longstreth for his letter of support.

Our deep thanks go to Robin Karson, executive director, Sarah Allaback, senior manuscript editor, and Carol Betsch, managing editor, at LALH, for their belief in the importance of this publication. We appreciate their patience, support, and enthusiasm over the years. Scholarship, and writing, take time, and more than once we were encouraged to feel that contributing the best book possible to the history of American landscape design trumps the meeting of deadlines. Jonathan Lippincott's superb design for the book showcases the rich visual imagery associated with the firm and its history, and we believe that Sid and Herbert Hare would approve.

As we researched Hare & Hare, we discovered that many of our favorite landscapes and spaces were designed by the firm. In hindsight, we should not have been surprised. Each place retained the characteristics that define Hare & Hare's work, and these were what instinctively drew us to it. We suspect that there are numerous projects across the country yet to be attributed to Hare & Hare. This book serves as an introduction. We hope that it provides the groundwork for a "rediscovery" of the firm that results in a renewed appreciation its work. Landscape stewardship is dependent on these first steps.

Finally, we are indebted to our friends and families for putting up with this project for so long. Children came to the point of rolling their eyes when they heard, yet again, "That's a Hare & Hare landscape!" and what became a running family joke—"What are you doing upstairs, Mom, still writing?"—will no longer be heard.

In closing, we dedicate this book to the memory of Sid J. and S. Herbert Hare for their contribution to American landscapes and places and to future research that will add to their legacy.

HARE & HARE, LANDSCAPE ARCHITECTS AND CITY PLANNERS

Introduction

While traveling on Cunard's RMS *Antonia*, amid "smooth sea and fair weather," Herbert Hare drafted a short letter to his Kansas City, Missouri, office, with comments about projects that were under way.[1] From April until mid-August of that year, 1924, he would be traveling in Europe gathering ideas, attending the International Town Planning Conference in Amsterdam, and purchasing works of art for the boulevards and the many neighborhoods of Kansas City's Country Club District planned by his firm. In his absence the office proceeded on projects as comprehensive as the new industrial town of Longview, Washington, planned in its entirety, and as specific as the setting for the Seventh National Flower Show where, in their forty-five vellum drawings, they envisioned an orchestra platform set among drifts of orchids and roses. Simultaneously his father, Sidney J. Hare, cofounder and partner in the firm, was at work on cemeteries in Virginia, Texas, and Tennessee. Within days of his return, Herbert headed to Houston, where he was serving as the consultant to its park and city planning commissions. This trip was to kick off a new phase of planning the suburban River Oaks neighborhoods for the philanthropist and businessman Will Hogg and his associate Hugh Potter. The range and number of that summer's projects, and the pace with which they were executed, is representative of the firm. By the following year, Hare & Hare had projects in twenty-eight states—from Massachusetts to Washington and from Wisconsin to Louisiana—and had completed its first international commission, in Costa Rica.

The history of Hare & Hare began in the summer of 1910 when the father-and-son team of Sidney J. (1860–1938) and S. Herbert (1888–1960) established the landscape architecture firm that carried their name for nearly seven decades. That summer they moved into offices in the downtown Gumbel Building, promoting their services and qualifications which Herbert described as "a combination of long experience and the best eastern technical training."[2] Sidney was skilled at civil engineering and well read in horticulture. A considerable knowledge of the sciences of geology and paleontology broadened his view. His background included nearly twenty years as a landscape gardener and over seventy commissions: residential subdivisions, institutional grounds, and parks, the last of which lent itself to the planning of cemeteries. One of the early proponents of the "modern cemetery" movement, Sidney worked across the country, from Monongahela, Pennsylvania, to Mitchell, South Dakota. An active member of the American Association of Cemetery Superintendents, he would become a Senior Fellow in the American Institute of Park Executives and was a charter member of the American Park and Outdoor Art Association (which later became the American Civic Association) devoted to the improvement of cities and public spaces.

Twenty-two-year-old Herbert brought a different set of skills to the firm. Where his father was grounded in the nineteenth century, the younger Hare would come to exemplify the twentieth. Trained for the bud-

Sidney J. Hare, 1912. JCHS.

S. Herbert Hare at nineteen, 1908. JCHS.

ding profession of landscape architecture and among the first students to study city planning at Harvard, he was also an adept draftsman with an interest in the art and history of landscape. To his college assignments—whether a planting plan for a rose garden, the grounds of a women's seminary, or a system of recreation areas—he devoted equal attention to detail. City planning projects considered the vernacular and monumental, useful space and adornment. Although he would admit design to be his real passion, his work would prove to be a balance of the artistic and the practical, going beyond the garden and the park, ultimately addressing comprehensive planning and issues such as bayou preservation, flood control, and land use. This formal training would serve as a foil to his father's varied background, and their partnership would contribute to the development of the profession in America.

For most of the nineteenth century, self-taught amateurs and professionals from varied fields contributed to the subject most often referred to as "landscape gardening." Engaged individuals, Sidney Hare among them, debated topics such as improved methods of fertilization, plant nomenclature, and the "fine art" of gardening, which would lead to the refinement of taste and, by extension, the landscape. They broadened their knowledge by reading A. J. Downing and articles in *Garden and Forest,* the journal dedicated to "horticulture, landscape art and forestry." It was not until the formation of the American Society of Landscape Architects (ASLA) in 1899 and Harvard and MIT's offering courses geared toward future practitioners the next year that landscape architecture began to coalesce as a profession. James Sturgis Pray, one of Herbert Hare's mentors at Harvard, described its beginnings as "so small, so scattered, and so little organized," but the discipline would attain a clear vision of its role and ideals over the following two decades.[3] By the early 1920s the landscape gardener began to be replaced by the licensed practitioner trained in the principles of comprehensive planning. This "before" and "after" are typically viewed as two distinct chapters in landscape history, yet both are evident in Hare & Hare's body of work.

The development of the "modern cemetery," the focus of Sidney's earliest commissions and an important facet of the firm's history, was a component of the evolving profession. A reform movement that embraced new technology and horticultural methods, the modern cemetery movement brought higher standards and professionalism to cemetery practice. Visually, it was a "cleaning up" of the picturesque aesthetic found in earlier rural cemeteries. Monumental gates, expanses of green lawn, and curving tree-lined avenues, like those in Sidney's plan for Monongahela

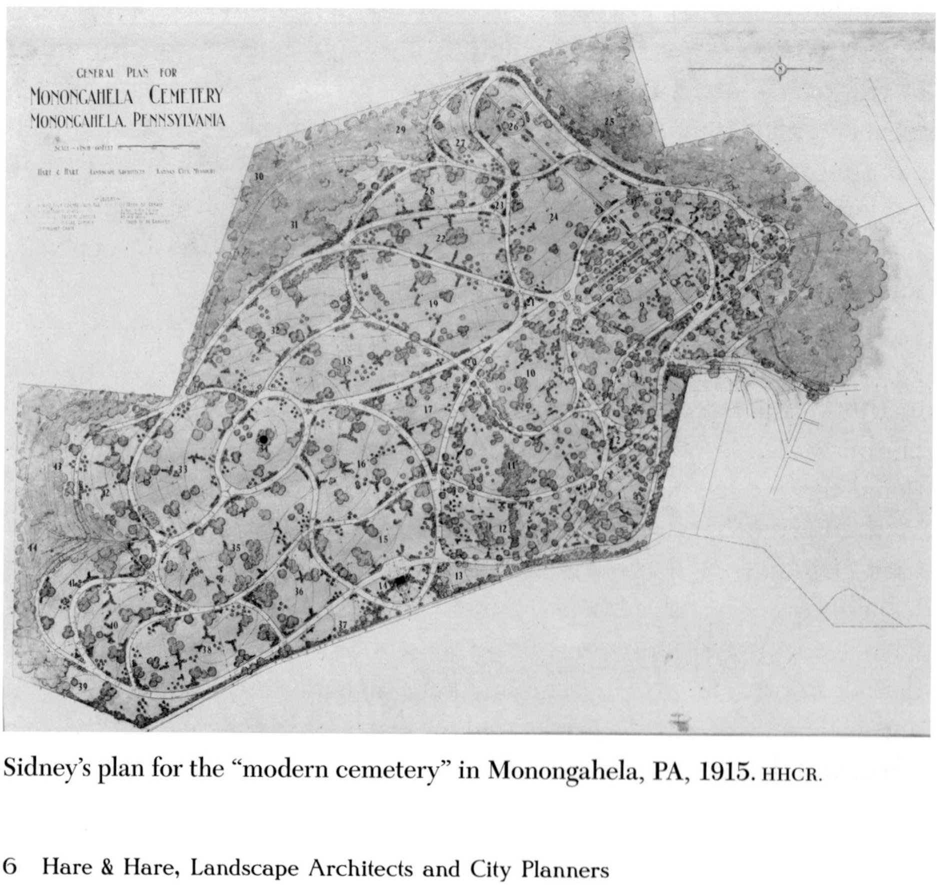

Sidney's plan for the "modern cemetery" in Monongahela, PA, 1915. HHCR.

Forest Hill Cemetery, Kansas City, MO, postcard, 1908. MVSC.

Cemetery, were the essence of the plan. Limiting the number of monuments cluttering the view, which created a parklike space rather than a "marble yard," was another priority. Sidney's proving ground would be Kansas City's Forest Hill Cemetery, where he began as superintendent in 1896. There he cultivated and curated a collection of trees and shrubs meant to delight and to educate people in an art he considered equal to painting or sculpture. But his commitment to the methodology of the modern cemetery demanded he also take on practical matters such as site grading and drainage and dealing with lot owners and the havoc inflicted by moles.

The emergence of urban planning as a profession also played a major role in the firm's success. This special field of study was codified by institutions of higher learning beginning in 1909, first at Harvard, when Herbert was enrolled, and then at MIT. That same year the first national conference devoted to the subject convened in Washington, D.C. Herbert would be in attendance eight years later when the American City Planning Institute was established at an organizational meeting in Kansas City. The foundation of the urban planning profession lay in the City Beautiful movement's vision of order and the Progressive Era's mandate of reform, but it would be honed into a discipline by the new social and economic needs posed by urbanization. Growth, public policy, and affordable housing were among the concerns to be addressed. One of

Herbert's drawing for the pavilion and garden at Point Defiance Park streetcar station, Tacoma, 1912. SHSMO-KC.

Herbert's strengths was such planning. The firm would be involved at the regional and state level and be commissioned, in numerous instances, to plan every component of a city from its streetcar stations to its civic center.

Sidney Hare believed the firm's work should speak for itself, and the quality of Hare & Hare's commissions do just that. Less patent are the two principal individuals behind those projects, although a sense of who they are can be drawn from company records and correspondence. We know both were fair, honest, and derived pleasure from hard work and diligence. Modest by nature, they shunned self-promotion and were more concerned with the quality of their work than the dollar figure attached to it. Each was progressive in his thinking and had a healthy skepticism of politicians—likely prompted by the tight hold that political boss Tom Pendergast had on Kansas City governmental workings in the 1930s. Both married for life. Deeply faithful, they were members of Kansas City's Sixth Church of Christ, Scientist and its mother church in Boston. Both likely abstained from drink, or "firewater" as Sidney called it, which he likened to "pouring in discord."[4]

Father and son may have shared mutual traits, but their personalities and physical characteristics were strikingly different. Slight of frame, and just over average height, Sidney had a head of curls that he cropped closer as he grew older and a full beard and mustache that he wore his entire life.

Even at the drafting board he dressed in suit-and-tie (which for decades was anchored by a favorite pin). Of the two he was the more high-spirited and admitted to being the extreme opposite of quiet. Straightforward, he was given to saying exactly what he thought, as when he admonished one client's suggestion as an example of ignorance and bad taste. Sid was bold enough to bill Mary Baker Eddy, the founder of Christian Science, for work at her Chestnut Hill, Massachusetts, estate. He could be described as a polymath. The geologist Richard J. Gentile has aptly noted his "diverse and unorthodox interests"—some of which could be considered eccentric.[5] Among these were his ongoing study of Giza's Great Pyramid (with the hope of locating the Ark of the Covenant in an inner chamber) and effort to compile and distribute evidence proving that the Icelandic explorer Leif Ericson had discovered North America. Visitors to his garden might find their conversations quickly "veer from things created to [the] Creator."[6]

Herbert was physically much larger than his father, with fair skin, heavy brows, and deep-set eyes. An image of him at nineteen, dressed in bow tie and jacket, reading "Man's Domination over Evil"—the text of a lecture presented by Edward A. Kimball at Harvard's Emerson Hall—suggests a seriousness that would lighten with age. Through experience and travel Herbert gained a greater sense of ease and polish: after his first trip to Europe there was an almost nonchalant and cosmopolitan air to his demeanor. The *Houston Gargoyle* magazine described him, at the age of forty, as looking somewhat like the family lawyer, "a little gray, with a close-cropped moustache and kind eyes, soft-spoken, hard-headed."[7] His close friends, who knew him as "Herb," characterized him as sincere and principled with "dogged perseverance in attaining his highest goals."[8] The sense of gravity he projected in his professional role belied his sense of humor and friendly personality. Somewhat of a contradiction, he was conservative in his personal life yet receptive to new ideas when it came to his work. Committed to a faith that eschewed the "embellishments of the person," he was a lover of the theater and a collector of American art who invested in corporate stocks.

Different, too, were the worlds that father and son lived in. Young Sid traveled by steamboat more than a week to get from his hometown of Louisville to Kansas City. With air travel Herbert could leave London one day and arrive home in Missouri the next. While Sid and his wife Mathilda traveled across the country, there is no evidence that they ever left it. Herbert and Aurel, on the other hand, traveled often and far: there were extended trips to Europe and a six-week tour where they lingered in Norway, Denmark, and Sweden. Summers were spent in Alaska, on Canada's Gaspé

Peninsula, and in the White Mountains of New Hampshire. Christmas trips were to the Bahamas and Hawaii, this last an example of mixing work and pleasure. During their two months in Hawaii, Herbert lectured on landscape architecture at the university while Aurel joined the Honolulu Print Makers club and began collecting art depicting Hawaiian landscapes and traditions.[9] In Havana, Cuba, on a month-long trip, Herbert presented on parks and public gardens at a conference of the Inter-American Institute of Municipal and Institutional History. The comfort of ocean liners was trumped, in Herbert's words, by the speed, and ease, of air travel.

Earlier in life both couples had lived in comfortable frame houses on the wooded residential blocks of Campbell Street, northeast of the Hyde Park neighborhood in Kansas City. But when time and workload permitted, Sid and his wife moved out past the city to the acreage they named "Harecliff," where they constructed a rustic house from rough-hewn logs, recycled bridge timbers brought from Colorado, and stone culled from the site. In the best sense of the word Sid and Mathilda could be described as "homespun." They spent decades coaxing native plants to volunteer—to create "happy accidents"—among the rocks. With the zeal of a missionary, Sid would expound on the value of grasses and forbs. Many of those who visited Harecliff (nearly nine thousand per Sid's calculations) were presented with a little souvenir booklet the couple had crafted. At night he trained his

Herbert and Aurel Hare in Pisa, Italy, 1924. SHSMO-KC.

Sidney Hare in his garden at Harecliff, c. 1927. SHSMO-KC.

telescope on the stars. He listened to birds in concert or watched the dawn break at the spot the couple had nicknamed "Wander Wonder Way." He summed up his life in nine words: "I am satisfied. I am happy. I am rich."[10]

The stark contrast between Herbert and Aurel's life and Sid and Mathilda's is evident in the places they called home and how they lived. Unlike his father, Herbert would never cultivate his own garden. The couple lived in a series of new apartment buildings, including the James Russell Lowell Apartment Hotel located at 722 Ward Parkway, designed by Nelle E. Peters, one of the country's few women architects. They then moved to the Sophian Plaza, an elegant high-rise adjacent to the Country Club Plaza, residing in an apartment on the top floor that provided the perfect backdrop for their art collection. Catholic in its range, it included the black-on-black pottery of Pueblo Indian artist Maria Montoya Martinez, a Paris street scene by the early modernist Stuart Davis, and an Aaron Douglas tempera study for "Aspects of Negro Life: An Idyll of the Deep South."[11] Directly across the street from the apartment building, the Nelson-Atkins Museum of Art stood on fifteen acres that, thirty years before, had been the site of Oak Hall, the mansion of *Kansas City Star* publisher and park proponent William Rockhill Nelson. The proportion and restraint of the sloping south lawn, designed to let the monumental architecture dominate, was the work of Hare & Hare.[12]

The first years after the establishment of Hare & Hare, father and son worked side by side as they had when Herbert was a "cub" draftsman during high school. One example of their joint efforts can be found in Tacoma's Point Defiance Park project. Sidney visited the site, photographed it, and made measured drawings. He then returned to confer with Herbert in devising the plan. For the preliminary report the younger Hare executed presentation drawings to accompany Sid's stereoscopic views. At the center of the report's cover is a tiny watercolor painting overlaid with vellum, depicting Puget Sound and statuesque pines, executed by Herbert. A 1913 park and boulevard system for the zinc- and lead-mining town of Joplin, Missouri, is another example of their collaboration on a major project. The proposed additions provided its 32,000-plus citizens a total of 443 acres of parkland and sixteen miles of boulevards. Included in these was McClelland Park, located in a rugged valley of Shoal Creek and meant to rival urban spaces such as Chicago's Jackson Park, and land around the perimeter set aside to protect the "open beauties of nature at her best."[13] Among the stereoviews in their report to the city officials were images of

Stereoviews of McClelland Park, Joplin: a picturesque outcropping and Herbert with plans in hand, 1912. SHSMO-KC.

Herbert seated on a rocky outcrop at the yawning opening of a cave, in topcoat and fedora, plans in hand.

Within three years there was less collaboration and a defining of roles. Equal in rank from the outset—only two instances have been found where Sid refers to his son as a "junior partner"—the Hares began to specialize in commissions that suited their strengths. Sid's focus remained primarily on cemeteries and parks, while Herbert attended to larger planning projects. The earliest of these were the neighborhoods of Kansas City's Country Club District, where, from the beginning, it was he, not his father, who worked alongside the developer J. C. Nichols. Although the firm's name implies two members working in unison, this would be the case for less than fifteen years. Sid remained actively involved until the mid-1920s, when he began to step back from full participation. Herbert's tenure would last for five decades, during which he would steer the firm through the Depression and a second world war.

Records from the earliest years indicate only "members of the firm," and the initials of two draftsmen—"AAL" and "FAO"—assisting in the office. A number of employees remain similarly anonymous, while others come to life through documents, drawings, and photographs compiled in a company scrapbook.[14] Ralph Reinhardt and Donald Bush, hired in 1916 and 1917, respectively, would play vital roles. Both were Kansas Citians, about a decade younger than Herbert, with complementary skills. Reinhardt was trained as an engineer, had worked with the U.S. Housing Corporation in Washington during World War I, and would become a member of the American Institute of Planners. His specialty was subdivisions and

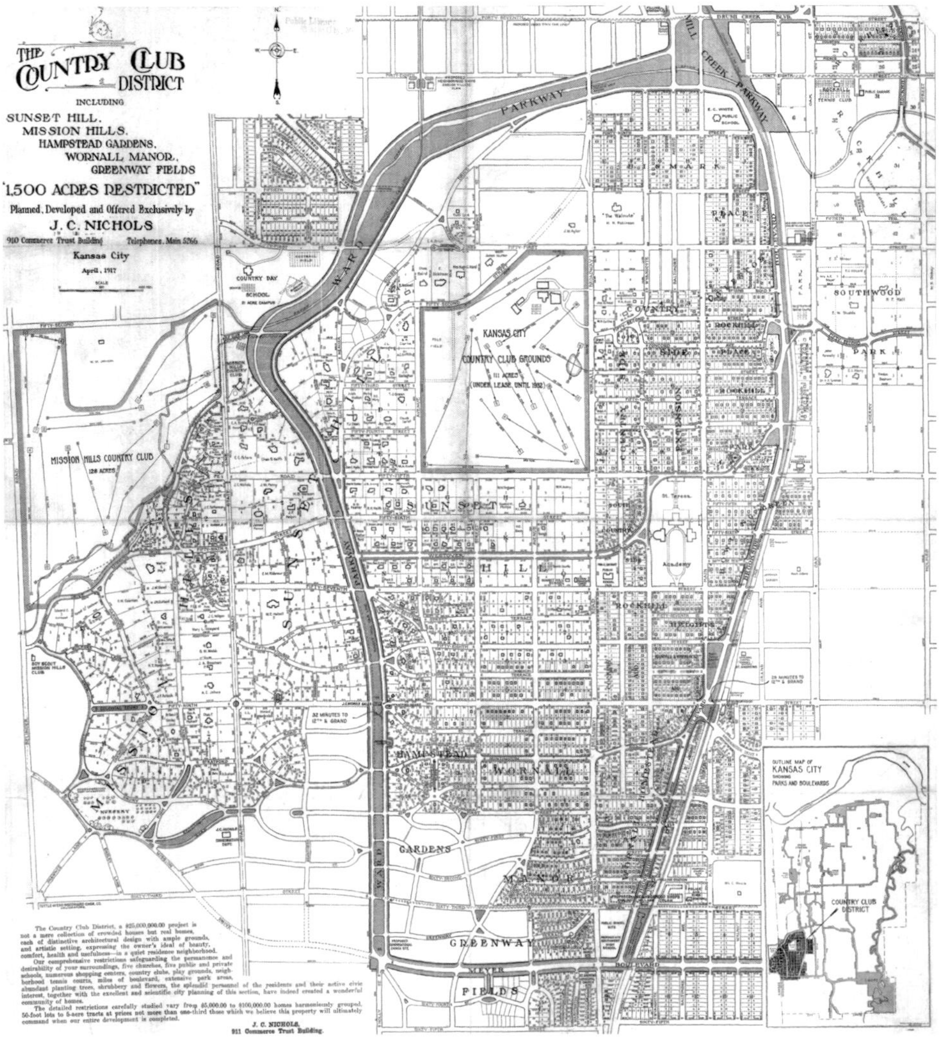

Map of the Country Club District, 1917. MVSC.

county planning and zoning, and though his initials appear throughout company files, his input is much harder to pinpoint than that of his associate Donald Bush. An able designer of parks and estates, with a degree in landscape architecture from the University of Illinois, Bush was affiliated with the American Institute of Park Executives and the ASLA, of which he became a fellow. In 1930, Reinhardt and Bush became principals of the firm, and Herbert would increasingly rely on them when he was away from the drafting table, traveling from project to project, as his role shifted to that of a liaison and the public face of the firm. The two remained with Hare & Hare for their entire careers, until Reinhardt's death in 1950 and Bush's retirement in 1970.

Draftsmen at work in the Hare & Hare office, c. 1930. SHSMO-KC.

The company photograph of Huldah Simms, c. 1930. SHSMO-KC.

Staff would be lost to both war efforts and, in one instance, to the "oil play" in Tulsa after drilling began there. By the 1920s there were typically three to five draftsmen on staff, numbers which remained constant through the 1950s. Valuable contributions were made by the intelligent and witty Eda Sutermeister, who had been employed by the landscape architect George Kessler prior to his death in 1923. Sutermeister was an excellent draftsman, capable of overseeing projects, of joking with park commissioners and coworkers, and of making decisions in Herbert's absence. And she would earn a wage equal to Donald Bush's. The only other woman employed (aside from Herbert's sister Nell, who acted as secretary in the early years) was Huldah Simms, of whom we know nothing except that Herbert credited her with running the office like clockwork for thirty years.[15]

The firm was built up slowly with hiring done incrementally, every decade, with few exceptions. Two of the next generation of professionals to join Hare & Hare had been groomed working for the National Park Service. The first of these, D. D. Obert, was involved in the early planning stages of Guadalupe Mountains National Park in Texas and arrived in Kansas City in 1930. Born in Washington state, he was a superb draftsman who executed numerous presentation drawings for Texas commissions and served as the firm's resident landscape architect during planning for the Texas Centennial in Dallas. After completion of this project in 1936, he became Fort Worth's city forester, a post he occupied during the decades Hare & Hare was involved with the city's planning and park development.

The next staff member, hired in 1935, was Ralph Ellifrit, who had worked with the Civilian Conservation Corps at Great Smokey Mountains National Park and Fort Pulaski on Tybee Island, Georgia, then returned to his hometown of Kansas City.[16] He, too, worked on Texas commissions—Houston's Civic Center, Hermann Park, and the University of Houston—before moving to oversee the firm's office there in 1939. The following year, Ellifrit was hired by Houston's mayor to head the city's planning department, a move Herbert approved of as it assured that the city would be in "good hands." For twenty-three years Ellifrit provided continuity and helped to guide growth, no easy feat amid an outspoken anti-planning constituency in a city that he would later characterize as "one of the last strongholds of rugged individualism."[17]

Herbert had always intended that the firm would stay small, so he could remain involved with the details, and it grew no larger than a staff of thirteen in 1943.[18] Eldridge Lovelace, a mentee of Herbert's who went on to work with the St. Louis firm of Harland Bartholomew, noted the deliberate hiring of apprentices and professionals at intervals of five or ten years in order to assure the firm's future. These would include H.

Ralph Reinhardt, Donald Bush, and Gordon Whiffen at the drafting table, c. 1950. SHSMO-KC.

Gordon Whiffen, a New Jersey native and one of the few members from outside the Midwest, hired in 1930 and Chalmer Cooper, who became part of the firm in 1940. Robert Lee Bell, Richard H. Kellenberg, and E. John Warren would join later (in 1948, 1951, and 1959, respectively). These last five individuals, led by Donald Bush, carried Hare & Hare forward after Herbert's death in 1960.[19]

Cultivating and maintaining relationships with clients was also one of the firm's strengths and a key to its success. At Greenwood Cemetery in

Aerial view of Philbrook Museum gardens, n.d. Beryl Ford Photograph Collection, Tulsa Historical Society.

Knoxville, Tennessee, for example, planning began in 1905, and Sid advised the directors and superintendents over decades. After his retirement the firm continued this practice, improving and enlarging cemeteries he had planned. Donald Bush's client relationships included Richard W. Norton Jr., for whom he spent nearly eight years designing the grounds of his Louisiana country house, adding pools, rills, and a lake accented by massive boulders hauled from west Texas. He worked with Louis W. Hill Jr. on the development of the "model village" of North Oaks outside St. Paul for more than two decades. Herbert was known for revisiting sites to enlarge gardens or add new plantings for residential clients and would move lilacs and live oaks to suit their requests, always keeping in mind the owners' personalities and changing interests. One grand example of meeting his clients' needs was the 1939 conversion of Villa Philbrook, and its "rare gardens," from the private residence of Waite and Genevieve Phillips into the first public art museum in Tulsa.

Often the professional relationships established by Hare & Hare grew into friendships. The Mount Hope Cemetery Association (near Joplin, Missouri) addressed Sid as "*Dear Friend*" in its letters, and his response was the same, also underlined. The salutations Sid used when writing suggest an informality not found in strict business dealings. The same ease is evident in Herbert's letters when he teased Texans about the weather ("Hotter than ——!") and in those written by Eda, who got away with subtle chiding about politics. Handwritten notes over the years suggest a genuine gratitude felt by all parties. There were tokens of appreciation exchanged—simple gifts, nothing expensive meant to persuade or influence. Pecans and colored pencils sent to Herbert by a park superintendent, cross-shaped crystals known as staurolites from Sid's collection donated to a city museum, and Eda's receipt of a Mexican cookbook are but three examples.

The commissions undertaken by the firm ranged from projects as singular as a water lily pool for a residential garden to those as comprehensive as the master plan for a city. Examples in Fort Worth bear this out. The firm planned park details, such as Lake Worth's picnic areas and shelters, but also prepared two park system master plans, in 1930 and 1957, to accommodate the city's tremendous growth. The firm addressed flood protection along a northwest tributary of the Trinity River, Marine Creek, but was also instrumental in planning the levee system for the whole of Tarrant County. Commissions included golf courses and country clubs but also a YMCA and a development program that improved fifty-four of the city's public school grounds. Greatest in scope was Hare & Hare's proposal for a

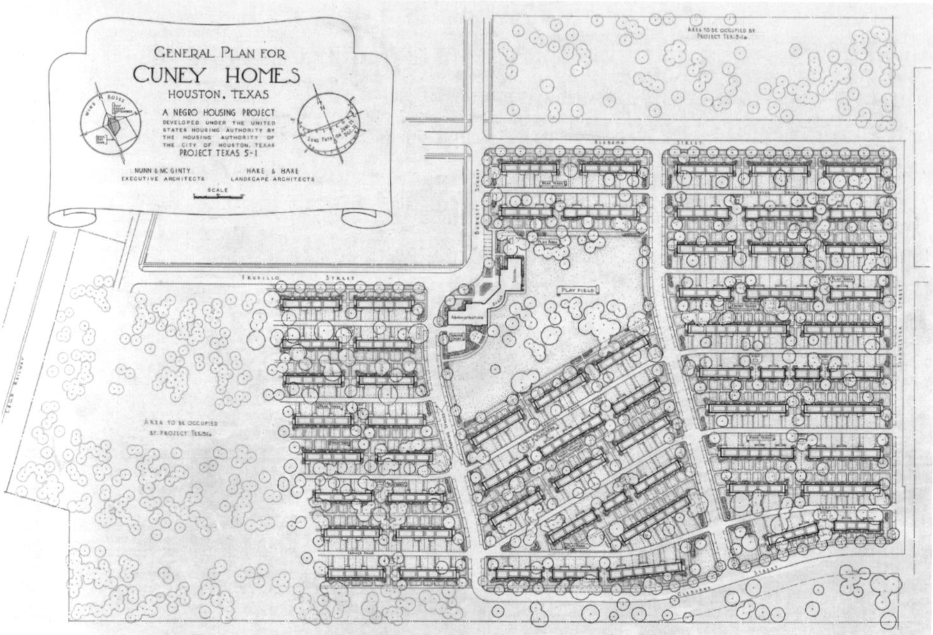

Plan for Cuney Homes housing project in Houston, 1939. HMRC-HPL.

regional plan encompassing Fort Worth and neighboring Dallas that would have guided growth and anticipated sprawl.

Devoting attention to detail, regardless of the size or the budget of a project, was also a hallmark of the firm. The placement of a sculpture at a five-acre Mission Hills, Kansas, estate, and how it should be oriented "just so" to best speak to the garden, would be indicated on the plans drawn for the clients. Equal attentiveness was given to Cuney Homes, a Houston low-income housing project for which the firm included front and rear yards, play areas, and curving tree-lined streets. To mitigate the lockstep effect of the rows of apartments, and to help catch the predominant breezes, Hare & Hare oriented the central group of buildings to the northwest. The presentation plan's scrolled cartouche identifies the project, a wind rose illustrates the predominant breezes by season, and an illustration shows how the paths of the sun will light the complex.

"Fitness" to the surroundings dictated the design aesthetic of each of Hare & Hare's projects and reflected the period in which a given work was executed. Sid's early "home grounds," densely planted to showcase color and texture, matured into the highly ornamental effect coveted at the end of the nineteenth century. Urban projects such as the Civic Center proposed for Houston and the Nelson-Atkins Museum of Art in Kansas City, 1929 and 1933, respectively, are both formal and monu-

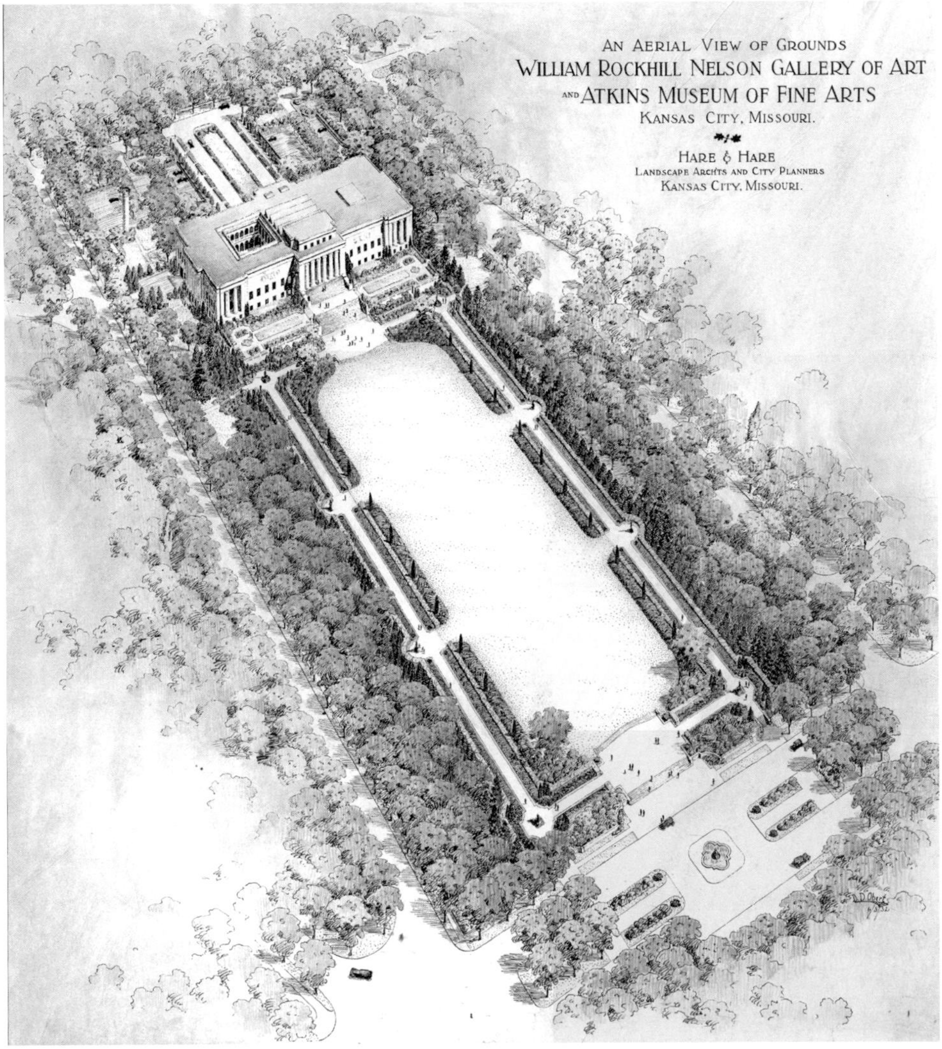

Aerial view of the Nelson-Atkins Museum of Art, Kansas City, drawn by D. D. Obert, June 3, 1932. SHSMO-KC.

mental, an appropriate context for the buildings they accompany.[20] In the mid-twentieth century several projects were designed in a contemporary idiom, such as the grounds at Hodges Gardens in Many, Louisiana, which provided the context for the midcentury-modern Lookout Tower. Likewise, the grounds of the Harry S. Truman Presidential Library in Independence, Missouri (completed in 1957), speak to the spare modernism of the building. In keeping with Herbert's insistence that a house and its grounds be related, for the Snower residence in Mission Hills, Kansas, designed by the modernist architect Marcel Breuer in 1954, the firm proposed elements compatible with the geometry of the house:

Harry S. Truman Library and grounds, c. 1959. Harry S. Truman Library.

arrow-straight walls of clipped evergreens and a row of hawthorns set parallel to the cantilevered south facade.

The firm played a significant role in improving and developing its hometown, and by the late 1920s had already planned and planted hundreds of residential, church, and school grounds, a long stretch of Ward Parkway (one of the most impressive in a city of many) and the subdivisions along it, and institutions such as the University of Kansas Medical Center across the county line. Hare & Hare would partner with the Olmsted Brothers firm on the setting for the iconic Liberty Memorial (years earlier Frederick Law Olmsted Jr. had referred to Herbert as his "man" in Kansas City) and serve as consultant to the city's park board (though it would be dropped briefly for refusing to pay corrupt politicians a percentage of its earnings).[21] For nearly fifteen years the developer J. C. Nichols worked exclusively with Hare & Hare in the planning of the Country Club District, which served as a model for the nation. Indeed, when Edward M. Bassett, president of American City Planning Institute, toured more than fifteen cities across the country in May 1927, his stop in Kansas City was, in his words, "not to teach but to learn."[22]

But Hare & Hare's work extended beyond the city, the state, and the Midwest. Its influence was multi-regional, spanning the central portion of the United States. Numerous midsize cities turned to the firm when taking initial steps toward urban planning. Projects, which varied in scope, were prepared for Grand Forks, North Dakota; Great Bend, Kansas; and Council Bluffs, Iowa. The many Nebraska commissions include West Lawn Cemetery, designed by Sid in 1909, and a plan for the Boys Town campus, both in Omaha, and contributions to today's University of Nebraska campus there and in Lincoln and Kearney. In Salt Lake City, Hare & Hare planned more than fifteen subdivisions between 1924 and 1955, many for the Ashton-Jenkins Company, and counted among its clients the Church of Jesus Christ of Latter-day Saints and the state prison. Other noteworthy commissions beyond the Midwest include Villa Philmonte in Cimarron, New Mexico (now owned by the Boy Scouts of America), the Denver neighborhood of Belcaro Park (named for the Phipps mansion it surrounds), the picturesque grounds of the Christian Science Sanatorium in Chestnut Hill, Massachusetts, and the University of Texas at Austin.

On a national level, Sid's foremost contribution was his participation in the ideological and physical shaping of a new type of cemetery, one fit for the twentieth century. A selection of his articles and photographs on the subject, published in specialized journals, were also included in *The*

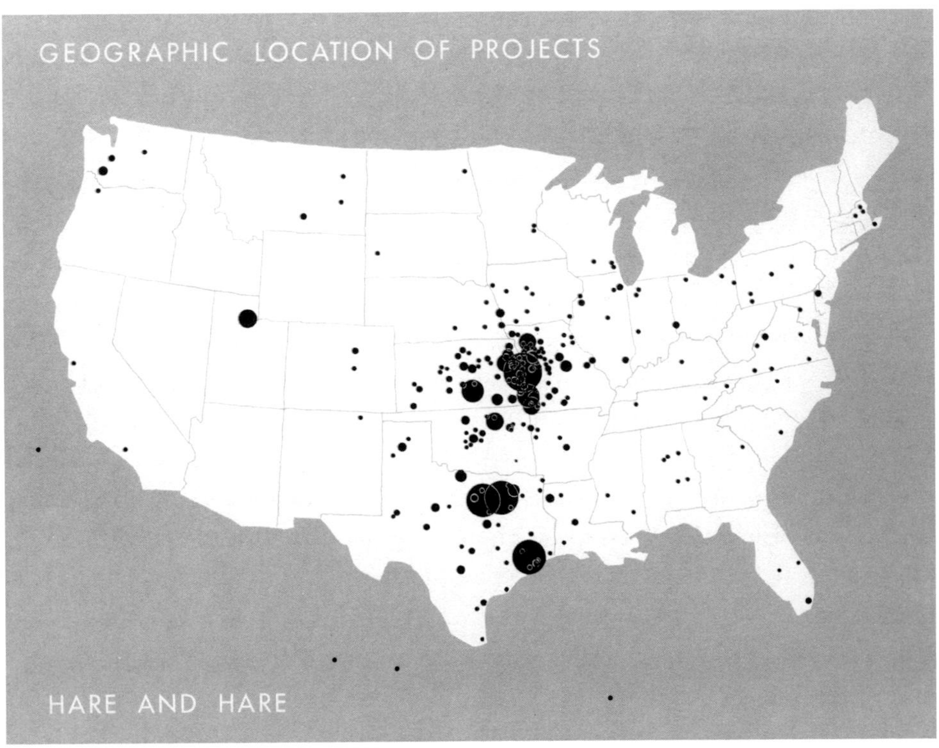

Map of Hare & Hare projects, c. 1960. SHSMO-KC.

Genevieve Phillips at Villa Philmonte, Cimarron, NM, c. 1930. Philmont Scout Ranch, Cimarron.

Cemetery Hand Book, the first assessment of the American cemetery. Professionals in the field knew Sid as an advocate for responsible water usage and the preservation of natural scenery. The landscape architect and environmental planner Warren H. Manning commended his "breadth of view" in thinking beyond the city when it came to park planning.[23]

Herbert's professional reputation exceeded his father's. Involved with policy and the setting of standards as a member of the National Resources Planning Board and the Federal Housing Administration, he believed planning to be the basis for "the intelligent expenditure of public funds."[24] Herbert saw the protection of natural resources as an obligation. He contributed to, edited, and reviewed national publications such as the ASLA's *Landscape Architecture,* the periodical *Planning and Civic Comment,* and editions of the Harvard City Planning Studies. As a member of the national competition jury charged to select an architect for the Jefferson National Expansion Memorial, better known as "the Arch," he sat alongside nationally known figures such as the architects Fiske Kimball and Richard Neutra. His years of board service included that for the Hubbard Educational Trust (established to further the study of the art and science of landscape architecture) and the correlative committee for the ASLA.

Level-headed and diplomatic, Herbert was courteous to individuals he disagreed with. He served a three-term tenure as president of the ASLA

Verona Columns Park, Mission Hills, KS. Photograph by Richard Welnowski, 2017.

in the early 1940s, representing the voice of reason in trying times. Both he and his father are among the American Planning Association's "National Planning Pioneers" for their contributions to education and practice on a national scale. Herbert dedicated much of his time to this last organization (known then as the American Institute of Planners), acting as its national membership chairman. Three months before his death he had been re-elected board vice president for a second term.

At the "Symposium on Placemaking," held in Kansas City in 2010 to celebrate the hundredth anniversary of the founding of Hare & Hare, the firm's current owner, Ralph Ochsner, acknowledged that the company was built on "a foundation of great places made by great people." This observation suggests the scope and number of outstanding commissions undertaken, as well as the character that makes them distinctive. Consistent within Hare & Hare's body of work is a sensitivity to utility and fitness, to nature, and to history. Sid and Herbert believed that good landscape architecture was both a science and an art and that a systematic approach to planning provided for "the welfare, convenience and happiness of present and future citizens."[25] Although they emphasized the practical, functional role of their profession, they firmly believed that if a city or a garden "is not to be a work of art, then it would be best not to build it."[26]

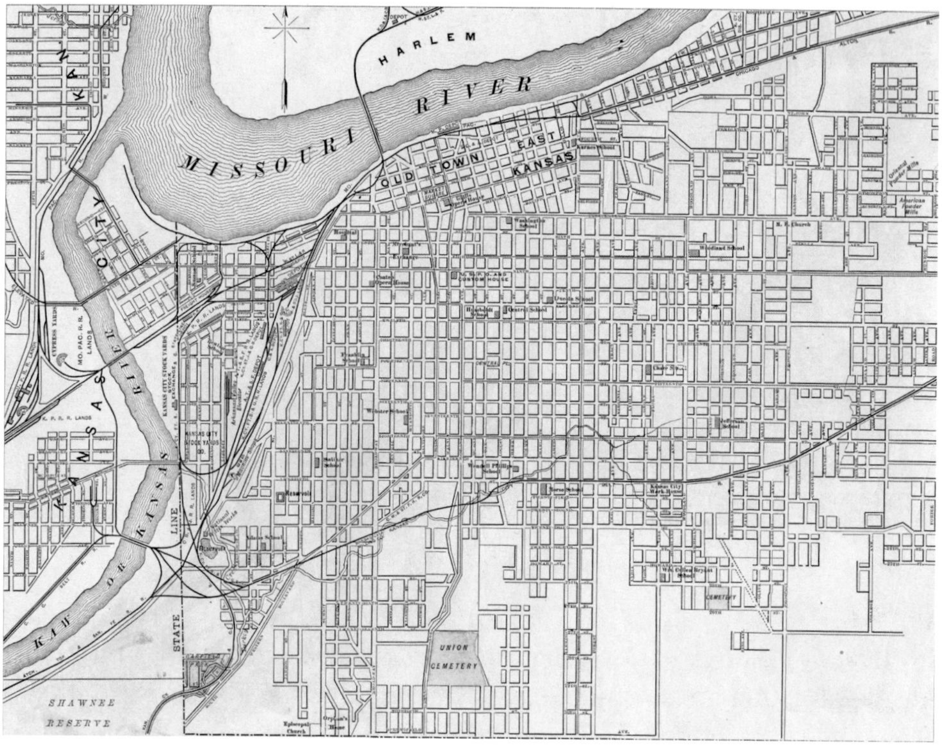

Map of Kansas City. *New Family Atlas of the World*, 1888. MVSC.

ONE

Early Kansas City, Sid Hare, and the "Fight for Parks"

Christopher Columbus and Isadora Bethurum Hare left Louisville, Kentucky, with their four children in the summer of 1868, bound for Kansas City.[1] It would take steamboats plying the Ohio, Mississippi, and Missouri Rivers eleven days to reach their destination. Their new home lay in a bend of the Missouri near its confluence with the Kansas River, also known as the Kaw. The location had long been a transportation hub, first for fur traders and then for settlers heading west. Above the rocky shelf that provided a natural landing for passengers and freight was the riverfront, by midcentury lined with a riot of warehouses, saloons, and hotels. The main business thoroughfare, Levee Street, had been widened and paved but the few other streets remained a sea of mud or a desert of dust depending on the season.[2]

Although early historians considered the place blessed by geography, its rocky topography in fact provided the early city its greatest challenges. From the channel cut by the Missouri, steep bluffs rose two hundred feet and then radiated in ridges alternating with ravines. This broken and uneven landscape, as described in contemporary accounts, posed "obstacles in the shape of elevations or depressions [which] were met at every turn."[3] Teams of laborers armed with pick and shovel cut through the bluffs, reduced the hills, and elevated the ravines in an effort to make the place habitable. This initial earthwork would be followed by a second round of cutting grids of streets at negotiable grades.

The antebellum population of Kansas City hovered under five thousand. By 1870, the number had grown to more than thirty thousand, due in part to the arrival of the Missouri Pacific Railroad. Both railroad and steamboat transportation provided vital connections north to south and east to west and helped establish the city as a key marketplace. By the mid-1870s the railroad became the principal means of transportation, and the center of enterprise shifted inland, away from the river proper, to a footprint of land crossed by railroad tracks called the West Bottoms. Within decades this low-lying farmland was transformed into the economic heart of the city and, when the Kansas City stockyards opened, the hub for cattle trade. It quickly grew from thirteen to fifty-five acres that straddled the Missouri-Kansas line. The hive of activity included cattle pens, sheep and hog sheds, loading docks, railroad yards, packing plants, and one of the largest horse and mule markets in the country. The families of meatpacking workers lived close by in shanties that clung to

Bluff grading at the corner of 4th and Grand, 1886. MVSC.

View of West Bottoms before major railroads, 1870. MVSC.

West Bottoms with Union Depot in the foreground, 1895. MVSC.

Stockyards, stereograph by Keystone View Company, c. 1897. Wikimedia Commons.

View of houses on West Bluffs looking toward Quality Hill, 1886. MVSC.

New York Life Building, n.d. MVSC.

the bluff while the well-to-do lived high above, on Quality Hill, removed from the mess.

Monuments to commerce went up—McKim, Mead & White's New York Life Building and the 1888 Board of Trade by Burnham & Root of Chicago—reflecting the city's leap from trading post to up-and-coming city.[4] These contrasted sharply with the shacks and billboards that lined the West Bluffs and greeted visitors arriving by train, suggesting that Kansas City was a backwater, or worse. Union Depot funneled railway passengers away from the West Bottoms to the cable car that climbed the bluff to downtown. There, the Blossom House and Delmonico Hotel, the Blue Goose Café, and the Coates Opera House communicated a different sense of arrival. By 1890, the population had grown to nearly 120,000. This was the burgeoning Midwest city that would prompt a young Sidney Hare to become "a friend in the fight for making Kansas City a better place to live."[5]

Christopher and Isadora Hare may have brought their family west wanting a fresh start. The Civil War had ended, and he had returned home from duty as a captain for the Kentucky Cavalry. The couple had recently lost an infant daughter, Lizzie, born the year before. Kansas City was booming, and there was ample opportunity for workers in the building trades. Soon after their arrival they moved into a house at the corner of 9th and Harrison, and Christopher started in the tin- and galvanized ironworks business on Main Street, a few blocks from the river. There he employed a "tinner" named C. R. Hare (perhaps a relative) and Sidney's older brother, Willy, part-time. "Sid," named for an uncle on his father's side, earned his money selling peaches for a dime to businessmen along Main Street and delivering the *Evening Bulletin*.

Sid attended public schools, first Morse Elementary and later Humboldt, where he would return as a teen to present to the students the "Centennial Orations" in honor of the country's one hundredth birthday. He developed an interest in the natural world and built collections of insects, birds, and Native American implements, the last of which included flint knives he would donate to the Smithsonian Institution in 1888. At Central High School his grades were good but not stellar. He studied civil engineering and photography, a skill he would master and apply later when working for the city. After graduation he took additional courses in engineering and surveying. Horticulture, a pursuit sparked by working with his mother in the family's old-fashioned flower garden in Louisville, was another course of study. Later in life he would be known for his cultivation of native plants and their habitats, and as a general lover of nature. All of these classes, and his interest in them, were a remarkable fit for what would become his lifework.

One of Sid's early and ongoing passions was the study of fossils. When he was sixteen his collection attracted much attention at a local exposition, and the following year he was inducted into the Kansas City Academy of Science as an honorary member. By twenty-one he was listed in the city

Central High School class picture with Sidney Hare, second row, to right of Miss Harmon, with books on his hip, 1882. JCHS.

directory as "geologist." He lectured on crinoids and published on trilobites and other rare fossils, illustrating his articles with his own drawings. When the public library dedicated museum space for the subject, he donated nearly half of his "geological treasures." In 1889, numerous Upper Carboniferous fossils, some yet unknown to science, were uncovered in the blue gray shale during construction of the Bullene, Moore, Emery & Company building downtown. The discovery revealed a new species that included eight crinoids; amateur paleontologist Sid Hare and Edward Butts, the city engineer, preserved the fossils and reported their findings to the scientific community. Two of the crinoids—*Aesiocrinus harii* and *Ethelocrinus harii*—were named for Sid Hare.[6]

Four years before the fossil discovery, Sid had married Illinois-born Mathilda Amelia Korfhage, the daughter of August, a Methodist Episcopal minister of Prussian descent, and Caroline, from Waldeck, Germany. Mathilda had also been raised in a family of six children but in circumstances perhaps more comfortable than his own. She was likely a pragmatic woman, having inherited this disposition from her mother who, in her will, admitted to being impressed with nothing more than "the uncertainty of life and the certainty of death."[7] At Sid and Mathilda's wedding, which took place at the Korfhages' Kansas City home, the bride was dressed in yards of silk and lace purchased from Roll, Thayer & Williams. She would bring to the marriage a house and property on Wyandotte Street deeded to her by her parents for the price of "love and affection and the sum of one dol-

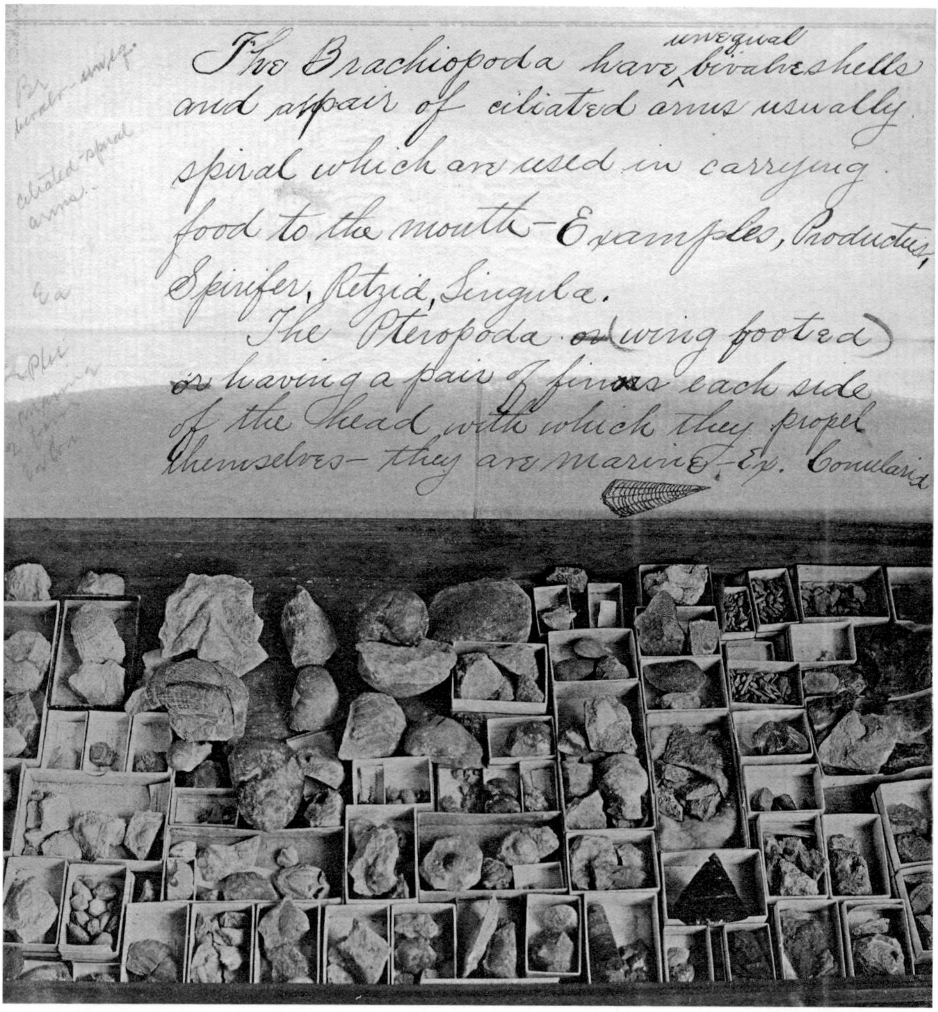

A portion of Sidney's fossil collection accompanied by his notes, c. 1900. JCHS.

lar."[8] The couple would soon have two children, first a daughter, Nell, and two years later, in 1888, a son, Sidney Herbert.

A portrait photograph taken in 1891 is among a handful of documents that convey a sense of this young family. Three-year-old Herbert is seated on his father's lap and Nell stands beside her mother. A pout can be discerned on little Herbert's face as he holds his father's forefinger with both hands for reassurance. His older sister, whom he will remain close with for life, appears somewhat wan. All are well dressed, if not fashionable: Nell in her ruffles, her brother with a floppy bow at his neck, Sid in lapelled waistcoat with his favorite pin stuck through a four-in-hand tie. Mathilda wears velvet and luminous satin, her pleated bodice cut to a deep V to accentuate her tiny waist. The alcove in which they are seated, with its Eastlake chair and drapes patterned with motifs drawn from nature, has all the hallmarks of the Aesthetic movement. One would expect to find it in London rather than Independence, Missouri, a town adjacent Kansas City, in the studio of photographer W. A. Hare (certainly a relative). The image speaks to the late nineteenth-century taste that will be the springboard for Sid's work.

In the 1870s, when Sid Hare was a teenager, there was not one municipal park in Kansas City, although the quest to establish them, and for community beautification, had begun years before. The 1856 dream of the millionaire mogul Kersey Coates, who invested in real estate in Quality Hill and planned a parklike boulevard encircling the city, was a beginning. But the first real step taken toward providing the restorative benefits of nature was not taken until 1879, with the city's improvement of the Old Grave Yard, centrally located and in easy reach of working-class neighborhoods. The next, a push by residents of McGee's Addition to gain city support in transforming vacant land (used as a circus ground) into a green space, failed to materialize. But increasingly a pro-park rallying cry could be heard, as from the merchant T. B. Bullene: "Now the pressing want, the imperative want is lungs for our proud, young giant metropolis."

Starting in 1872, editorials in favor of beautification outlined the economic and social pros of parkland in the *Kansas City Times* and *Kansas*

The Hare family portrait taken by W. A. Hare, Independence, 1891. JCHS.

City Journal. They promoted awareness of parks as healthy alternatives to brawls and brothels, as a draw to attract newcomers, and as having a positive effect on real estate values. But these talking points were countered by a general indifference to aesthetics by the public and city officials alike. Investing in open space when sewers and streets had yet to be built made little sense to them. The newspapers returned with the argument that the city's booming population would soon demand parks—if simply for breathing room—and boulevards that could ease traffic. And the purchase of park land should happen sooner rather than later, before land values increased.

The debate over civic improvement was played out in the *Times* and the *Journal*, but it was William Rockhill Nelson's *Star* that was the loudest on the subject. His tirades, and those written by staffers as "letters to the editor," appeared regularly from its founding in 1880. Stocky and overbearing, the "bluff, gruff, fearless" newspaper man pushed through long work days, making demands by way of a thunderous voice. The seemingly unrefined Nelson had in fact attended college at Notre Dame, passed the bar exam, and traveled Europe. And, he believed in reform. For Nelson, new to the city at the age of thirty-nine, "betterment" was a civic duty. As an ally of the pro-park faction, he galvanized public interest by publishing on every aspect of the issue. His domineering character helped push for-

William Rockhill Nelson, n.d. MVSC.

ward the idea of a park and boulevard system, which would be a "badge of municipal maturity."[9]

Nelson's neighbor August Meyer was another fierce advocate in the battle for parks. Having moved from his native St. Louis in his early thirties, he was aware, as Nelson had been, of the opportunities Kansas City presented. Educated in schools of mines in Freiburg and Berlin, he first worked in Colorado (where he helped found Leadville) as a mining engineer and investor. He became a multimillionaire from the smelting plant he started in the nearby Argentine industrial district of Kansas. A father of five, at once dapper and earnest, Meyer was devoted to work, charity, and church, and he was a foil to Nelson's bluster and autocracy. He believed in teamwork, was an able public speaker nimble under fire, and was an outdoor enthusiast who came to know the outskirts of the city by riding horseback. Meyer shared German heritage and a love of rugged terrain with the up-and-coming landscape architect George Kessler, with whom he would work on park planning. Meyer took notes as he traveled Europe and wrote to New York, Boston, and Buffalo inquiring about park statistics, information to be used in his pursuit of civic improvement. He would ultimately be credited with coauthoring the park system that resulted, setting the stage for planning carried forward by Hare & Hare.[10]

"The street question, the park question, the boulevard question," as

August Meyer, n.d. MVSC.

George Kessler, 1914. Kansas City Museum.

the *Journal* put it, ultimately became a question of state legislation and multiple city charters that played out over twenty-five years.[11] The debate had much to do with the parties invested in the outcome. Besides citizens groups, Meyer, and Nelson, park supporters ranged from the Commercial Club (predecessor to the Chamber of Commerce) and the Municipal Improvement Association, to James Pendergast, the political boss and city alderman whose First Ward and Climax Saloon lay in the West Bottoms. The anti-park faction was made up of a nebulous mix of county officials, professionals, and businessmen in real estate, insurance, and banking, including the president of the Taxpayers' League, a formidable player in the fight against parks. Referred to by Nelson as "fossils" and "mossbacks" for their resistance to change, all were cautious of reform and preoccupied with money, fearful of how increased taxes would affect their pocketbooks.

Because of these divided interests, private initiatives failed, as did those proposed by civic-minded mayors and council members. Although the city had been granted power to condemn land for public use in 1875, no parks were established. A decade later a citizens group, appointed by the mayor, was set up to consider the park and boulevard issue, which was slowly gaining traction. Its charge was to make a recommendation on whether to consider implementation of a farsighted plan—one that addressed the city's growth—or establish small parks in existing neighborhoods. The most earnest political tug-of-war began in 1888 when a park bill sponsored in the state legislature, which passed in the senate but died in the house, was revised and passed the following year, though without immediate funding. An 1889 charter, amended in 1892, finally created a "durable and effective" board, one with the authority to issue bonds to fund projects.[12] This success was qualified a year later when its funding of $25,000 was reduced to $5,000 and the Missouri Supreme Court threw out earlier legislation that had empowered the board to issue bonds.[13] The park commission would not acquire the authority, autonomy, and fiscal power it needed to withstand legal challenges until 1895, when it welcomed yet another charter amendment. Crafted by the cunning and skillful Delbert James Haff, general counsel to the park board, who forged "the legal structure for [Kansas City's] City Beautiful movement," this last amendment met with overwhelming public support. After a ward-by-ward push by the board, the amendment passed with 10,298 votes for and 1,784 against.[14]

The "durable and effective" park board appointed by Mayor Benjamin Holmes on March 5, 1892, was made up of moneyed laymen who were reformers and fervent supporters of beautifying the city. The board's president and "driving force," August Meyer, had toured and researched parks in Europe and in the East. Appointed commissioners were Simeon B. Armour, of the meatpacking firm, whose family was from New York and who, with his brother Andrew, had also been in banking in Kansas City; Louis Hammerslough, railroad speculator (one of the first trains through the city bore his name) and successful clothier who had immigrated from Hanover in 1858; William C. Glass, his fortune made in wholesale liquor and cigars; and Adriance Van Brunt, noted local architect. George Kessler was hired as secretary, with pay of $200 per month, and served in the capacity of engineer "without pay." Not until a year later did he officially become the board's landscape architect, the timing of which may have been a conscientious move to calm critics by suggesting that improvement preceded aesthetics.

The board quickly set to work assessing topography, land values, and population density, appointing a committee that visited parks in Chicago, St. Louis, and Boston, Baltimore, Washington, D.C., Brooklyn, and Buffalo. It assessed park statistics, including those collected by Meyer and others published by W. H. Eckman in his 1888 pamphlet on park history and facts.[15] As their ideas developed, letters of advice went back and forth between Meyer, Kessler, and the Olmsted firm. The board's activities were given credence by a nod from F. L. Olmsted Sr., when he visited in the fall of 1892. In August of the following year, Charles Eliot, a partner in the Olmsted firm who was cited by newspapers as being the board's consulting engineer, came to bestow his blessing and met with the mayor, Meyer, and Van Brunt. Such a system, assured Eliot, "judiciously planned and wisely carried out," would help right the city's patchwork of "ragged" and inconsistent neighborhoods and would fix "definitely the character of the improvements."[16]

The final report, officially titled the *Board of Park and Boulevard Commissioners of Kansas City, Missouri, Embracing Recommendations for the Establishment of a Park and Boulevard System for Kansas City*, was submitted to Mayor W. S. Cowherd on October 12, 1893. Ambitious and progressive, this first written plan for a comprehensive system was an eighty-page illustrated document. Its opening statement, addressed directly to the mayor, stated the "guiding facts" at all times before the board members. These were, first, their "duty of developing a plan that shall not only meet present, but future wants" and, second, "that to undertake important work in a half-hearted manner is the poorest economy, and that it is far better to plan comprehensively and broadly and proceed

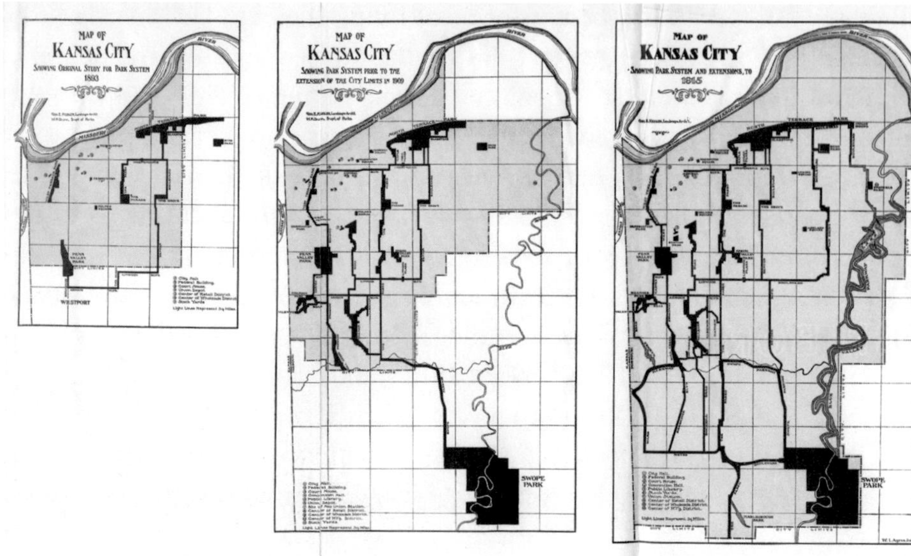

Map of Kansas City showing its park system in 1893, 1909, and 1915. MVSC.

with actual construction leisurely, than to attempt economy in the original plans."[17]

A general report from the park commissioners—a justification "in favor of parks"—followed, describing the aims and duties of the city and commission, the value of beauty, and the effect of parks and boulevards on real estate values, as well as providing park statistics from New York, Boston, Chicago, and elsewhere. Next came a detailed discussion of the "erratic and tantalizing topography" of the city with recommendations addressing function and aesthetics related to the placement of boulevards and pleasure and play grounds. The final section was the "Report of the Engineer," Kessler's technical comments on design, construction method, and the use of appropriate materials and plants.

Creation of the three major parks proposed in the report—West Terrace, North Terrace, and Penn Valley—would transform blighted districts and reclaim underused areas whose landscapes, "diversified and intricate to a degree," lent themselves to park improvement. West Terrace Park would clean up the scruffy West Bluffs, which had been a source of concern since the arrival of the railroad, and dress them with stone staircases capped with viewing pavilions. The rugged terrain along the city's north edge, considered a "squirrel pasture" too steep for even a goat to climb, would become North Terrace (now Kessler) Park. Cliff Drive would echo the route of the river below and ribbon through woods and Argentine limestone outcroppings. The third major project, Penn Valley Park, would transform a neglected area in the southwest portion of the city, which had been described as a "topographical enigma" of forked ravines and stone ledges.[18]

In addition to these three major parks, smaller tracts of land were reserved for playgrounds and neighborhood green spaces, resulting in a hierarchy of parks that served the varied needs of the city's residents. All would be knit together by a system of boulevards and parkways connecting older and newer portions of the city. Hundred-foot-wide boulevards would include forty-foot drives flanked by thirty-foot-wide green spaces densely lined with elms, maples, poplar, and lindens. A parkway

Kersey Coates Drive in West Terrace Park, n.d. MVSC.

Drive in Penn Valley Park near Santa Fe Trail marker, 1920. KC History Collection, MVSC.

named the Paseo, with a series of terraces, fountains, and a sunken garden anchoring intersections along the route, was the most formal element proposed.

By the time the park and boulevard report was submitted to the mayor in 1893, Sid Hare had been employed in the Kansas City engineer's office for twelve years. Hired at the age of twenty-one, his first assignments were as a chainman and levelman assisting in determining elevations, and in survey work as a transitman and draftsman. Engineering projects included surveying for a major roadway, Southwest Boulevard, and portions of a stone retaining wall along Bluff Street. Sewer repairs and installation along downtown's Main Street were within his purview, as was the OK Creek (in the valley where, in 1914, rail lines would lead to the second largest Union Station in the country). He began recording conditions, photographing pollution shrouding the city from atop City Hall and testing a "smoke consumer device" intended to correct its effects. With his camera, he documented streets in need of repair, the rail yards, the "shanty town," and billboards scattered along the West Bluffs—all of which would be addressed in future improvement. The collection of photographs later served to illustrate Sid's "before" and "after" lectures on civic progress.

When the city engineer's office began the comprehensive survey at the request of the newly appointed park commission, Sid and George Kessler found themselves working side-by-side (a practice that would continue years later with Sid's son).[19] Each brought complementary skills to the job at hand. Kessler had a German education in botany, forestry, and landscape gardening, while Sid's strength was his practical experience and knowledge of the topography gained from living in the city for

Bluff Street wall from 4th Street. Photo by Sid Hare. MVSC.

West Bluff from Union Depot. Photo by Sid Hare, 1892. MVSC.

Bluffs and cow path before construction of Cliff Drive, North Terrace Park, 1903. MVSC.

Cliff Drive, North Terrace Park, n.d. MVSC.

twenty-four years. Kessler served on the park commission and Sid represented the engineer's office, taking notes and recording data related to the park survey as plans progressed. Sid conducted early surveys for park development, the first of which he had undertaken a decade earlier (in 1882), at a tiny, city-owned wedge of land named West Prospect Triangle (today Andrew Drips Park). It was Sid who took Kessler to the rustic woods with panoramic views of the Missouri River, which would become North Terrace Park, and pointed out the possibilities. Together the two walked the cow path that became Cliff Drive, the "pièce de résistance" of the entire system.[20]

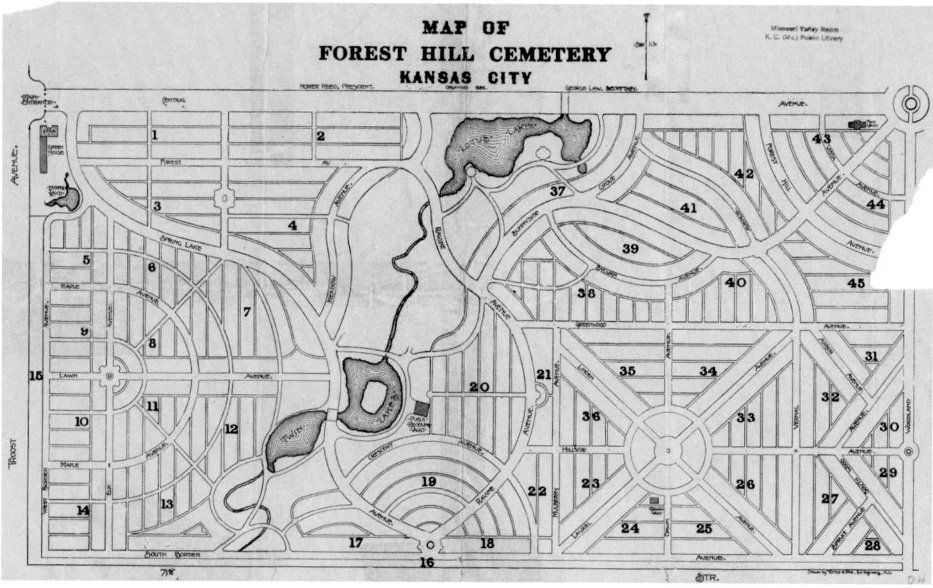

Forest Hill Cemetery plan, drawn by Tuttle & Pike Civil Engineering, 1888. MVSC.

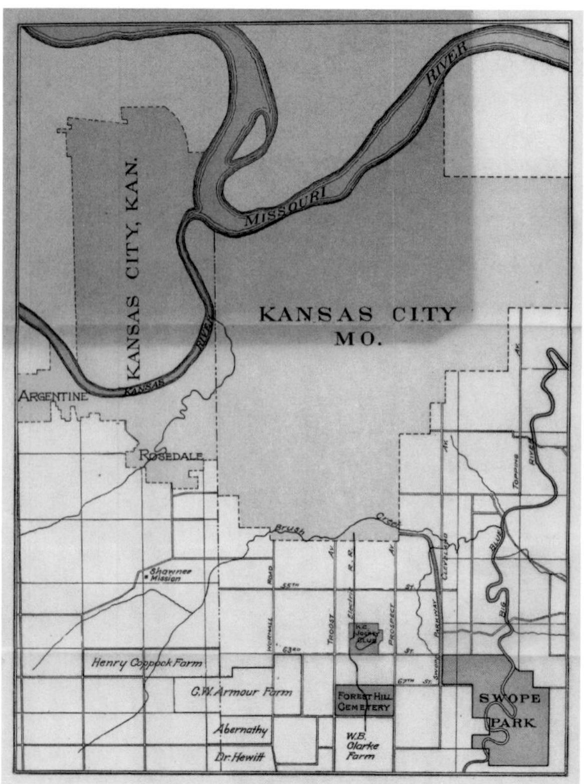

Map of Kansas City with Forest Hill Cemetery indicated in lower center, c. 1900. JCHS.

TWO

Sid Hare and the Development of the Modern Cemetery

Perhaps eager to work with landscape in a more artistic way, Sid resigned from his position with the city in 1896 to become the supervisor of Forest Hill Cemetery. Located on Troost Avenue, it was far beyond the southeast edge of the city limits whose southern boundary lay at 31st Street, forty blocks to the north. Developed in 1888, Forest Hill was owned by the Troost Avenue Cemetery Company. George Kessler had worked with George Law, the company secretary, in laying out the plans and Law oversaw the initial plantings. Sid's business cards bear his elaborate scrolled signature and identify him as superintendent and "landscape engineer"—with a share (albeit small) in the cemetery company stock.

As superintendent, Sid planned to transform Forest Hill. Working from the inventory in the cemetery's nursery, and ordering new specimens from Thomas Meehan & Sons in Philadelphia, he planted more than six thousand new trees and shrubs within the year. These included ginkgo (*Ginkgo biloba*), various species of beech, and a collection of Japanese maples (*Acer palmatum*) newly introduced to the country. Each was identified with zinc and aluminum labels bearing the scientific and common names. Forty kinds of water lilies and a multitude of goldfish were added to the cemetery's lakes; five thousand bedding plants provided summer color; and plans were made to stock a new two-acre lake with black bass for fishing. Hare intended to create a place for the living as well as the dead, one that would attract students of botany, to rival Henry Shaw's garden (today's Missouri Botanical Garden) in St. Louis.[1]

As late as 1938, Forest Hill's collection of trees remained the most varied in the city. *Trees of Forest Hill, Kansas City, Missouri,* a guidebook to "tree study" at the cemetery, provided identifying characteristics of bark, twig, flower, and fruit for each species (tagged with numbers to aid in identification). Encouraging critical examination, it suggested one "observe closely, study, compare and read," thus encouraging appreciation for its subject. Woven throughout the guide are drawings and photographs—likely by Sid—of great specimen trees included in the collection, along with a list that cites botanical and common names. Forest Hill's more than one hundred species and varieties included exotics like golden rain tree (*Koelreuteria paniculata*), European larch (*Larix europaea*), and pagoda tree (*Sophora japonica*)—some found nowhere else in the city—as well as cucumber tree (*Magnolia acuminata*), Osage orange (*Maclura pomiferum*), and yellow wood (*Cladrastis lutea*), "common native trees that may here be studied to advantage."[2]

The move to Forest Hill signaled a change in direction for Sid, from surveying and documenting sites to managing and planting a designed landscape, with the attendant change in job requirements. It was there that

Forest Hill Cemetery, c. 1910. Forest Hill Cemetery Collection.

Sidney Hare's copy of *Trees of Forest Hill*, c. 1930. JCHS.

he became an expert on "what and where to plant."[3] Curating the collection of trees (and shrubs) during his tenure, Sid oversaw an arboretum so impressive that President Theodore Roosevelt praised it as one of the finest he had ever seen.[4] Although Sid remained in the position of superintendent for only six years, his foresight during that period would be lauded in the cemetery's guidebook in the decades that followed. He, and the firm, returned often to make improvements. Sid's contributions in the early 1920s include planting plans executed on linen (a practice that would end with him) and a vellum plant list over six feet in length. Twenty planting plans drafted by the firm document the addition of thousands of bulbs, hundreds of perennials—larkspur, bleeding heart, and dianthus—oaks, and evergreens through 1930. Forest Hill became Sid's proving ground and the springboard for decades of cemetery work, where he would have an active voice in cemetery reform.

In his position at Forest Hill, Sid would join with members of the American Association of Cemetery Superintendents (AACS) in defining a new type of burial landscape and ultimately be credited with "the progress of the Cemetery profession everywhere."[5] The organization's first meeting had been held in October 1887 at Spring Grove Cemetery in Cincinnati, the finest cemetery in the Midwest and, according to the consensus of progressive professionals, in the entire country. Founded in 1845, and based on a plan by Howard Daniels, Spring Grove attracted the Prussian landscape gardener Adolph Strauch a decade later. He began the process of simplifying the landscape—editing the view—by sweeping away fences and promoting a seamless pastoral scene in contrast to the picturesque (some would say cluttered) effect it was acquiring over time. Strauch, who had passed away four years before the AACS meeting, was lauded as a visionary—"the fountainhead"—and the originator of the "landscape lawn plan."[6] Led by president Charles Nichols, the superintendent of Fairmount Cemetery in Newark, New Jersey, the group of twenty-five attendees considered Spring Grove the ideal birthplace for the organization and the perfect context in which to address the "modern cemetery."

"Map and Views of Spring Grove Cemetery," published by H. C. Ruggles, 1867. LC.

"The Lake in Spring Grove Cemetery," Detroit Publishing Company, c. 1906. LC.

"Chapel in Spring Grove Cemetery," Detroit Publishing Company, c. 1906. LC.

AACS members sought to achieve an improved version of the cemetery, different from the one defined in the first half of the nineteenth century. Rural cemeteries—the first designed outdoor spaces and the precursors to public parks in this country—were a response to the health hazards of crowded city burial grounds, changing perceptions of death, and epidemics (such as cholera) that swept through urban spaces. They contrasted with the gloomy graveyards of the past, lined with brittle headstones, in their soothing parklike spaces planted with willows and evergreens and ornamented with urns and sculpture. Andrew Jackson Downing wrote on the subject in *The Horticulturalist* in 1846, suggesting that rural cemeteries were more than mere burial grounds. Downing described them as "solemn places of meditation for the friends of the deceased" and places of retreat where the "united charm of nature and art . . . [provides] the double wealth of rural and moral associations."[7] The models for this movement were established: Mount Auburn, in Cambridge, Massachusetts (1831); Laurel Hill, in Philadelphia (1836); and Green-Wood, in Brooklyn, New York (1838), so popular it became a tourist attraction second only to Niagara Falls. To the west were Graceland in Chicago (1861) and Bellefontaine in St. Louis (1849), overseen by Almerin Hotchkiss, who had come from Green-Wood

"Mount Auburn Cemetery—burial place of Longfellow," stereograph, Underwood & Underwood Publishers, c. 1914. LC.

in Brooklyn.[8] These resting places of the dead became inclusive landscapes where gender, age, and class mattered little. Family members could bond with nature, each other, and loved ones who had left this world.

But not long after midcentury the rural cemetery, as a type, became a victim of changing taste and aesthetics. Landscape advocates, many of whom would become allied with the AACS, believed cemeteries were reaching "their lowest ebb" and called for reform. One egregious practice was the excessive use of monuments, "the vulgar fashion of using stone," for the mere love of display. And over time, the absence of rules—varied types of fencing, plantings (some successful, others not), inartistic memorials, and accrued offerings made by family members—resulted in a lack of "harmony with and subordination to nature."[9] Strauch's landscape lawn plan, understood by visiting Spring Grove firsthand or communicated through his 1869 writings on the subject, was a method gaining currency with designers and practitioners, among them his friend Jacob Weidenmann.[10]

At Cedar Hill Cemetery, in Hartford, Connecticut (1863), Weidenmann adopted Strauch's revised and edited approach to cemetery planning. He set swards of grass, specimen trees, and an artistically arranged body of water against the backdrop of nature to provide a "serene frame of mind"

"Greenwood Cemetery, Brooklyn," stereograph by George Stacy, c. 1865. LC.

for visitors.[11] Echoing Strauch's landscape lawn plan, Weidenmann termed his approach the "open lawn system."[12] Fences, walls, and curbs were not permitted, each plot had a single monument framed by shrubs, and individual graves were marked solely by stones flush with the ground. Interest in this approach became evident in later additions to Graceland Cemetery in Chicago when O. C. Simonds and Bryan Lathrop worked there in tandem beginning in 1881.[13] On newly opened sections they adapted the ideals and features of the Cincinnati model by creating wide sweeps of lawn, rejecting the use of fences, restricting the number of monuments, and insisting that headstones be kept low to the ground.[14] This shift in taste and type became evident in the Bronx, in additions to Woodlawn Cemetery after 1867, and in Minneapolis at Lakewood Cemetery, a "model of modern lawn plan development," in the 1870s.[15]

The modern cemetery movement included a push for higher standards and greater professionalism on behalf of superintendents and cemetery associations, a goal Sid would later promote in his presentations and articles. In its constitution, the AACS defined its primary objective as "the advancement of the interests and the elevation of the character of the cemeteries of America."[16] The reform of cemetery practice was tied directly to management; it must address economics and efficiency and keep abreast of new technology and horticultural methods.[17] Ongoing education, and dissemination of information, were imperative. To address this need, annual AACS meetings covered subjects such as provisions for perpetual care,

"Entrance to Cedar Hill Cemetery, Hartford." Detroit Publishing Company, 1900–1906. LC.

Lake Willowmere, Graceland Cemetery, Chicago. Photographic Print Co., 1904. Trustees of Graceland Cemetery Improvement Fund.

cost accounting, and new hygienic methods of burial; proper drainage, soil type, and roadbed materials; technology and products such as casket-lowering devices, grave vaults, and sterile grave liners. Implicit in the group's objective was knowledge of landscape—practical and aesthetic—as a requisite for those in charge.

At the 1890 annual meeting held in Boston, AACS members voted on twenty-one rules or standards meant to "maintain the dignity and character of a city of the dead."[18] These rules outlined appropriate types of planting and materials, set grade and height limitations, and defined methods of construction. Although lot owners and the public had the privilege of providing input, authority lay in the hands of trustees (representing stock companies or corporations) and superintendents—experts in landscape gardening and the special needs of burial grounds who were charged with their care "for all time." Adherence to these rules meant that lot owners were restricted from planting or otherwise ornamenting plots, ensuring a unified and "approved" effect that benefited the cemetery as a whole. Action of the AACS prompted a decade of sweeping change in cemetery planning, and the rules they codified would guide the modern cemetery into the next century.

The increasing specialization in cemetery reform led to the publication of numerous journals focusing on the cemetery profession, each with a different perspective. *The Cemetery Beautiful* reported on the "cemetery as a business . . . how to maintain, develop and beautify at a profit." *Monument and Cemetery Review* considered itself "the exponent of Art in the Monument Field" and, along with *The Monumental News,* was allied closely with companies that produced and marketed granite, bronze, and marble monuments.[19] With the aim of the landscape lawn plan to use fewer large headstones, vaults, and mausoleums—to create, in the words of one Massachusetts cemetery superintendent, "a park, rather than a marble yard"—these last two journals may have seemed more a sales tool than an objective means of information.[20] But another publication, *Park and Cemetery,* published from Dearborn Street in Chicago by R. J. Haight (and Allied Arts Publishing Co.), developed its mission to encompass the improvement of cemetery landscapes and management. In less than a decade Haight and Sidney Hare would become not only business associates but friends.[21]

Park and Cemetery, an illustrated monthly, began publication in 1891, first under the title *Modern Cemetery* and later as *Park and Cemetery and Landscape Gardening.*[22] True to its name, it included articles on state and national parks, playgrounds, and recreation areas, but foremost it addressed the needs of "the cemetery man" and was the "official organ" of the AACS. Many members, "among the most prominent Landscape Architects, Engineers, Horticulturalists, Park and Cemetery Superintendents in the United States," contributed to the publication, providing practical and aesthetic advice along with plans and illustrations. The wide range of articles included "The First Experiments in Cemetery Management" by Arthur Hobert, superintendent of Lakewood Cemetery, Minneapolis; the nurseryman Thomas Meehan's 1894 "Suitable Trees and Shrubs for a Modern Cemetery"; and "Cemeteries on the Western Plains and Their Ornamentations" (1894) by J. Y. Craig, superintendent of Forest Lawn Cemetery in Omaha.[23] Numerous articles, on subjects from administration to ground cover, were contributed by founding member O. C. Simonds.

Ultimately, select articles that appeared in *Park and Cemetery* were compiled to create a summation of the subject, *The Cemetery Hand Book,* published in the 1921 (with a 1932 reprint edition). "The First Encyclopedia of the Cemetery Field" featured over seven hundred pages of articles and four hundred illustrations—"a thirty years' collection of facts and methods"—dealing with all aspects of the modern cemetery. Contributors were superintendents and landscape professionals, among them William

Salway and Carl E. Kern (Spring Grove Cemetery), Frank Eurich (founding member of AACS and designer of Woodlawn, in Detroit), John Noyes (Missouri Botanical Garden), O. C. Simonds, and Hare & Hare.[24]

In mid-September 1897, with barely a year of experience as superintendent at Forest Hill, Sid Hare attended the annual AACS meeting held at the Grand Hotel in Cincinnati. The organization had returned to its "birthplace," and that of the modern cemetery, to celebrate a decade of advancement and education. During an evening session Sid delivered the first of the many papers he would present to the group, titled "The Influence of Surroundings." In it, he notes the relationship of cemeteries to parks and boulevards. The ability of these landscapes to "educate the people in an art equally as grand as the art of painting or sculpture" prompts them to "adorn their home grounds, to plant trees and shrubs, and to study nature, the mother of all true art." He warned, however, that an appreciation of nature did not justify a "do-it-yourself" approach. Landscape improvements should be made "under the guiding hand of one who has made a study of landscape gardening and knows the uses and beauties of trees and

"Landscape Pictures in Cemetery Lots," one of Sidney's visual lessons in the artistic arrangement of nature from *The Cemetery Hand Book*, 1921.

shrubs when planted according to a well studied design." Sid then turned to the subject of cemeteries, noting that "everything done should be toward adornment of the ground as a whole." By "adornment" he meant the arrangement of nature—"velvety" lawns, curving walks, mirror lakes, and long vistas—rather than art. Best to "let one plan, one carefully studied plan, govern all planting of trees and shrubs, and this alone will make harmony and beauty of landscape."[25]

Sid understood more than aesthetics. His background in geology and paleontology, as an amateur botanist, and in his work in the city engineer's office grounded him in the technical aspects of dealing with nature. He had, for several years, been compiling data on "trees and shrubs adapted to landscape work" and was insistent that one must know "their value either for flower or foliage for spring effects, summer and fall effects on the lawn. . . . Their rapidity of growth, height and spread, winter effect of stem and bark, whether they form suckers or not, when and how to prune, best soil adapted, best location to insure success, whether open or protected, sunny or shady, high or low, moist or dry . . . how to propagate, and lastly, yet first to us, how to use them."[26] With the presentation of this paper, Sid joined the ranks of landscape gardeners and cemetery men—the "us" he refers to.

In the fall of 1900, while in Cleveland, Sid was approached by J. R. Vernon, secretary of the Salem Cemetery Association, about its project seventy miles to the southwest. The association had purchased land—the second farm beyond the railroad—for a new cemetery intended to replace the "disgraceful" burial ground near the depot.[27] Vernon, on behalf of the board, insisted that Sid "come soon," which he did.[28] Platting was postponed in hope of purchasing land that would provide a better approach, but within months Sid had submitted multiple plans—watercolor and ink on vellum and linen—and plant lists, accompanied by detailed instructions. The result was Grandview Cemetery, in Salem, Ohio, Sid's first independent design executed while still employed at Forest Hill.

Twenty acres of land were platted into a series of ovoid and kidney-shaped burial sections, some more densely platted than others, arranged around a center section, a perfect circle. Sid insisted on no sunken walks or extensive grading and wanted the placement of drives along low points in the topography—following the general contours of the ground—which would "throw the burial sections above."[29] Both sides of the thirty-foot macadam drives were to be sodded and planted to contribute to a

"Grand View Cemetery, Salem, Ohio," 1900, by Sidney Hare, "Civil and Landscape Engineer." SHSMO-KC.

parklike effect and prevent a line of headstones from pressing up to the roadway as at the town's old cemetery. From the south drive one passed Willow Lake and continued along streets named Cypress, Catalpa, Chestnut, and Linden, which looped around and back again to the entrances.

Sid suggested that all plant material, of which he included a list with prices and sizes, come from Meehan & Sons. Specific (if somewhat complicated) written directions were sent to supplement his drawn plans. His "formula," keyed to the planting plans, referred to plant type and number, lot and block location. "A2 1/NW cor./W of 1," for example, indicated one *Acer* 'Wieri' (silver maple) to be planted in the northwest corner west of Block 1. A Mr. French was instructed to begin laying out the grounds, to start a nursery in the cemetery's southwest corner, and to purchase plants and trees by the hundreds or thousands. Such "small stock to draw from . . . will grow into *value*," wrote Sid, and after one or more years, could be moved to their permanent locations.[30]

As a modern cemetery, the intended result at Grandview was to have less marble and stone and more nature—unbroken by fencing, trellises, and plantings by lot owners. Its booklet of regulations specified monument size, number, and placement (in the center of the lot) and that trees and shrubs be planted "in accordance with the general plan for the ornamentation of the grounds by the superintendent or cemetery employees only." Trustees, represented by the superintendent, retained the right to "exclude or remove" any headstone, monument, tree, or plant that was considered "injurious to the general appearance."[31] Despite regulations, lot owners requested exceptions. One local church, having purchased an entire section, questioned the central plantings proposed for it. They desired instead a large cross on the site's elevated mound. Sid's response—"best to stick to the plans"—pointed out that his arrangement provided a necessary (and naturalistic) backdrop and screen; "remove it and you will eventually have a stoneyard in full view."[32] The modern approach of a single monument per plot, with gravestones flush to the ground, was also challenged by several families. Writing to Sid, vice president of the association W. H. Mullins noted that, although progress was being made at Grandview, he feared there might one day be "a village of vaults" on the hill.[33]

The work at Grandview was complete by 1902. The final bill submitted by Sid on February 11, 1902, was for 370 hours (at sixty cents per hour) plus two visits to Salem at the rate of $10 per day. That, including plant lists and colored plans, came to $242. Sid's first independent project had been a success and, just as important, it appears that he, association vice president Mullins, and secretary Vernon became friends. Letters between them reveal a mutual respect, shared sense of humor, and genuine concern for one another. They joke with each other (there is a reference to "sister Hare" who dared leave Ohio's "lone dreary winter"); Mullins sends thanks for the gift of a rubber stamp embossed with a hare; Vernon sends condolences on the death on Sid's "dear" brother, Will.[34]

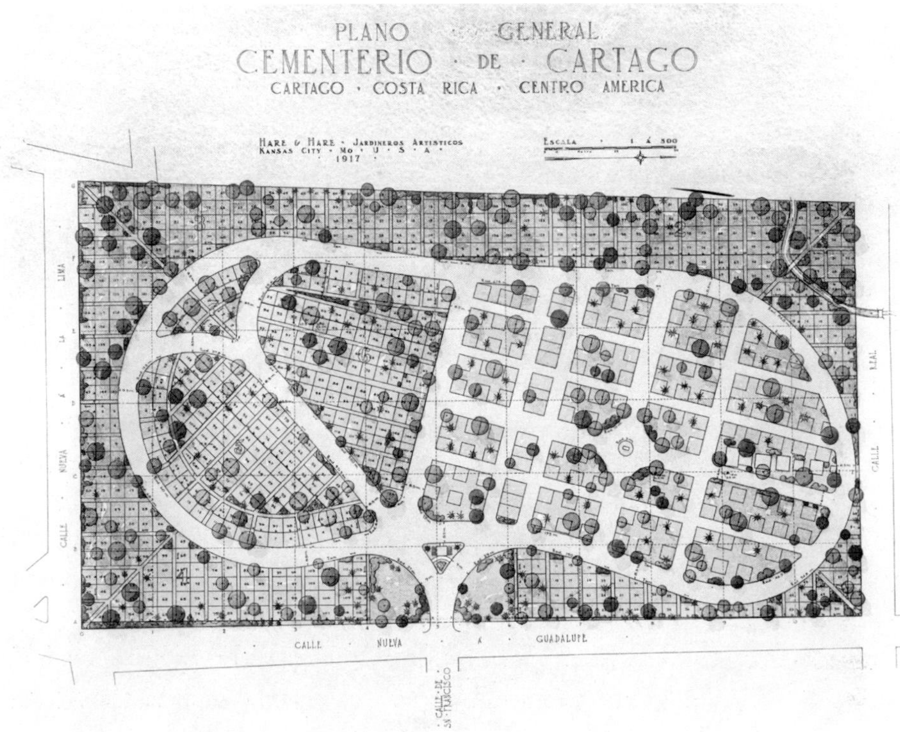

Cartago Cemetery, Cartago, Costa Rica, plan by "Hare & Hare, Jardineros Artisticos, Kansas City, MO, U.S.A.," 1917. SHSMO-KC.

Nine years later, with the purchase of the thirty-acre McMillian Tract including "all that beautiful ravine running through it," there was an expansion and filling in of the grounds. Sid's first instruction was to clean up and remove straggly undergrowth but to leave clumps of native shrubs. A new lake, rimmed with golden willow and yellow birch, was proposed, as was a new pergola, abloom in three seasons, draped with Chinese wisteria, the double pink rose 'Dorothy Perkins,' and fall-blooming *Clematis paniculata.* Dozens of purple and white common and Persian lilacs lined the drive. Last, Sid instructed, "put a moon vine on the shelter."[35]

In total, Sid Hare and his firm designed (or added substantial grounds to) fifty-four cemeteries in the United States and one in Cartago, Costa Rica. There, at 4,930 feet above sea level, they reshaped the south slope of an earthquake-wrecked volcano, and its demolished catacombs and mausoleums, into a modern cemetery planted with palms, bamboo, and eucalyptus.[36] It was a tropical version of what Sid thought the best cemetery should be: a "botanical garden, bird sanctuary and arboretum."

Herbert Hare as a toddler, c. 1890. JCHS.

THREE

The Founding of the Firm

Early in his childhood Sidney Herbert Hare and his family lived on East 13th Street in a house shared with his grandparents, Christopher and Isadora. Sidney H. (the name he would go by during his youth) told an interviewer that he had been brought up on botany, landscape, and solitude.[1] In the backyard his father, Sid, taught him about the plants he cultivated "under glass." This early education also included lessons about the fossils in his father's collection such as the lilylike crinoids (their name derived from the Greek word for the flower) and ferns preserved in stone. Sidney H. attended the newly opened Webster School, a public institution two miles west of their house, which educated students from neighborhoods as varied as Quality Hill, known as "Silk Stocking Ridge," and those near the pawnshop district. When Sidney H. was almost nine, the family moved beyond the city, to 69th and Troost, to be near his father's new job at Forest Hill Cemetery. Because of the distance from school, he and his sister stayed over at their grandfather Korfhage's house at 27th and Main Street when inclement weather threatened. The house lay near open country dotted with fruit trees and barns. There, and in the solitude of rolling wooded hills at the cemetery, Sidney H. first experienced the capacity of landscape to inspire and provide a sense of well-being.

As a youth Sidney H. excelled in art, and especially enjoyed sketching intricate and colorful images of horses. His father cultivated his talent in drawing (indeed the ability came from Sid), and his teachers often displayed his work. At the Manual Training High School he chose courses in freehand and mechanical drawing, portraiture, and math. Drawn toward commercial design as a calling, he was critical of uninspired packaging—cows on butter cartons and lackluster figures in newspaper ads—and he felt he could improve on the poor and stereotyped imagery used in advertising. The opportunity presented itself when his teacher referred him to Cusil Lechtman, a Russian-born businessman who had arrived in Kansas City by way of St. Joseph, Missouri, and owner of Lechtman Printing. An image of a hog for the label of a lard pail was the assignment and, according to Sidney H., he drew a "real living hog." A hard lesson in what he considered "the great world of bad commercial art" followed when criticism came back from the packinghouse, scribbled in bright red pencil: "Take your artist out and show him a hog." With time he decided that the bar was set fairly low and that commercial art was not for him.[2]

Sidney H. worked as a draftsman for the architectural firm of Shepard & Farrar in the summer of 1906. During the school year, afternoons were spent drafting at his father's office in their house on Campbell Street after he attended morning classes in freehand drawing, portraiture, and applied design. The last of these, which he thought would prove least valuable, transformed his thinking. He began to see that the fundamentals of art—line, texture, proportion, color—were the soul of the design, whether in a painting or a work of marble or metal. While at his desk sketching a flower, as his handling of line and mass gave form to the petals, he observed that the image was "like a landscape with hills and valleys."[3] With new eyes he reiterated his observation, "like a landscape." His father had long understood the link between nature and art, observing that parks are "an art equally as grand as the art of painting or sculpture."[4] Years later Sidney H. would remember the moment at his desk when he recognized the relationship between landscape and the fine arts for himself.

After 1900, Sid Hare considered himself experienced in cemetery planning and began to branch out, promoting himself as a designer of home grounds and parks. The move was logical, based on the aesthetic and practical relationship of cemetery and park planning. The progression was part of a process that dealt not only with design concerns but also with how this self-taught practitioner would define his work and communicate his qualifications. One senses Sid experimenting with the image he wished to project to clients and fellow professionals, both visually and in terms of his title. His early advertisements published monthly in *Park and Cem-*

Sidney Hare's decorative logo, c. 1900. SHSMO-KC.

Sidney Hare seated at his desk, c. 1920. SHSMO-KC.

etery, his business cards, and his letterhead were crisp and modern but became more decorative in later years. In his spare, graphic ad of 1904, he called himself a "civil and landscape engineer" with myriad abilities from landscape planting to park design. Three years later, using his charming hand-drawn image of a hare, he promoted himself as a landscape architect, noting his ability to preserve the natural features of a property. At once a visual and verbal play, his florid signature, turned over, becomes a hare reflected in a pool.[5] Implicit is Sid's personality and sense of humor, as well as his artistic abilities, which would be applied to the landscape.

The title Sid used on finished projects varied to suit the job at hand. Cemetery projects were often signed as "civil and landscape engineer"; residential work (referred to as "home grounds") was signed as "landscape gardener" or "planting designer"; and planning projects of various sizes identified him as "landscape architect." Sid Hare's alternating use of title in the 1890s and early 1900s illustrates the fluidity that existed in landscape study and practice, which was shaped by a layering and commingling of disciplines. Horticulturalists, geologists, artists, and authors all brought disparate training and points of view. One's education could just as likely come from a school of botany, grand tours of Europe, or, in Hare's case, engineering and work on the land. Although these landscape gardeners were experts, they were not yet specialists.[6]

As landscape architecture became a more specialized field in the early years of the twentieth century, professionals were increasingly engaged with new problems related to urban growth and planning. Many felt the need for a proper title to represent this new role and differentiate it from the past. Charles Eliot, a pioneer in regional planning and land conservancy, wrote of landscape gardening *and* landscape architecture. He did not view these hierarchically but rather as related activities, stating that landscape architecture "includes and covers" engineering, gardening, and forestry.[7] When the writer Mariana Griswold Van Rensselaer applied her aesthetic sensibilities to the discussion, she found landscape gardening to be the "older, equally dignified, and exacter term" for what she considered the fourth fine art after architecture, painting, and sculpture.[8] Frank A. Waugh, who established the undergraduate program in landscape gardening at Massachusetts Agricultural College in 1903, also preferred the older term, in part because it reflected his background in horticulture. To him the newer title (which he finally came to accept in the mid-1920s) seemed "ponderous" and implied "princely and magnificent undertakings."[9]

Waugh's comments underscore the fact that the discussion of proper terminology touched on larger issues of ideology and alliance. A growing contingent considered any reference to gardening old-fashioned and an indication of one's amateur status. Further, so this thinking went, it implied a delight in plants and decorative effects over comprehensive planning. Yet many continued to associate themselves with "landscape gardening" as a means to emphasize their background or distinguish their approach from that of the emerging profession. The sorting out of titles and roles continued through the first decades of the twentieth century.[10] For Hare & Hare, this professionalization is represented by the addition, in 1922, of "city planner" to their title. By 1930, the ASLA (and the public) had a clearer sense of the profession, and the title "landscape gardener" was virtually nonexistent among American practitioners.

During Sid's early career, he actively participated in the AACS and submitted work for its publication *Park and Cemetery*.[11] Although committed primarily to cemetery work, the magazine in its broader mission was devoted "to the advancement of art out-of-doors, in the improvement of public ground and home surroundings"—a stance that acknowledges the increasing overlap of cemetery planning and design of the larger landscape. Sid's first paper, presented at the organization's Cincinnati meeting in 1897, addressed the beauty of the modern cemetery—its vistas, well-kept lawns, and bright foliage—and how such landscapes could drive from the

"Snap Shots of the AACS Convention at St. Louis taken by Sid J. Hare," from *Park and Cemetery*, 1914.

mind all the gloom of death. He went on to acknowledge the link between cemeteries, parks, and planted boulevards and to note that nature, "the mother of all true art," can transform the viewer when properly designed.[12] Organizing the AACS annual meeting in Kansas City in 1908 (and again in 1911), Sid invited George Kessler, with whom he had worked in the city engineer's office, to present to the group. Kessler's talk, titled "The Cemetery," noted that these places of rest are "an essential portion of the park system of every city in the country."[13] Increasingly, Sid's presentations also addressed the landscape-at-large, dealing with topics such as the integration of rural qualities into urban spaces, the linking of viewsheds, and city street planting.

Besides organizing and presenting at annual meetings, Sid photographed the AACS field trips (always "snapping" pictures, according to a fellow member), thus acting as de facto historian for the group. One meeting report describes a focused Hare shielding himself from drizzling rain with a giant water lily pad as he takes a time-lapse photograph of the scene. These images appeared in *Park and Cemetery,* as did articles about his work, such as at Greenwood Cemetery in Knoxville (1904) and Elmwood in Birmingham, Alabama (1906). He was a regular respondent to the magazine's "Asked and Answered" column, in which, according to the magazine, questions were answered promptly by the ablest talent. Subjects were as varied as how to kill moles (Sid suggests a three-pronged tool), how to get rid of blackbirds, and proper methods of grading and road alignment.

Herbert Hare's ink on waxed linen sketch for the entrance of Elmwood Cemetery, 1912. SHSMO-KC.

Meanwhile, he and the journal's publisher, R. J. Haight, began to correspond, Sid writing to Haight about his pleasure in "transforming the unsightly into the beautiful" and on bringing out "harmony and beauty where discord and ugliness has held forth."[14] In addition the two exchanged letters about the tenets of the Christian Science church, of which the Hares were members.

Projects from these years of Sid's independent practice reveal his design process and the refining of his method and aesthetic. Continuing to use photography, as he had for the city when documenting newly paved sidewalks and brick streets, he began recording residential improvements in before-and-after photos. His photographs of a given site were both "memory aids" (to refer to in the planning process) and illustrations for potential clients and for projects he published in *Park and Cemetery*. For presentations he made lantern slides from his own negatives, hand-tinting them to create color images. Depending on the circumstances he used two types of cameras, a high-quality Premo 5 x 7 Reversible Back, manufactured by the Rochester Optical Company, which could accommodate both film and glass plates, and a Kodak Hawk-Eye No. 2 stereoscopic camera, which he found especially useful to document the date and continuation of bloom on shrubs and flowers. The Hawk-Eye was also helpful in documenting types of bark and contrasting forms as revealed by the winter landscape. A new idea he considered, in a letter to Haight, was whether using a halftone stereoscopic image in publications and presentations would reveal distances not perceived otherwise.

Watercolor plans, overlaid with sheer tracing cloth indicating the names of trees and shrubs, were provided to clients of several early projects to educate them in "the pleasure" of knowing plants. Working on linen and vellum, Sid built up varied shades of green with layers of water-

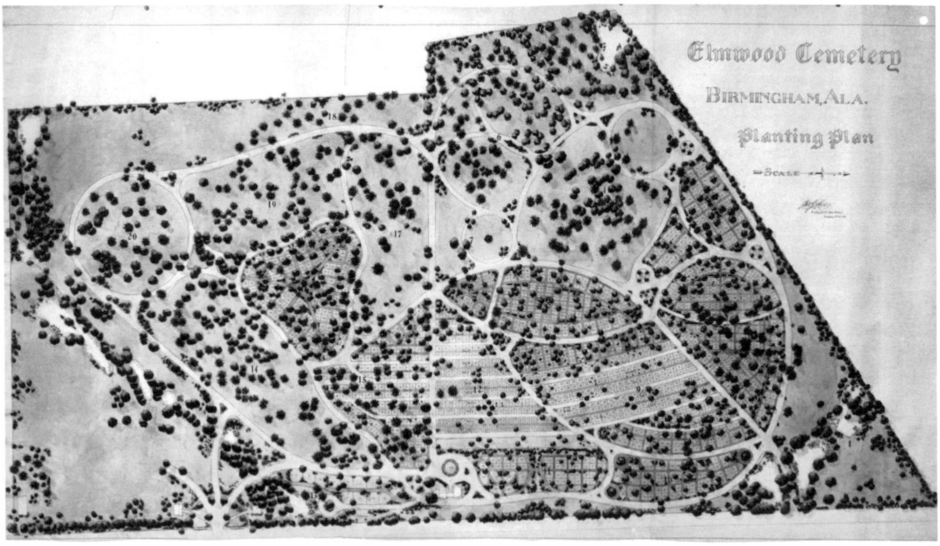

Planting plan for Elmwood Cemetery, Birmingham, AL, 1906. SHSMO-KC.

color, delineating plant names and directions, such as "Border the creek with *Spiraea vanhouttei* to the bridge," in black ink. Much of this work, particularly for cemeteries such as Grandview in Salem, Ohio, reveals a delight in the ornate visual aesthetic of the late nineteenth century. One senses Sid's reveling in a plan's presentation: an unfurled ribbon or cartouche bears the project name, spelled out in a bold script, and all is accompanied by his scrolled and florid signature, the rich presentation a match to the rich plantings he proposes. This decorative quality—like a fingerprint that identifies Sid's work—would, however, eventually disappear. His son would craft a more modern presentation, suited to twentieth-century sensibilities and the standards of the profession established after the founding of the firm.

Around 1900, clients began to approach Sid with ideas for large projects. Potential commissions included a forty-acre hotel ground in Kansas, with a ten-acre lake and sulfur and salt springs, meant to be "the Saratoga of the West," and a "model farm district" in Arkansas. By his own admission, he chose to turn down work, preferring to do fewer projects rather than slight any or delegate them to "inferior" subordinates. Besides part-time help from his son, no records indicate Sid had employees to assist him (the firm would grow to a staff of thirteen in 1943). Although he enjoyed rising early and working late into the night, it was still difficult to handle the dozens of commissions he landed between 1900 and 1910. Of these, projects in Missouri and in Texas set patterns that continued throughout the firm's career. A single commission in a given city would lead to the firm's returning to oversee an entire range of projects (in several cities, more than a hundred). The resulting network of personal connections not only brought commissions from returning clients but established Sid Hare and his son as links in a chain, part of a larger picture, carrying forward the work of predecessors and fellow professionals. Hare & Hare's work in Joplin, Missouri, in the southwest corner of the state, illustrates this pattern of obtaining commissions, as well as the firm's significant influence in shaping the development of numerous midwestern towns.

The mining of lead and zinc (called "blackjack") gave birth to Joplin and the neighboring towns of Webb City and Carthage. The two minerals—"joint kings of the district" according to investors—produced a $6 million output in 1897, and a few years later the region's zinc production was a full 83 percent of the U.S. total. The quarrying of limestone there was equally important, and running through the beds of stone were veins of marble—a pearly grey that sparkles white in the sun. This "Carthage marble" was used in buildings across the country, from the county courthouse and state capitol to New York City's Guaranty Trust Building. After 1890, the area's population boomed, and Joplin nearly tripled from under ten thousand to over twenty-six thousand citizens. Mining brought not only cash to the territory but, according to Sid, "a demand for good things."[15] By 1900, growth and increased wealth prompted an interest in civic improvements that ranged from libraries and schools to parks and a YMCA. Affluent citizens built residences with grounds in need of planting and funded new cemeteries, worthy of their social standing, where they would be laid to rest.

Cunningham Park (1907) was Joplin's first public park and the first of Sid's projects there. The seven acres of ground along Maiden Lane, donated by the city's mayor in 1897, came with stands of mature oak and native trees. The linen and vellum planting plans, which incorporate Sid's numerical and alphabetical coding system to indicate plant type and location, illustrate what would become his signature combination of perennials planted with attention to color, time of bloom, and habit. The plan addressed both active and contemplative forms of recreation, proposing both a tennis court and circuit walks for strolling along the park's main greensward. In the northwest corner it included a pond rimmed with cattails, willows, and clumping bamboo, and a chain of fountains and circular beds, planted in rings of bold contrasting colors, provided a formal effect. Soon the park became one of the city's favorite and most used green spaces.

Mineral Park followed in 1909, and Sid's proposal again included space and facilities for active recreation—a wading pool, sand court, an "outdoor gymnasium," croquet or tennis lawn, seesaws and swings. The perimeter was defined by banks of Persian lilacs, silverberry (*Elaeagnus angustifolia*), mock orange, and pea shrub (*Caragana arborescens*). One entrance was flanked by ginkgo trees (sheared into pyramidal forms!) which blazed brilliant yellow in autumn. A playful use of color served as ornament: the creek meandering through was edged in spiraea and backed by red barberry; walks were anchored by clumps of pink and white honeysuckle (*Lonicera tatarica*), widely used before its rapacious nature was known, and hedges of

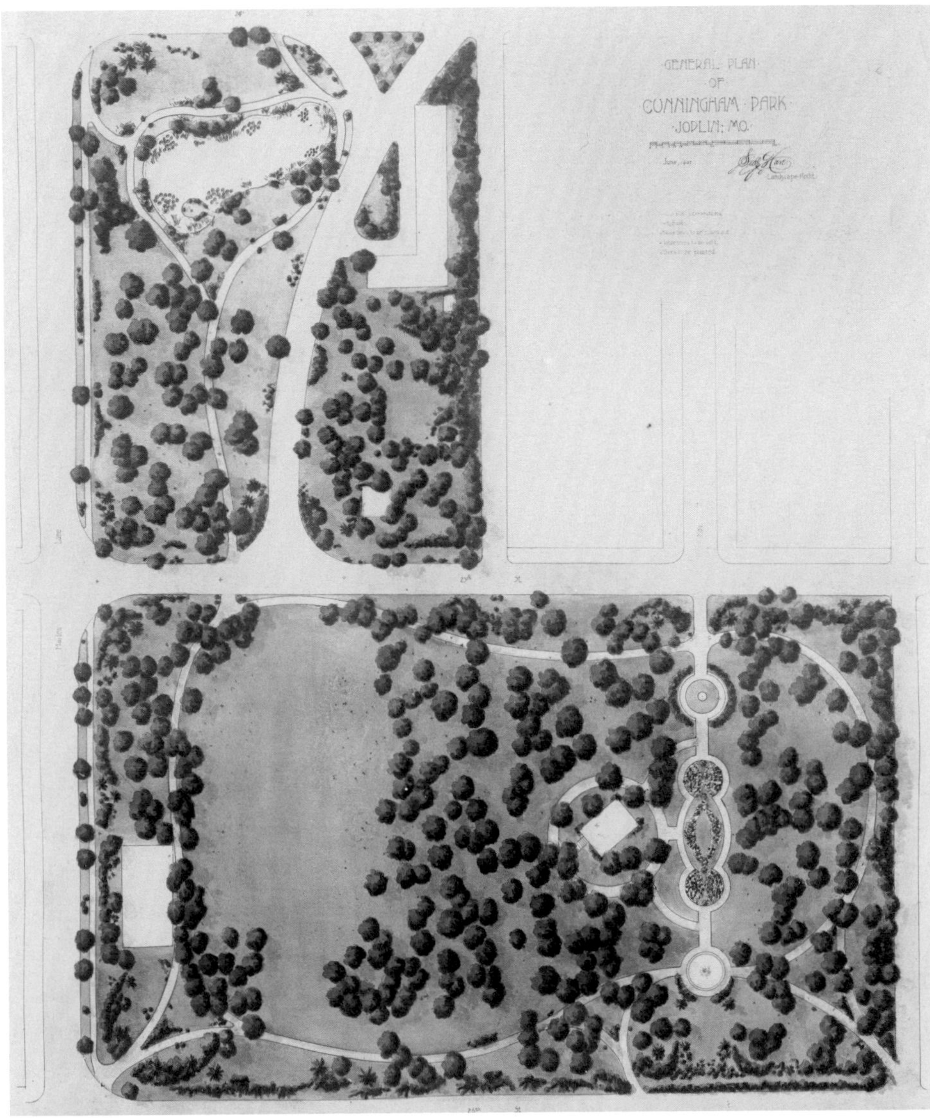

Sidney Hare, "General Plan of Cunningham Park, Joplin, MO," 1907. SHSMO-KC.

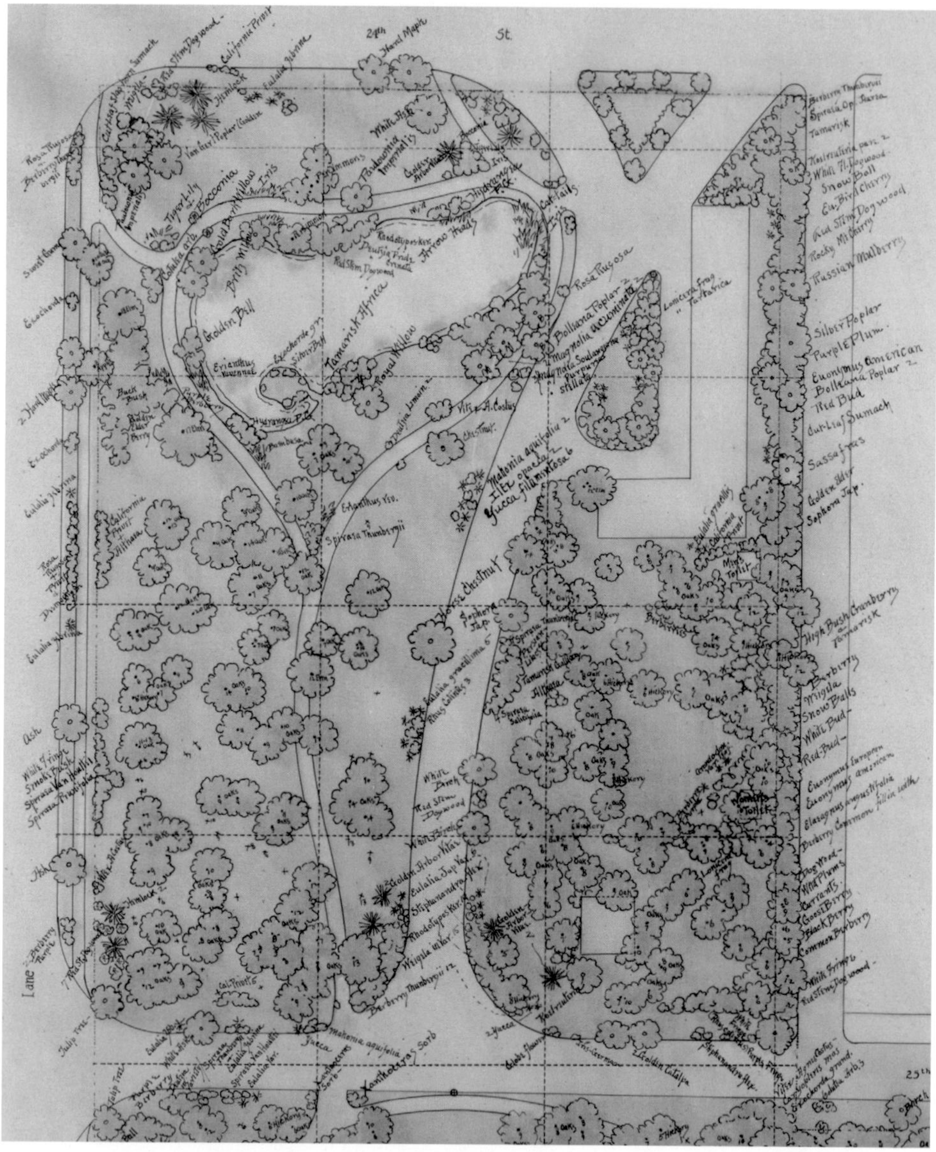

The Cunningham Park planting plan with names and locations of each new tree, shrub, and perennial, as well as trees to be retained or removed, 1907. SHSMO-KC.

alternating green and purple barberry were planted to define spaces. The same year he drew plans for Schifferdecker Park, which was also called "Electric Park" for its Moorish pavilions ablaze at night with thousands of incandescent bulbs. It grew from its original 40 acres to 160, to include the "Dazy Dazer" roller coaster, a zoo, and the city's first public swimming pool. These improvements were meant to fit into the larger park and boulevard system the firm would draft for Joplin in 1913. The thorough report, illustrated with eighteen pages of stereoviews taken by Sid, addressed the city's positive and negative aspects (weighing its wealth of trees and natural scenery against its mining district and the "unfortunate" location of the railroad tracks). The outer parks it proposed were likened to a "People's Country Club."[16]

During these years Sid implemented multiple home grounds and neighborhoods in Joplin, Carthage, and Webb City. He also designed Park Cemetery, in Carthage (1907), and Mount Hope Cemetery), between Joplin and Webb City (1908, both incorporating the circuit drives that skirt swards of green and corner entrances flanked by gates. They were then planted with Sid's signature choice of trees which included oaks, maples, and evergreens. He supplied more than forty pages of plans to guide planting at Park Cemetery, and he suggested a sundial, seats for rest, and entrance gates ornamented with acanthus-leaf carving "or the like." Mount Hope, which began as a "tumble down, uncared for farm with briars and weed patches," was given a Lily Lake and Bog Garden (aquatics were to be ordered from Dreer Nursery of Philadelphia).[17] Sid proposed drifts of crocus across the lawn for spring color and softened a low spot with clumps of snowball bushes, red- and whitebud trees, and dogwoods. Willows—with yellow, brown, and red bark—were planted to contrast with colors in the

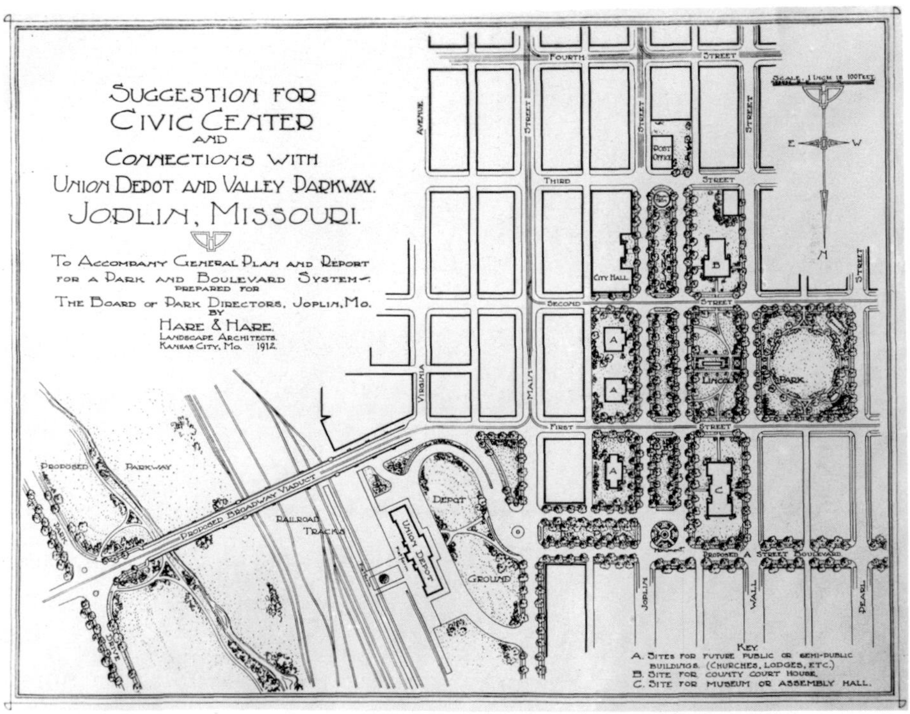

Hare & Hare's Civic Center, a component in the comprehensive planning report prepared for Joplin, 1912. SHSMO-KC.

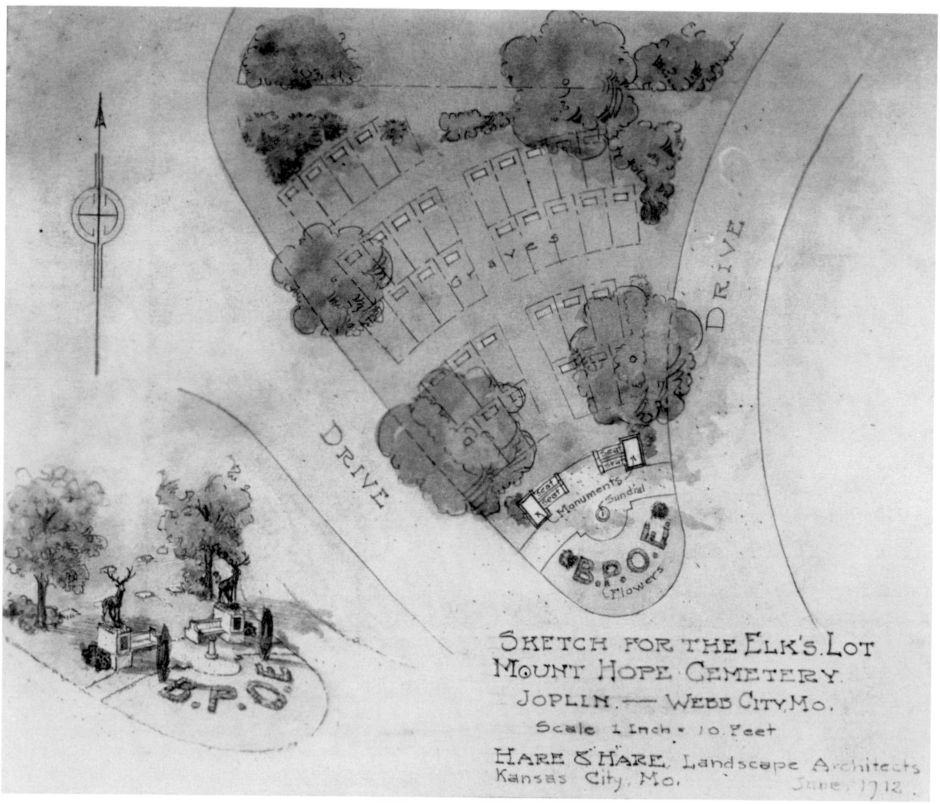

Proposals for pergola-flanked chapel and section dedicated to a fraternal order, Mount Hope Cemetery, near Joplin, 1912. SHSMO-KC.

winter landscape. According to Sid, it would be "a pretty place to be buried in, [and] a desirable place to visit and study rare trees, shrubs and flowers while we live."[18]

Of the two cemeteries, the earliest section of Park Cemetery hews closest to the modern cemetery as a type, with a single monument per plot and footstones and lot markers flush to the ground. Mount Hope yielded to popular taste, allowing a number of monumental Art Deco, Egyptian, and Greek Revival mausoleums on its sweep of rolling ground. These were planted according to modern dictates, with a frame of shrubs and small trees and lawn to the front to retain artistic settings.[19] Sid backed the Rogers mausoleum with "native woodland" and placed banks of hydrangea, weigela, and lilacs in the foreground. Mount Hope became the eternal resting places of the local elite including the Schifferdeckers, the Nobels, and the Orrs.

The horticulturalist responsible for implementing the Mount Hope planting plans was a local nurseryman, Edward Teas, born in Carthage. His father, John C. Teas, had run a well-known nursery business there since 1868. He was especially known for the Teas weeping mulberry (*Morus alba* 'Pendula'), a chance seedling of Russian mulberry stock grafted to create an ornamental form. (Liberty Hyde Bailey's *Cyclopedia* cited Teas's contribution and described the tree as one of the most popular small weeping lawn trees in the country.) Following in his father's footsteps, Edward opened a nursery with greenhouses in Joplin, ultimately becoming known for hybridizing roses and orange trees. Sid's work with Teas at Mount Hope coincided with another of his projects just under way in Texas, west of Houston between Buffalo and Brays Bayous. This was a garden suburb to be named "Bellaire," for its Gulf breezes and ideal environment, and just to its west, a "white city," with library, school, theater, city hall, and game grounds, all ordered on principles of the City Beautiful. Having built a close working relationship with Teas, Sid brought him in as a "man on the ground" to oversee the extensive plantings. For two years Teas traveled back and forth, ultimately pulling up stakes in Joplin and relocating to Houston.

Bellaire was conceived and financed by William Wright Baldwin, president of the St. Louis, Keokuk & Northwestern and the Chicago, Burlington & Kansas City railways and of the South End Land Company. Baldwin had recently purchased the 9,449-acre ranch of William Marsh Rice, benefactor of Rice University. Capitalizing on the opportunities and growth associated with Texas oil, Baldwin wanted to create a suburban resident farm district, named Westmoreland Farms, which included a town to serve as an agricultural trading center. Baldwin hired Sid to draft a proposal for three thousand of his acres. The 1908 plan divided the parcel into truck farms with approximately three hundred acres in the center reserved for the town of Bellaire. Although the development would be linked with Houston's Main Street via streetcar, six miles of prairie served as a buffer from the city. A 16,500-foot parkway "just steps away" from one's doorway would provide, according to Sid, a place where "the travel of teams and the splash of mud would not mar the pleasure" of walking. For purchase in the town were one- to five-acre lots, with rich earth, good drinking water, and room for gardens. Promotional brochures described "homes of contentment" on spacious lots, with land to raise cows and chickens (which provided fresh eggs to "the delight of the housewife"), and noted that pecans and figs did especially well in the black soil.[20] Sid called its artesian water "as fine as you [will] ever drink."[21]

Baldwin lived in Burlington, Iowa, and though he made trips to the site, he handled much of the venture from afar. Sid admitted the difficulty of his client's working "at arm's length," and the push-and-pull between Baldwin's interest in Bellaire as an investment—"making the dollars last"—and Sid's in achieving proper results is evident in their communications. Rushing things was not Sid's way. When Baldwin pushed the project, insisting that the plan be done "next Wednesday," Sid lamented to nurseryman Teas, "I believe he is not appreciative of landscape art or what it means to prepare a plan that will result in the 'best' and have continuation of bloom, harmony of color, contrasts in foliage and something attractive for every day in the year."[22]

Moreover, Baldwin decided to "rearrange" Sid's plan for Bellaire—to plat its lots in a rigid grid rather than fit them to the land and its conditions, a dramatic change prompting a response that outlined, in no uncertain terms, every point Sid found objectionable. In a lengthy letter he explained that the plan was outdated, that it spoke not to the future but to the "dead past," that the changes indicated a lack of taste and good judgment, and that its organization and spatial planning suggested the rankest ignorance of true art.[23] Nevertheless, the project's civil engineer, Frank Dormant, platted the land into a grid set to points of the compass. Ostensibly the change was to provide better drainage for excessive rainfall, but certainly it resulted in a greater number of salable lots. There was also disagreement between the two about street names, drawing the comment from Sid, "I had planned to name the streets for *trees that grow in Texas*."[24] Having registered his various objections, Sid acquiesced, and all came together, from surveying to planting, in a mere five months.

Sid's planting plan tempered the angles of the grid with grouped trees and shrubs, giving a parklike effect on the prairie. With proper planting, he envisioned sunshine and shade, vistas and screens, nooks and corners, light and air, all necessities for a modern southern city. The main axis was the Paseo (now Bellaire Boulevard), a 250-foot-wide boulevard connecting with Main Street which was to be shaded with willow oak, enlivened with subtropical beds of croton, tamarix, and aralia (*Fatsia*), and edged with a privet hedge backed by cannas massed in single colors.[25] Hedges of yucca and of rugosa rose were interwoven with groupings of shrubs. At right angles was Floral Way, a pedestrian green space anchored by a small lake with planted walks on all sides designed to serve as the heart of the community.

Edward Teas leaned on Sid to include many oaks and sycamores in the plan (noting that he would retain the native willows). On fifteen acres Baldwin had given Teas for his nursery, he raised plants suited to the South: palms, crape myrtle, grasses, and cape jessamine (*Gardenia jasminoides*). Following Baldwin's instructions, he planted five acres fronting the main boulevard with rose gardens. Baldwin also insisted on a brilliant and alluring show of color and growth along the boulevards of Bellaire to

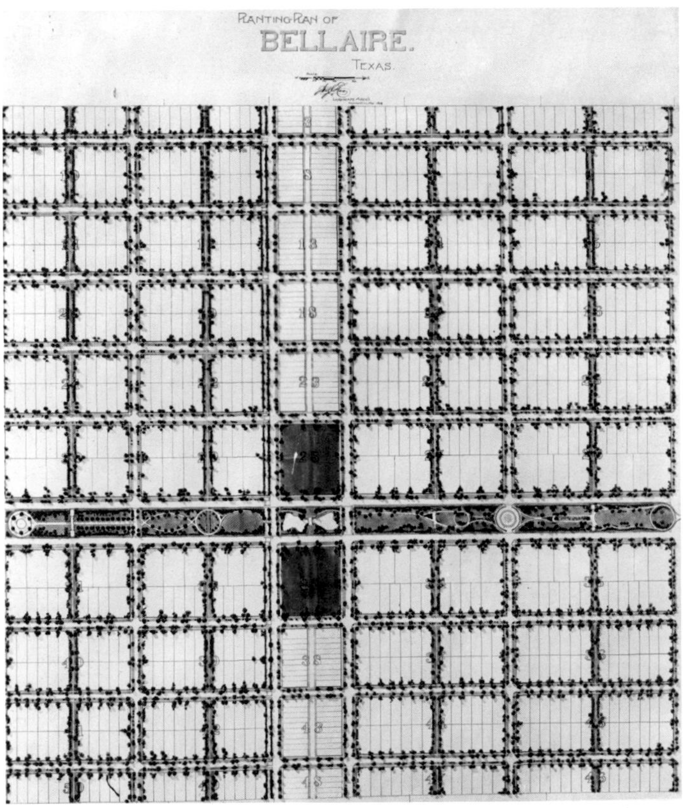

Sidney Hare's 1908 planting plan for Bellaire. SHSMO-KC.

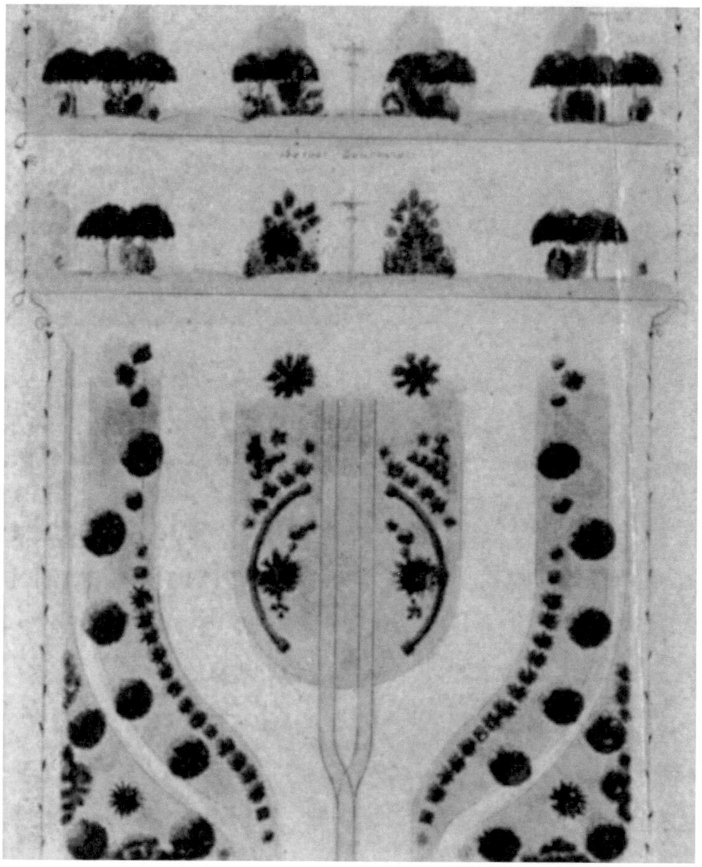

Hare's stylized drawing of Bellaire's entrance, 1908. SHSMO-KC.

Edward Teas's crew transplanting a pittosporum shrub in Bellaire, c. 1913. Woodson Research Center, Fondren Library, Rice University.

greet visitors and prospective buyers. He built model farms at each side of the entrance, and instructed Teas to plant them and the seventy-five adjacent acres in strawberries, onions, and cow peas to suggest the land's abundance.

Working with Sid at Bellaire was advantageous for the nurseryman from Missouri. Teas and his family settled permanently in Westmoreland Farms. He built greenhouses where he raised thousands of trees, shrubs, vines, and roses. Teas's specialty remained the beautification of home grounds, and his ads and handbills, illustrated with charming drawings and photographs of houses snug with plantings, included the catchphrase "It's Not a Home Until It's Planted."[26] Sid and Teas's partnership is representative of the links and connections that recur with regularity throughout the history of the Hare firm. Sid's work at Bellaire forecasts the firm's future community-building effort a decade later, when it would return to Texas to virtually remake Houston and Fort Worth.

Out of school, barely eighteen, and working full-time for his father, Sidney H. applied his increasingly discerning eye to commissions that came through the office. Rather than using plans to judge a project, he chose instead to walk the site, realizing that "on the ground" and "on paper" were two very different experiences. He noticed details such as walks lacking "grace," acceptable on a plan but visually clumsy when installed. And he recognized that good design was achieved both over the drafting board and in the field, not by one or the other. With youthful confidence, the younger Hare began to pose alternatives to his father's design decisions, as he did at the start of the project for Matt A. Foster, a book dealer who owned considerable real estate in downtown Kansas City. The property on Armour Boulevard was on one of the many wide shady boulevards proposed in the park and boulevard plan. The finest residences would be built along these axial drives flanked by formal rows of elms, maples, and lindens, and Foster's was one of these.

The 1908 plan called for transplanting maple trees to provide shade and quickly improve the place. Sid coaxed Boston ivy and clematis across the facade, softened the grounds with clusters of quince, magnolia, and dogwood, and hedged the east periphery with purple barberry (*Berberis*). The mix of plants—snowberry bushes, yucca, and a single Teas weeping mulberry—was both charming and bold, and likely spoke to the personality of the owner. Garden beds included red cannas, caladium, and dusty miller for summer; in spring, a rock garden of ferns, lilies, and columbine bloomed on the cool north side and crocus were sprinkled across the lawn. An old-fashioned garden of hollyhocks, larkspur, foxglove, and rhubarb lay next to the stable; the rear of the property was enclosed by a screen of mock orange, lilacs, and white fringe trees (*Chionanthus virginicus*). In the margin of the plan Sid included the recipe and instructions for fertilizing the lawn.

The plant list for the Foster property must have met with the younger Hare's approval, but the placement and curvature of the front walk sparked a debate between father and son. Sidney H. insisted that a spiral reverse curve would be more graceful than what had been proposed.[27] Though he backed up his observation by explaining that he'd studied the subject, he felt a nagging uncertainty about how to prove his point. Years later he remembered that moment as a turning point: what he had wanted then was to further his education under "advanced thinkers" of the newly formed field of landscape architecture.[28] Sid acknowledged the opportunity that such an education could bring and even considered relocating his family to give his children educational advantages. Writing to his friend R. J. Haight, he inquired about any positions open near Boston, New York, or Washington to which he might apply. Ultimately, the family remained in Kansas City, but the following year, when Sid attended the August AACS meeting in Providence and Newport, he was accompanied by his wife, daughter, and son. One of their stops was Pine Grove Cemetery in Lynn, Massachusetts, where they placed a blossom on the grave of the former superintendent, their friend William Stone. In Sid's words, "Brother" Stone was now doing the business of eternity. Their next stop was Boston, likely with a visit to Cambridge and Harvard University.

The landscape architecture program at Harvard officially began in 1899, the same year the ASLA was founded. University president Charles W. Eliot was an ardent advocate who considered landscape a fine art with redeeming social value. He believed that professionals could improve the environment and increase mankind's appreciation for its mountains, watercourses, and the "autumn tints of nature."[29] Instruction, according to Eliot, should balance the practical and the technical with "art for art's sake." Nathaniel Shaler, professor of geology and dean of Harvard's Lawrence Scientific School, lectured on the earth sciences, linking the vast and the minute while instructing his students in the exercise of truly *seeing* the landscape. Other colleagues lectured on the relationship of landscape to botany, the fine arts, and horticulture.

From his Harvard education, Eliot's son Charles gained a view of landscape that addressed turn-of-the-century concerns such as the principles of the City Beautiful movement and environmental conservation. His awareness of the power and beauty of landscape, and the need for stewardship, led to the founding of The Trustees of Public Reservations. He saw landscape not as a patchwork of discrete spaces but holistically. His approach to planning was equally comprehensive and his method systematic. In articulate essays the young Eliot spoke of "fitness," preservation of the rough and wild, and the need for special study in order to solve landscape problems. He was envisioned as the ideal candidate to head Harvard's program, but with his untimely death in March 1897, Frederick Law Olmsted Jr., although busy as a partner in the firm begun by his father, accepted the job of shaping the scope and methodology of this first degree program in *arte topiaria,* or landscape architecture.[30]

Twenty-year-old Sidney H. was accepted as a special student in Harvard's newly formed master's degree program in 1908 based on his proficiency in drafting and drawing and his familiarity with plants. He lived at 63 Gorham Street, a mile walk down Oxford Street from Robinson Hall, where architecture and landscape studies were housed in the recently completed Beaux-Arts building designed by McKim, Mead & White. The year he arrived, recent changes in the department included Olmsted Jr.'s return to private practice—though he came back regularly to lecture—and the appointment of Harvard-educated James Sturgis Pray, who had served as Olmsted's teaching assistant in prior years, as chair. Pray continued the pedagogical method and the curriculum—the teaching of landscape as a fine art—established by his predecessor, and in 1909 added the program's first course on city planning, which would provide Sidney H. the ability to move from site-specific to large-scale projects.

Only a handful of students (all male) had preceded Sidney H. in Harvard's program. His fellow students included William Lyman Phillips, who would spend decades involved with Florida's native landscapes and ecosystems; Charles P. Punchard Jr., the National Park Service's first landscape architect (employed under the title of landscape engineer); Frederick Noble Evans, park superintendent in Sacramento, California, for twenty-six years; and Bremer Whidden Pond, who taught at Harvard for thirty-five years and helped pioneer the education of women landscape architects at the Cambridge School of Architecture and Landscape Architecture. Also enrolled at the time was Fletcher Steele, the iconoclast who would become a key figure in the transition from formal to modern landscape design who later shaped Mabel Choate's estate, Naumkeag, in the Berkshires.

Two years of coursework began for Sidney H. with the introductory "Principles of Landscape Architecture." The course was formulated by Olmsted Jr., who had lectured on subjects such as Italy's Villa Lante (a model that Sidney H. would draw on in the future) and the French chateau Vaux-le-Vicomte, of which he found the lack of ample shade and seclusion a shortcoming. The course was meant to ground students in garden history and aesthetics by indelibly fusing the two and to underscore the connection between landscape architecture, art, and civilization. By analyzing works of art, students honed critical thinking skills and methods of problem solving that could be applied to design. The course went on to balance fine art with broader themes of environmental history and cultural

One of Herbert Hare's Harvard projects, a system of parks and playgrounds linked by boulevards for Brockton, Massachusetts, June 1910. SHSMO-KC.

geography, ending with the study of parks and public spaces in the proximity of Boston.

The curriculum also included construction drawing (practice with grading plans, profiles, and drainage) and two sections on the art of design—Sidney H.'s strong suit—which built on the instruction he had received in high school. The courses were taught by Pray, with occasional instruction by Olmsted Jr. and teaching assistants Henry Vincent Hubbard, Frederick Evans, and Bremer Pond. In addition, four courses related to horticulture—the basics followed by a focus on plants and design—were led by Benjamin M. Watson (newly transferred from the Bussey Institution, which specialized in agricultural and horticultural instruction). Stu-

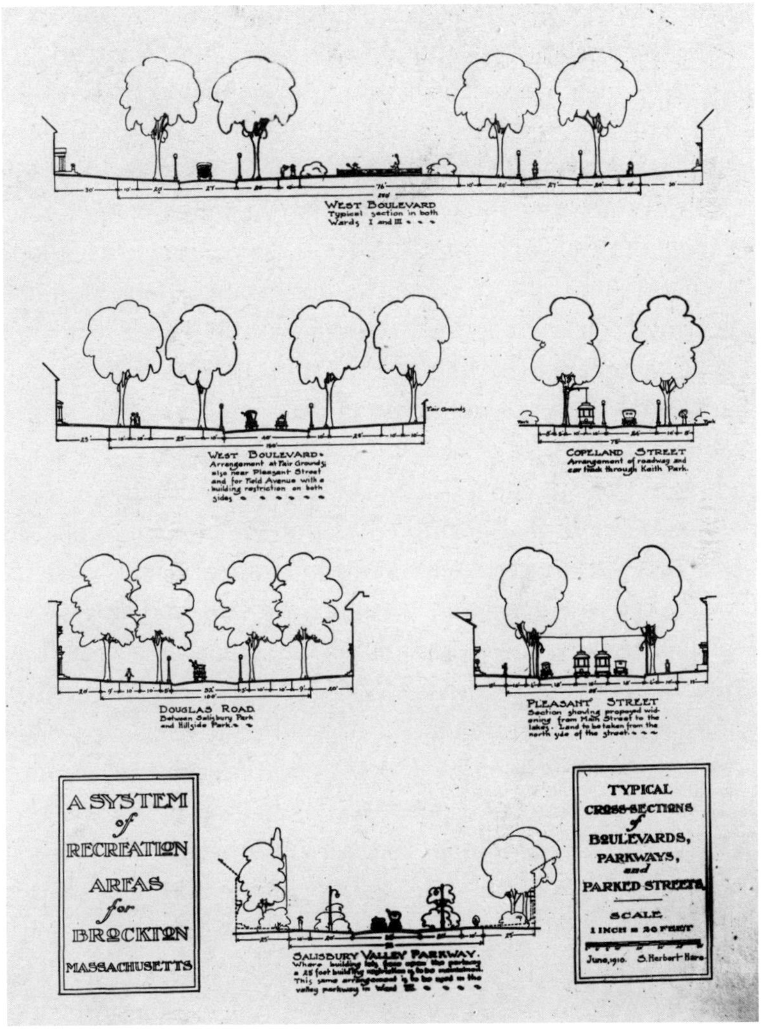

Boulevard, parkway, and street cross sections for Herbert's Brockton project, 1910. SHSMO-KC.

dents had access to hands-on experience at the school's Botanic Garden under head gardener Robert Cameron. Drafting and Pray's "Principles of City Planning," "illustrated by a critical study of examples," which included classes led by Olmsted, rounded out Sidney H.'s course load. He spent about fifty hours per week on his studies during his second year.[31]

Complementing these classes were field trips in and around Boston that allowed landscape students to sharpen their observations, with their boots on. Sidney H. participated in the Harvard practice of making studies of public squares—his include Chester Square in Boston and Monument Square in Charlestown—an exercise he continued throughout his career with studies of Honolulu's Thomas Square and the Place de l'Étoile in Paris from the 1940s and 1950s. Required readings provided a firm foundation in the liberal arts that ran the gamut of art and science. Classics included writings on British landscape practitioners William Kent and Lancelot "Capability" Brown, Charles Eliot's essay "What Would Be Fair Must First Be Fit," Pray's article "The Italian Garden," philosophy professor George Santayana's chapter "Form" from his book *The Sense of Beauty* (1896), and *A Theory of Pure Design* (1907) by Denman Ross, who taught painting in Robinson Hall and was an expert in color theory. The inclusion of Shaler's writings on nature and culture and a chapter from his book *Man and Earth* (1905) confirmed the ongoing link to the natural sciences.

Sidney H. completed the master's program in 1910.[32] He kept portions of his coursework and class notes throughout his life, which may indicate how he valued his Harvard education. Among his papers are copious plant lists including botanical names and varieties (apparently those used in horticulture courses taught by Benjamin Watson). He held on to planting plans prepared for his "Landscape Architecture 8" course, among them plans for Longfellow Park, a rose garden for Ernest Bowditch, and an estate at Fresh Pond (all in Cambridge). Pages from his city planning project for "Landscape Architecture 10," the capstone course of the program, record the twenty-two year old's observations on the elements of an effective city. He writes of traffic patterns, the siting of buildings (noting both vernacular examples such as cab stands and monumental ones such as market halls), and the nature of "useful" space and adornment. That he left a positive impression on his mentors is certain. Seven years after graduation he and James Sturgis Pray, who had guided much of his research, worked together planning cantonments (military housing) for Fort Riley, Kansas.[33] When Sidney H. applied for membership in the ASLA at the age of twenty-five, Olmsted Jr. described him as a "good man," commenting to the examining board that his work at Harvard had been "exceptionally favorable."[34]

The Gumbel Building, 801 Walnut Street, Kansas City, Hare & Hare's first downtown office. MVSC.

On June 17, Sid Hare was in Boston to pick up his son. They returned home to Kansas City and Sidney H. moved in with his parents and sister at 3224 Campbell Street. Years before, when the family had moved into the large frame house, his father described it as more modern and convenient than their previous homes, with room enough for an office where the two spent hours drawing and drafting. Whether the plan to establish the firm of Hare & Hare was conceived when Sidney H. left for Harvard is not known, but it was a certainty before he finished his course work. The previous March Sid had written to R. J. Haight about the large amount of work he was involved with and noted how glad he would be to have his son, "who will become a partner," back in Kansas City. That June they were associated in business under the name of Hare & Hare, and they proceeded to "divorce the office from the home," in Sid's words. The firm moved into a downtown office on Walnut Street, where it inhabited the top floor of the elegant Gumbel Building. In a way, the choice of location echoed the personalities of the two men. Designed by the local architect John McKecknie, the Gumbel was sheathed in richly ornamented terra-cotta that spoke to tradition but employed a new construction technique using reinforced concrete. It was the perfect blend of historic ornament and modern function.[35]

At the beginning of partnership, the division of labor in the office placed Sid, whose name and reputation was established, out in the field while his son held down the office, executing drawings and plans. Sidney H. jumped right in, returning calls for his father and advising clients on his behalf. By midsummer all communication referred to "we" and "us." The firm was at work on six cemeteries from Nebraska to Alabama. In Texas, Bellaire was under way, as was Mission Burial Park and the subdivision of Riverside Park in San Antonio. There were new types of commissions undertaken as well, such as the sunken water garden that transformed a blighted area of downtown Kansas City, Kansas. Increasingly, these were large projects involving a great amount of planning. The design of neighborhoods, with "resident parks," where "landscape, art and nature are combined to get the best result" were a part of this growth.[36]

Kansas City commissions continued, often coming from previous clients. A simple order of ferns (from the Edward Gillett Nursery in Southwick, Massachusetts) for Henry Corwin Flower, founder of Fidelity National Bank and Trust, led to a major project at Flower's new residence. Round Hill, in the Hyde Park neighborhood, was the architect Henry Hoit's "very radical remodeling" of an existing house with its back to the private street of Janssen Place just east. For Flower's four acres, the firm undertook a comprehensive rearrangement of the property to create a close relationship between house and grounds, thereby making "the latter more useful and livable."[37] Multiple terraces linked indoor and outdoor spaces and overlooked sloping lawn to the south and, to the east, the main garden: a 140-foot grass panel edged with perennials and shrubbery that terminated

The sunken garden at Waterway Park in Kansas City, c. 1912. *Park and Cemetery* (March 1913).

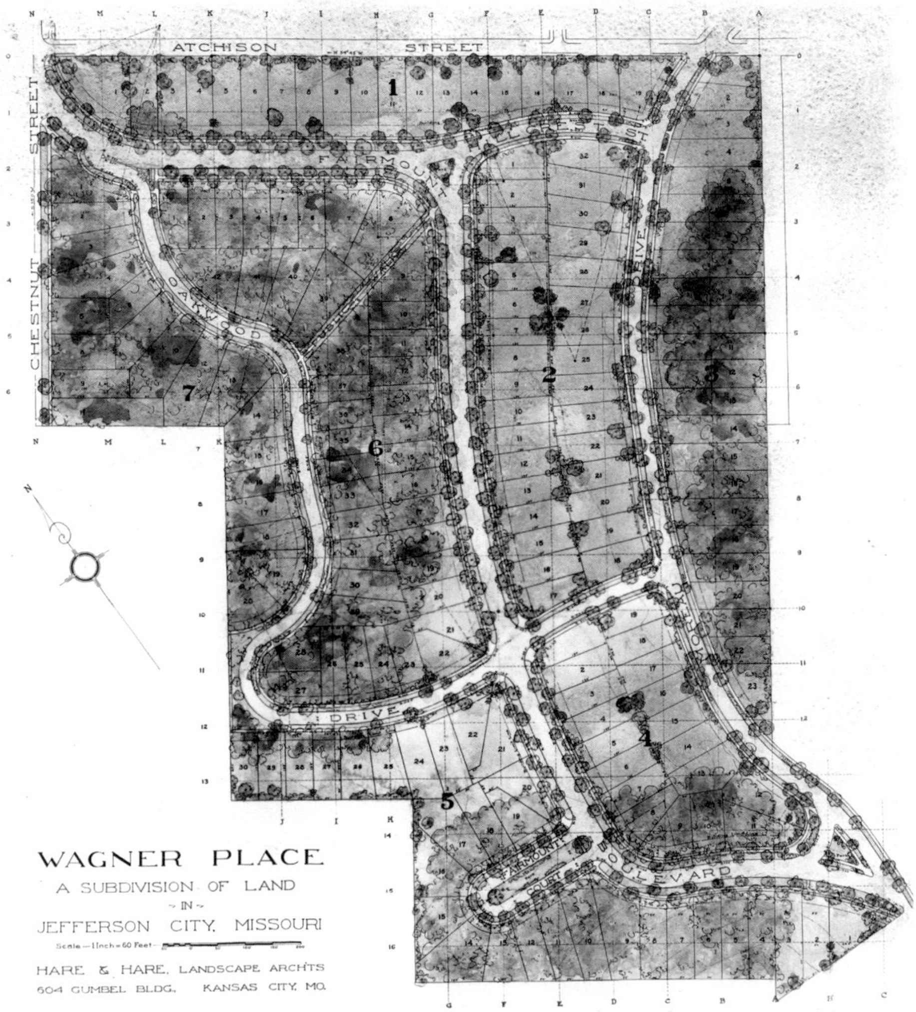

Wagner Place, a subdivision Sidney referred to as a "resident park," 1912. SHSMO-KC.

in a dense screen of Lombardy poplars. Beyond the main garden was a cutting garden with a brass sundial and to the rear of the house were vegetable gardens. Teams of gardeners spent days planting, eventually adding 1,697 perennials, 1,400 bulbs, 289 shrubs and evergreens, and 2 catalpa trees to complete the grounds. The owner was instructed to use the formula devised for Spring Grove Cemetery to control algae in the pond. The flower plans and presentation drawings, ink on linen, are some of the first evidence of Sidney H.'s hand, the mode of representation that would become the firm's trademark. Yet the view signed "S.H.H." is one of the last to indicate a specific delineator. With rare exceptions all future work would bear the name of Hare & Hare.[38]

Sid spent fifteen days in October and early November 1910 in Chestnut Hill, near Boston, assessing the estate grounds of Mary Baker Eddy.[39] Plans to improve the grounds had begun that summer in letters to Adam Dickey, a former resident of Kansas City who lived at the house and served as her secretary.[40] "The natural beauty of the place should not be greatly disturbed but rather improved upon," Sid wrote, best to reflect "the one who lives within."[41] The firm reorganized the service areas—stable, laundry yard, garage—in relation to the residence, and proposed a lily pond and summer house, with a view to open pasture with grazing cattle. Sid followed his son's advice and suggested contacting the able Boston civil engineer Frank E. Sherry to prepare the topographical map. Eddy's death on December 3 ended the project, but working relationships had been established. The following year the firm designed the grounds for Dickey's house near Nantasket Beach in Hull, Massachusetts, and, in 1917, those for his house in Cohasset. Also in 1917, church representatives chose Hare & Hare to design the grounds of the Chestnut Hill Benevolent Association. Twenty-five plans on vellum and linen and eight planting plans would guide the project.

In the fall of 1910, while Sid was in discussion with Mary Baker Eddy's representatives, a letter arrived from George A. Hill of Tacoma, Washington. Hill, the superintendent of the Tacoma park system and a former employee of the city cemetery, knew of Sid's work, in part, from his articles in *Park and Cemetery*.[42] His letter explained the need for a man of experience, capable of drafting a new master plan for Point Defiance Park, a tract of just under 640 acres jutting into the tidal waters of Puget Sound. The park offered views of Mount Rainier, the highest mountain in the Cascade Range, and the snow-capped Olympic Mountains. Its native madrone trees (*Arbutus menziesii*) and thousands of old-growth fir, cedar, and hemlock contrasted with willows and colonies of ferns hidden beneath a dense understory. On its north tip, more than a mile of beach met the ocean where thousands came to swim in the summer.[43] The superintendent's proposal prompted Sid's immediate reply. Writing to Hill, he assured that his expertise provided "the best service in all parts of the work" and that he would protect both the natural landscape and the pocketbooks of Tacoma citizens.[44]

According to the recently established Metropolitan Park District, 125 park acres had been developed in a haphazard manner—stripped to accommodate a jumble of buildings and services that included a zoo, natatorium, greenhouses, stables, superintendent's lodge, and picnic grounds. The park board's requirements were twofold. The new master plan must

View of Puget Sound from Point Defiance Park shoreline, postcard, c. 1906. Swanson Collection, Metro Parks Tacoma.

Point Defiance Park, postcard, c. 1910. Swanson Collection, Metro Parks Tacoma.

provide "an entirely new scheme" for the location of important features, and, most critically, it must preserve the natural wildness of the forest while increasing its accessibility for public use. "You have a rare opportunity," wrote Frederick Heath, the acting president of the park district.[45] Certainly Sid agreed; within two months the contract was signed.

The following March, Sid headed west, stopping in Denver, San Fran-

"Zoological Gardens, Point Defiance Park," postcard, c. 1910. Swanson Collection, Metro Parks Tacoma.

cisco, and Portland along the way. Once in Tacoma he spent two weeks working out of the Stanford White–designed Tacoma Hotel located on the city waterfront and meeting with Hill and Heath. Sid hiked the park, observing its landscape features—its shoreline, bluffs, and sandy soil—and recording them, in pencil and ink, on a large topographic map. On it he also noted numerous recommendations and caveats, among them where to clear brush to capitalize on the view of Puget Sound and where stands of madrone trees were to remain untouched. After documenting the site with photographs and measurements, he returned to Kansas City to work on the project.

Hare & Hare's illustrated preliminary report presented to Tacoma's Metropolitan Park District board in 1911 began by insisting on the prudent removal of underbrush and the avoidance of "ignorant clearing or denuding [of] the land." Strict rules and "zealous watching" would be needed to protect the park's choice native specimens, and the report appealed to the citizens of Tacoma, and their sense of civic duty, to become "guardians" of Point Defiance Park. By dividing the park into three zones (or "Functions and Natural Divisions"), the plan accommodated active sports and the zoo at the very southeast tip, leaving much of the remaining 525 acres as natural landscape. It promoted the increasing of "flower, fern, shrub, and tree" native to the Pacific Northwest, such as kalmia, rhododendron,

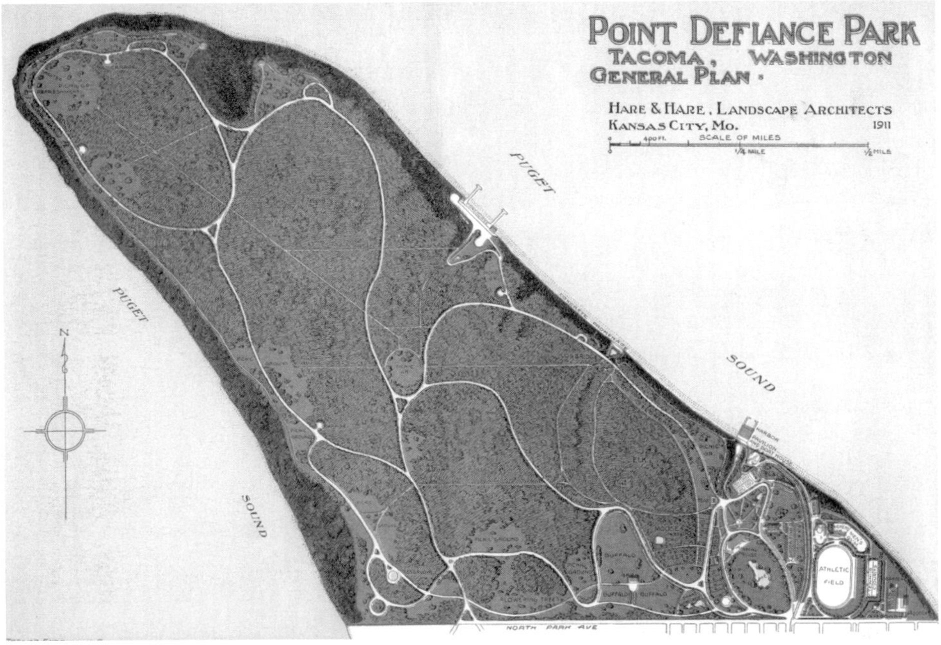

"Point Defiance Park, Tacoma, Washington, General Plan," 1911. Metro Parks Tacoma.

and trillium. Proposed were "vista walks" providing long views through the arching woods and a promenade following the long sweeping curves of the beach. Plantings for fifteen new picnic grounds included Oregon grape, red flowering currant, and pussy willows (with instructions to cut back old growth for larger catkins). One formal element, the Concourse, was a broad walk linking twin pavilions and lined with linden trees (*Tilia argentea*) pruned into broad flat heads, a device straight from European models that must be credited to Sidney H.[46]

Ornamental beds were limited to the street car station and the boulevard, the Hares noting that the indiscriminate placement of such formal arrangements not only was a waste of money but detracted from the restfulness of the landscape. By restricting decorative plantings to the entrances of main thoroughfares, they hoped to increase the sense of a gradual change from formal to informal. All architecture within the park—the car shelter, Concourse pavilions, shelters along the Promenade—was to be consistent. Designed in a "Japanesque" style inspired by the Kinkaku-ji Temple in Kyoto, and still a key feature in the park today, it would be executed by the local architectural firm of Heath & Twitchell. Electric lines were to be buried underground, and providing water for fire protection was considered an essential feature of the plan. To that end, the firm advised that it would be wise to prohibit smoking.

The street car station, still in use today as a community gathering place, c. 1915. Metro Parks Tacoma.

In the Point Defiance project one senses father and son working together, not only in terms of planning and design, but in the visual aspects of presentation. One particular plan reveals the hand of both: the building up of layers of green watercolor, rich and deep, that Sid mastered in his early cemetery plans, with graphic modern lettering executed in a bold shade of red, which is certainly the work of his son. The firm's report to the Metropolitan Park District combined their work as well. The report was bound in dark brown board, its cover incised with black lettering, and at the center Sidney H. placed a tiny watercolor view of the park overlaid with vellum. Inside, pages of Sid's stereoviews, slipped into cuts in the paper, illustrated the site, and narrative outlined the proposed plans. Once the park was completed, the firm photographed a view of the broad concave lawn just inside the Pearl Street entrance and its backdrop of "wild wood." Pleased with the results of the Hare plan, the park district used a drawing of this image as its letterhead for years to come.

The success of the Tacoma project coincided with Sid's acceptance as a member of the ASLA in November 1912. And with this first large-scale project the father-and-son team stepped into the arena of planning on a national level. Point Defiance Park was the beginning of their ongoing interest in park work, such as that implemented by the Civilian Conservation Corps during the Depression. Stewardship of park resources and the devising of plans to guide future development, first formulated for the Tacoma park, become ever more important themes in the firm's work.

At the entrance to Point Defiance Park, postcard, c. 1912. Swanson Collection, Metro Parks Tacoma.

It was at this juncture that Sid's son began to be known as Herbert rather than Sidney H., in part to avoid confusion, but more importantly as a means to define himself and his role within the firm. The two men were, in a sense, bookends. The father was self-taught and grounded in the nineteenth century, an amateur who had begun practice when cemetery and park design were nearly seamless processes, with an artistic sensibility from the same era and a penchant for native plants. Herbert was the Harvard-educated professional trained in city planning, with knowledge of European models, whose thinking and design aesthetic represent the twentieth century and the cusp of change. He recognized his father as a mentor as he, too, became an authority in the field. The two brought to their projects divergent abilities and backgrounds that reflected their individual strengths—a dynamic that strengthened their work as a partnership.

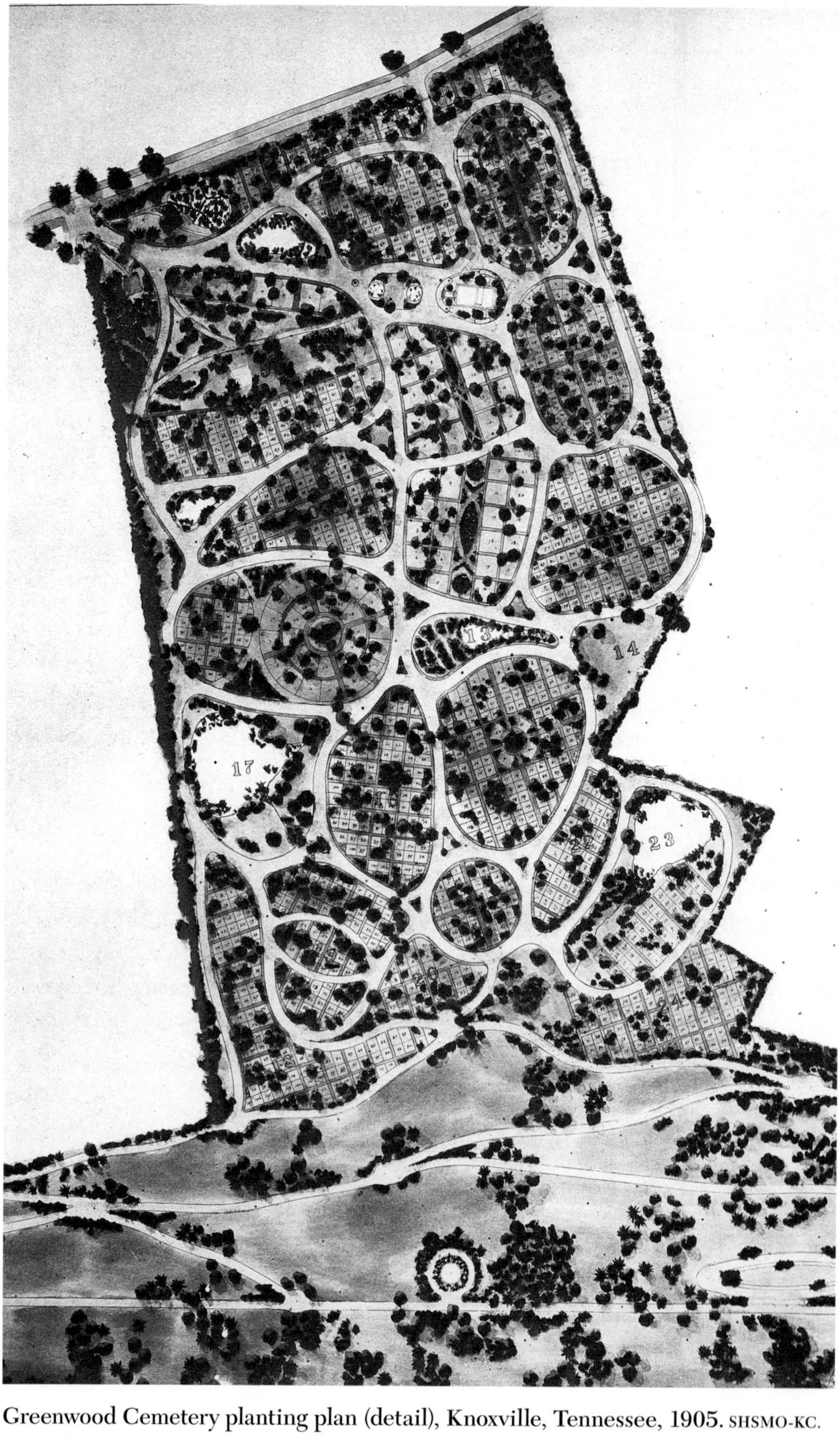

Greenwood Cemetery planting plan (detail), Knoxville, Tennessee, 1905. SHSMO-KC.

FOUR

Kansas City's Country Club District and the "New Industrial City of the Pacific Northwest"

"We are very busy," Sid wrote to his friend R. J. Haight in the spring of 1913, "working nights in an effort to [keep] up."[1] Despite their grueling schedule—Sid's habit was to work from five in the morning until eleven at night—some ongoing jobs had to be returned to as time allowed. One such project was Greenwood Cemetery in Knoxville, Tennessee, which had been under way for nearly a decade. It had begun in 1905 with a long train ride south, which seemed to stop at every bale of cotton, during which Sid vividly recorded the landscape and culture along the way. In his letter to "My Dear Ones at Home" he wrote of cypress swamps and bright red soil, of cattle grazing on cane and cornstalks. He passed magnolias, yucca, and a red-berried plant that reminded him of the Missouri native shrub "Wahoo" (*Euonymus atropurpureus*). Everywhere there was "cotton—cotton—cotton" planted in undulating rows to catch and hold the rainfall. He questioned why there were no orchards on such ideal ground, wrote of meadowlarks, and recorded (with emphasis) seeing crinoids, like those he collected, embedded in the rusty chert soil. In closing, Sid instructed his family to "*keep these notes.*"[2]

At Greenwood, Sid adhered to the principles of design he had followed since his tenure at Forest Hill Cemetery, aiming for harmony of color, continuation of bloom, and contrasts in foliage (and bark) that would provide interest every day of the year. For each section of the cemetery he proposed key features such as small lakes for goldfish and water lilies, but he also let the character of the site guide the plan. He designed an ornamental garden with beds reserved for "rare historic plants," likely the collection that had come from Edith (Mrs. Theodore) Roosevelt's White House garden.[3] He took into account vistas, water supply, and the best location for roads. All was arranged against a backdrop of mountains "outlined against the sky."[4] During Greenwood's evolution, Sid and R. N. Kesterson, the local dentist who had started the cemetery company, worked as a team and became friends. Sid dictated aesthetics and promoted the tenets of the modern cemetery, warning against "flocks of tomb-stones" or at least hiding them behind dense plantings so as not to mar the parklike effect.

As Greenwood developed, Herbert began cultivating new clients in Tulsa, Oklahoma, most of whom were involved in the petroleum industry and were building houses with grounds in need of improvement. The first of these Tulsa clients was Harry Ford Sinclair, founder of the oil company that bore his name, who wrote to Herbert in 1914. In his response to Sinclair's letter, Herbert mentioned "the local private places" they were designing—the suburban homes of people he suspected the businessman might know. More important, he went on to emphasize the firm's strengths: a combination of long experience and "the best eastern technical training."[5] He stressed their ability to work "intelligently" with Sinclair's architects to ensure the proper relationship of house and grounds. On January 10, five days after he had written to the Oklahoma oil man, Herbert arrived in Tulsa to assess the project.

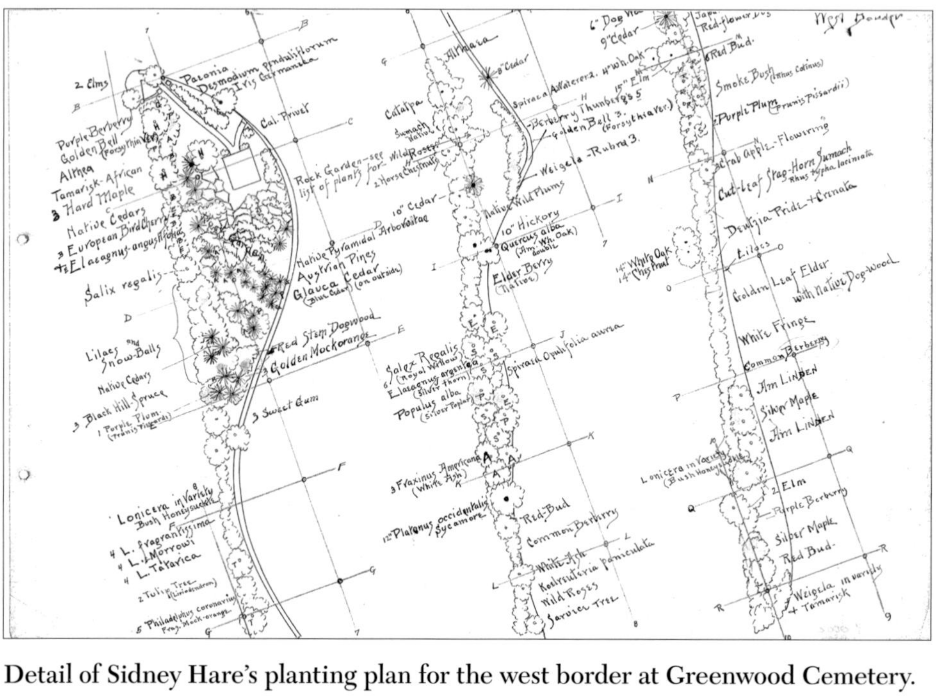

Detail of Sidney Hare's planting plan for the west border at Greenwood Cemetery.

One of the finest lots in Tulsa, graced by a giant post oak (*Quercus stellata*), overlooked the Arkansas River. Years earlier, the Locapoga clan of the Creek Indians had settled the area, starting anew in Indian Territory as a result of the Removal Act. They chose this spot for their "busk ground," their spiritual center and place to conduct business, blessing it by placing ashes from earlier council fires—brought from their ancestral home in Alabama—beneath the great oak. No longer used by the Creek community when oil was discovered near Tulsa, Sinclair purchased the property and had a house, designed by the Hoggson Brothers firm of New York City, constructed on the site.

Herbert's plan balanced the Sinclairs' request for livable grounds that

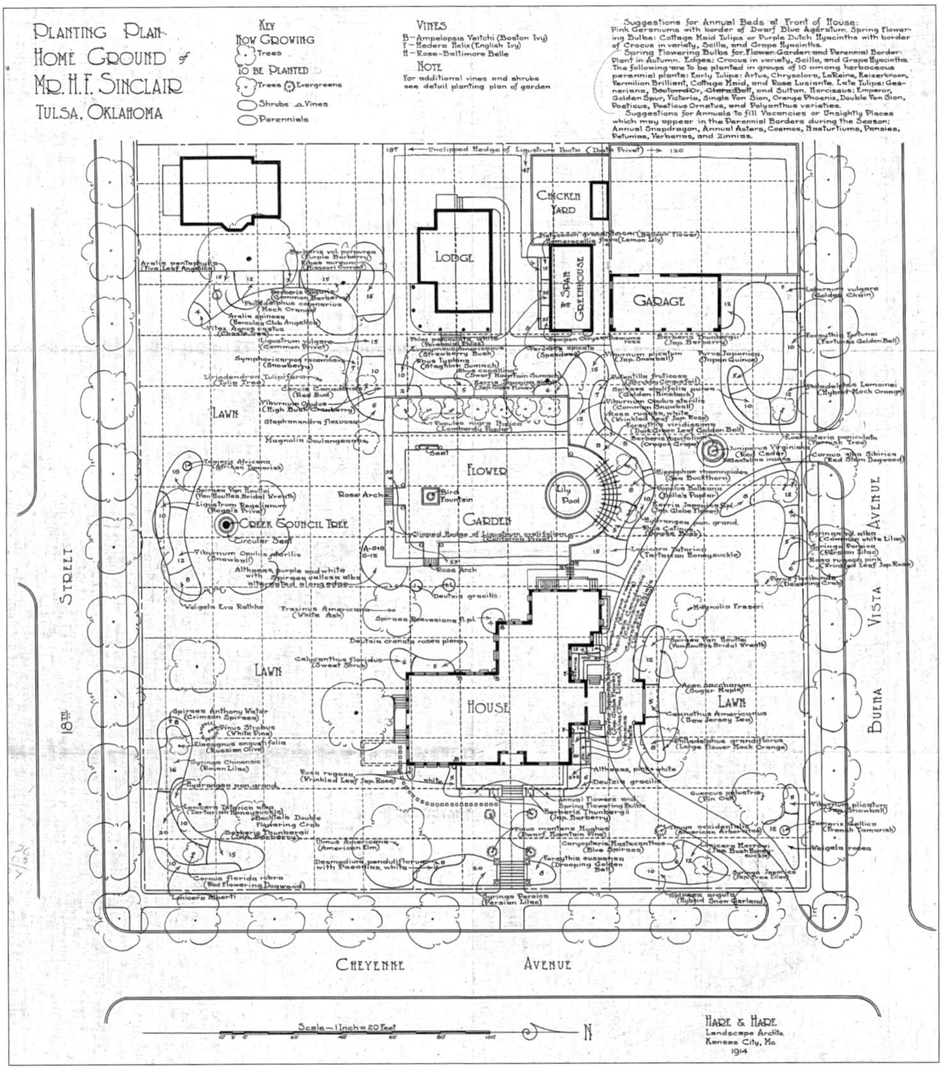

"Planting Plan–Home Ground of Mr. H. F. Sinclair, Tulsa," 1914. SHSMO-KC.

would not be too costly with his professional eye for improvement. They wanted a practical hothouse—nothing ornamental—with a plot behind it for Elizabeth Sinclair's chickens. In addition Herbert suggested a drying yard and a 3,700-square-foot vegetable garden (large enough to include flowers for cutting). He provided a four-page plant list, particularly heavy on shrubs and perennials (over 1,200 of each), and paid keen attention to the placement of gardens and associated views. Rose-covered arches were placed on axis with the living room, with the couple's bird fountain serving as a focal point. The flower garden was located so that the principal rooms of the house had glimpses of it and open lawn beyond. The owners were advised on the placement of the drive, that it be one broad natural curve from the street to the porte cochere. And the Creek Council Tree, valued by both the owner and the landscape architect for its historical significance, anchored the south side of the property.[6]

Soon after arriving in Tulsa, Herbert took on various projects, from home grounds to subdivisions, for other wealthy clients. The Sinclairs' neighbors in the city's Riverview section included the family of Pennsylvania-born J. H. Markham Jr. Herbert worked directly with Maud Markham, suggesting that the bare ground adjacent the Georgian Revival–style house be adorned with nearly seven hundred trees and shrubs and twelve hundred perennials. The Kansas City architect Henry Hoit, with whom Hare & Hare partnered on a regular basis, was proposed as the designer for the vine-draped arbor in the walled flower garden. In the northwest corner was a play yard that included not only a slide, swing, and sand court but a diminutive tea house for the children.

Progress on the Markhams' grounds had barely commenced when Herbert met with Joshua and Ottille Cosden, the neighbors across the street who, it appears, were not to be outdone. The Cosdens' oil refinery had recently become the largest in the Southwest, and when Herbert met with them, they were moving from a Craftsman bungalow into a Classical Revival mansion (the first in the state with an indoor swimming pool). He proposed a tasteful series of outdoor rooms defined by latticework screens and ornamented with pergolas. Late in the planning process the Cosdens decided to add a tennis court to the grounds.

Within days a letter from Herbert went out to the En-Tout-Cas Company of Syston, England, via their office on Water Street in New York City. Their fast-drying tennis courts, made of a special mix of Leicestershire clay, had been installed at Long Island estates and the St. Louis Country Club. The company's promotional booklet featured the duke of Devonshire's double courts at Chatsworth on the frontispiece. The firm would

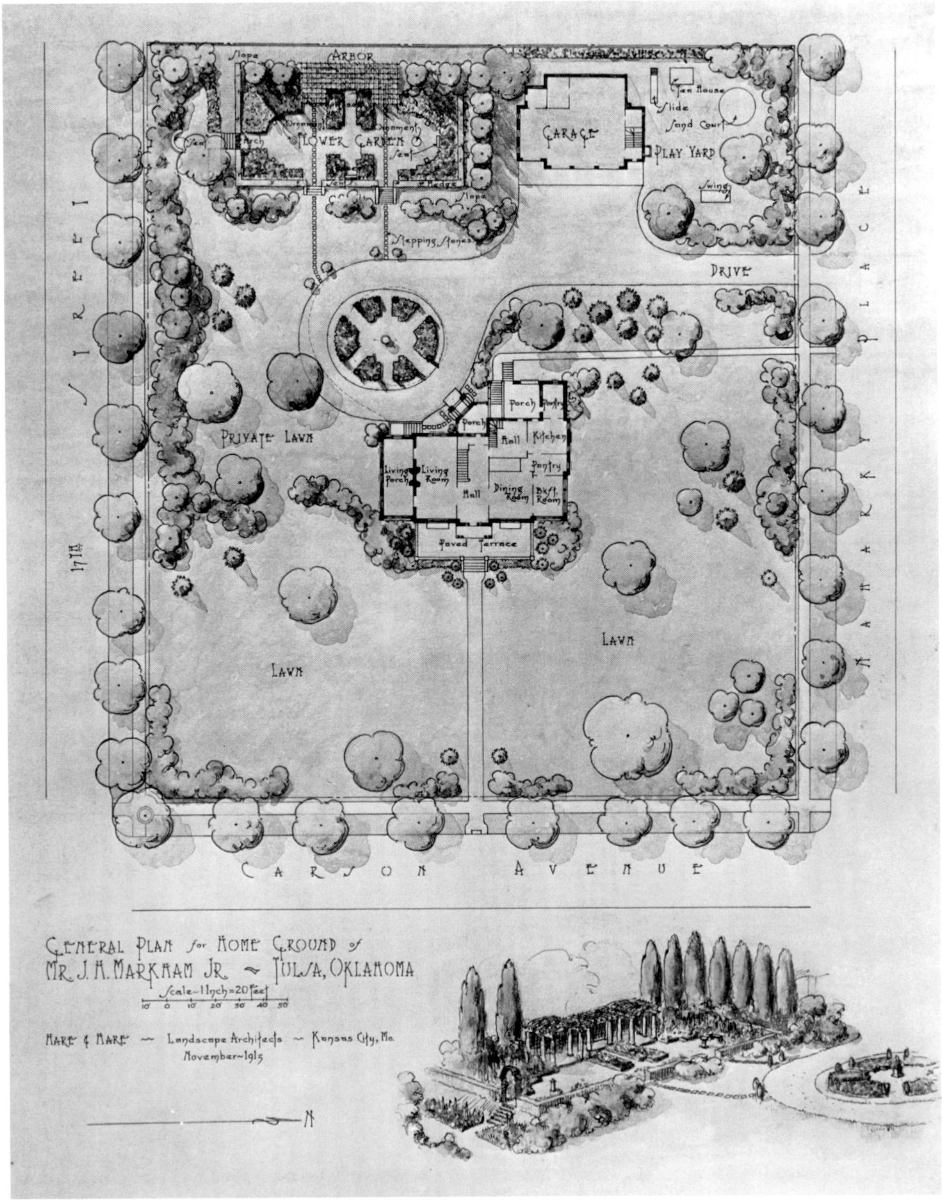

Plan and proposed view for the J. H. Markham Jr. residence, Tulsa, 1915. SHSMO-KC.

send an expert foreman to supervise construction and would provide instruction to the groundskeeper or gardener responsible for its care. Before the ink was dry on Herbert's drawing of the view toward the house from the proposed addition, he received a telegram: "Want two courts instead of one. Please arrange accordingly."[7]

In the spring of 1914, when Sid was fifty-four, he and his wife Mathilda purchased twenty-one acres of property. In a postcard to Haight, Sid described the land as wild and as rugged as one could find within forty miles of the city.[8] It sat to the southeast, beyond Swope Park—the city's largest at 1,334 acres—atop a high ridge. They named it "Harecliff." The house Sid eventually built, which they called "Timber-tent," would be perched overlooking the stream that wound along the edge of the property and be constructed of stone collected from their acreage and heavy hewn pine timbers recycled from old wooden bridges no longer in use. Not far from the house a rustic cedar pergola, inscribed "To Linger Long," would offer shade; next to it a well, with an oak bucket and dipper, provided cool water. The long curving drive, lined with glacial rocks, would be planted with lavender moss phlox and just beyond, redbud trees and banks of forsythia that bloomed in the spring.

The couple envisioned Harecliff as a refuge for wildflowers and birds, not merely for themselves but for others to enjoy (in later years they opened it to the public every Sunday).[9] It was to be a lesson in the value of native plants (considered "weeds" by those who preferred the exotic and pedigreed) and a chance to experience the landscape's constant shifting

Harecliff and Timber-tent, autochrome by Frank Lauder, 1934. MVSC.

Mathilda Hare next to a monolithic rock incorporated into Timber-tent's facade, 1927. Sylvia Mooney.

The fireplace at Timber-tent. On and above the mantle are references to the founding of Kansas City and the nearby Santa Fe Trail, 1927. Sylvia Mooney.

Sid and redbud tree at Harecliff, autochrome by Frank Lauder, 1934. MVSC.

of color and shadow. Sid likened it to "nature in her everyday garments," a place where ironweed, flax, and mullein were allowed to self-seed and scramble down the hillside and others, such as goldenrod and vervain, to colonize in sociable groups. In the spring, masses of pink bloom gave way to yellow. In the winter, reeds and vines stood out against the snow and water rushed through tangles of gray-green stems.

In the summer of that year, on July 11, Herbert married Aurel May Murty, a Radcliffe student from Wabash, Nebraska. The two had met during their college years in Cambridge when she was living on Hammond Street around the corner and a few blocks away from Herbert's Gorham Street apartment. Three years his senior, the bright and creative Aurel had studied both Latin and art. The week after their wedding in Lincoln they headed west to Seattle and Tacoma, visiting Point Defiance Park and nearby Mount Rainier (which the newlywed landscape architect and new member of ASLA considered the "most stunning" of sites) before heading to the Southwest.[10] They were treated royally by the entire Tacoma park board, in particular George Hill, the superintendent of the system, and his wife. Besides satisfying an interest in revisiting the Northwest, the trip may have been an unofficial call to follow up on a potential project envisioned by his father the year before. In a letter, Sid had assured Hill that Hare & Hare stood ready to prepare a park and boulevard system for his city and posed an important question, one that spoke to Herbert's strengths: "Is Tacoma ready for a city plan?"[11]

Now twenty-six, Herbert was quickly becoming comfortable with his role as a landscape professional. He mentored potential students and recommended Harvard for what he called its "superior advantages" and the course work it offered.[12] Writing to his own mentor James Sturgis Pray, he mentioned a young man he believed would prove both "interested and thorough." One of the many others he helped in this manner was Eldridge Lovelace, who grew up in a Hare & Hare–designed neighborhood and eventually became a city planner with Harland Bartholomew's firm in St. Louis. Herbert spent "innumerable hours" of his time advising Lovelace on his choice of university and the progress of his studies. Writing of his mentor some years later in *Landscape Architecture*, Lovelace called Herbert "an inspiring example of what it means to be a real professional."[13]

The following fall Herbert began teaching classes at the University of Kansas, lecturing every Thursday to a group of about sixty students from the architecture, art, and botany departments (the last of which listed Herbert on its letterhead).[14] On Friday afternoons he taught at the Kansas City Art Institute, which was housed on the grounds of park board president August Meyer's former estate. Herbert's lectures were rooted in the tradition taught at Harvard, a blending of landscape history and aesthetic theory. He covered the gardens of Renaissance Italy, the "culmination of splendor" at Versailles, and the English landscape movement of the eighteenth century. American subjects came next: Colonial gardens, and the work of A. J. Downing, Frederick Law Olmsted, and Charles Eliot. Texts he cited for further reading included Mariana Griswold Van Rensselaer's *Art Out-of-Doors* (1893) and, after its publication in 1917, Hubbard and Kimball's *Introduction to the Study of Landscape Design*.

In terms of aesthetics, Herbert spoke of "fitness," "the spirit of the place," and "the charm of seclusion." He warned against excess ("variety overdone means confusion") and addressed the issue of good taste by, in one case, using the old-fashioned rockery as an example. Sugarloafs of rocks and soil set in the middle of a lawn, he explained, had gone the way of "wax flowers and jigsaw porch decorations." The value of beauty in unadorned nature should never be "pawned," he stressed, for a series of cluttered spaces lacking in organic development. Good design took into consideration the natural conditions of a site and, when possible, preserved them.[15]

In the buildup to World War I, Herbert's teaching took a backseat and the firm became involved in new kinds of projects. The first of these came in June 1917, when Herbert assisted James Sturgis Pray in conceiving a plan for the Fort Riley, Kansas, cantonment named Camp Funston. One of the largest of sixteen divisional cantonments built for the war, the Fort Riley camp housed and serviced more than forty thousand individuals. Herbert served there as camp planner for the War Department through November, seeing that the project was completed within three months. In June of the following year he left for Washington—Aurel joined him in September—to work for the U.S. Housing Corporation as one of seven district town planners. Duties also included inspecting cantonments in the South, assisting in planning hospital additions and overseeing fire protection. For her part, Aurel sent newspaper clippings—"voluminous envelopes" of them, according to Chalmer Cooper (later a senior vice president of the firm)—to employees enlisted in military service overseas.[16]

Sid described the office as having been depleted by the "call to colors." All current employees (including the draftsman Ralph Reinhardt, who would later become a partner in the firm) had gone to Washington to work for the U.S. Housing Corporation, and three former employees were serving in the armed forces. Private work had been given up, and Sid vowed he was willing to close the office in order to make "this old world free from Kaisers and bosses."[17] With the end of the war on November 11, 1918, things began to return to normal. The first week of December, Sid traveled to Washington to represent the firm at what turned out to be a largely attended, and enthusiastic, meeting of the ASLA. Herbert's decision to forego the annual meeting suggests the workload that awaited him back in Kansas City. The number of commissions would double within the months that followed, many of them in the neighborhoods of the city's Country Club District.

One of the firm's largest, most important projects spanning the pre- and postwar years was in Kansas City for the developer Jesse Clyde Nichols. A phone call from Nichols to the Hare & Hare office in February 1913 began this collaboration, and Herbert would record it in his diary as a "pleasant and I hope profitable talk."[18] The conversation marked a turning point in the firm's history. Over the course of nearly forty years, Hare & Hare would plan approximately 2,500 acres of individual but contiguous subdivisions collectively known as the Country Club District. Nichols had

J. C. Nichols, c. 1912. Ansel Nichols Mitchell Family Papers, SHSMO-KC.

chosen the name to suggest quality and value by association, but in spite of the exclusivity implied, the district would include not only grand houses on large lots but neighborhoods of modest houses intended for middle-class families.[19] Called by the historian William S. Worley "a bringing together [of] the best thinking available at the time," the Country Club District helped crystallize interest in high-quality suburban design in the early twentieth century.[20] Hare & Hare's contributions were an essential component of what Nichols described as "planning for permanence."

Kansas-born Jesse Clyde Nichols had become familiar with the topography of Kansas City in his mid-teens when he worked delivering chickens, butter, and eggs from his hometown of Olathe. In 1900, between his junior and senior years at the University of Kansas, he and a fellow student traveled to Europe. Biking through England, Nichols noted the charm, orderliness, and what he described as the "stability" of its villages. As he recalled in his memoir, "it was then that the spark was struck that ultimately brought the Country Club District into being."[21] The next year, he graduated with honors and was awarded a one-year scholarship to Harvard (six years before Herbert was to enroll). In an industrial history course taught by a leading monetary economist, Oliver M. W. Sprague, he learned about how "development could generate as well as respond to land values and

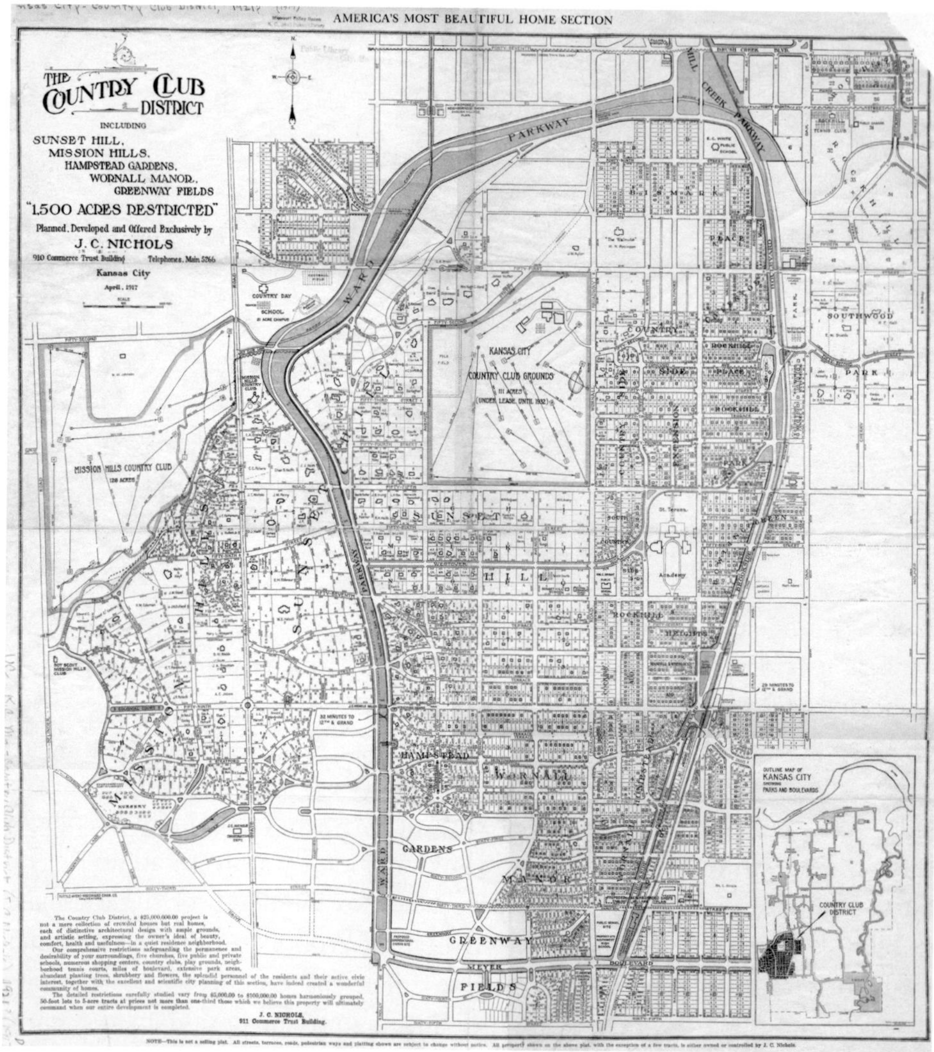

Early plan for the Country Club District, 1917. MVSC.

should be of long-term benefit to the community."[22] A few years later Nichols applied Sprague's theory by developing well-designed neighborhoods that attracted homeowners and balanced profit with civic good.

Nichols arrived at his unique approach to planning by synthesizing ideas from fellow planners and real estate operatives. These ideas were often gleaned from meetings of the American Civic Association and the National Association of Real Estate Boards, where the younger and less experienced Nichols met, among others, Edward H. Bouton. A former Kansas Citian who was overseeing the development of the Baltimore suburb of Roland Park, Bouton had come to be considered the "dean of American real estate developers."[23] Their meeting was the beginning of a friendship and exchange of ideas that lasted nearly three decades, a relationship that would overlap with Nichols's association with Hare & Hare.

Nichols borrowed two vital planning tools from Bouton, which the latter implemented first in Kansas City and then at the Maryland suburb.[24] The first was deed restrictions that "run with the land," legally binding regardless of who the future owners or sellers may be. Meant to ensure the "perpetuation of a high level of quality," restrictions could (and did) stipulate the minimum cost of construction and materials to be used, building widths and minimum setbacks, and the required amount of open space per lot. Other important restrictions precluded inappropriate activities or industry and placed architectural control—the review and approval of plans to ensure consistency of scale and visual harmony within a neighborhood—in the hands of the developer.[25]

Restrictions were also used to ensure more than a neighborhood's visual homogeneity. Nationally, it was accepted practice to prohibit the sale or occupancy of property to blacks and Jews. Nichols ultimately adjusted his view regarding the sale of property to families of the Jewish faith, announcing his decision at a conference of Developers of High Class Residential Property, calling such a restriction "un-American, and undemocratic, and so unfair."[26] Racially restricted covenants—legally binding agreements meant to protect property values—would not be challenged in this country until the 1948 U.S. Supreme Court case *Shelley v. Kraemer.*

The second vital planning tool borrowed from Bouton was mandatory homeowners' associations to oversee the enforcement of restrictions and neighborhood concerns such as garbage collection, sewers, snow removal,

J. C. Nichols Company sign on Brookside Boulevard, 1912. NCS.

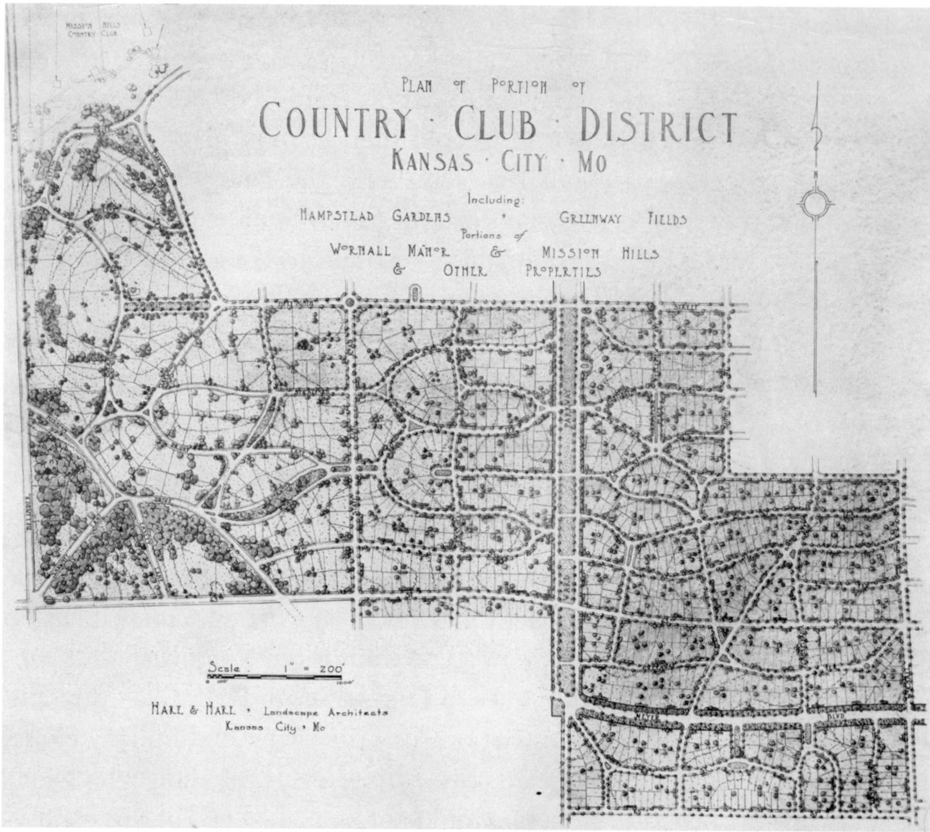

Country Club District plan illustrating the adjacent neighborhoods of Hampstead Gardens, Greenway Fields, Wornall Manor, and the first blocks of Mission Hills, c. 1920. SHSMO-KC.

and the maintenance of improved and vacant property. To finance the expenses of these activities, property owners were assessed annually based on the total square footage or frontage of their property. Women—housewives and mothers—played a significant role in these associations from the start and dealt with issues such as noise, speeding, and neighborhood aesthetics. The Mission Hills Homes Company, chartered on August 18, 1914, was an effective early model; over the following decades its activities and responsibilities were fine-tuned to best suit each subdivision. As the architectural historian Richard Longstreth has pointed out, "the scale and degree of synthesis" of Nichols's approach to planning was a departure from earlier methods.[27] Yet even such effective business policies could not account for the "physical excellence that made the Country Club District by general consensus one of the finest residential sections in the United States."[28] Credit for that must be given to Herbert Hare and his firm.

Crestwood is an early and representative example of the Hare & Hare–

Nichols collaboration that created the picturesque imagery envisioned for the entire Country Club District. Named for the site's old-growth forest and broad southern slopes, it lay just south of the Rockhill neighborhood that the *Kansas City Star* owner, William Nelson, had developed a decade before. The middle-class homeowners who purchased property in Crestwood—teachers, butchers, and salesmen—were attracted by the complete package it offered: lots with charming houses, paved streets with sidewalks, utilities, and even financing.[29] In addition to "beauty, comfort, health and usefulness," the neighborhood also offered convenience. Only steps away from home were the Crestwood Shops—a set of buildings residents described as "unobtrusive and of service to the community" which included drug and hardware stores,

Road paving, n.d. SHSMO-KC.

Brookside Shopping District, 1919, NCS.

"Parklet" at convergence of Huntington Road and Brookside Boulevard, c. 1943. J. C. Nichols Company Scrapbooks, SHMO-KC.

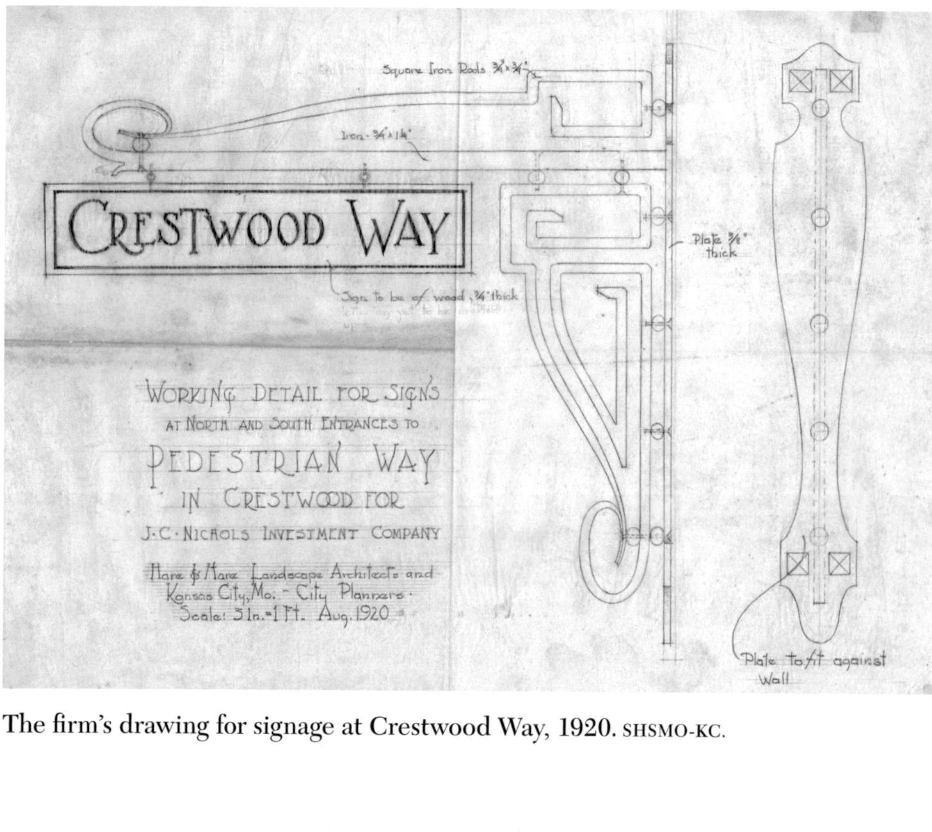

The firm's drawing for signage at Crestwood Way, 1920. SHSMO-KC.

a tea room and beauty shop, and the Piggly Wiggly Grocery.[30] Every District neighborhood also included playgrounds, schools, and churches.

Hare & Hare incorporated existing pasture and woods into its plan for Crestwood. Intersections of narrow winding streets were softened with masses of flowering shrubs—white and carmine red spiraea, Japanese rose (*Kerria japonica*) with single and double blooms, and *Deutzia gracilis*, whose willowy branches were covered in white blooms midspring. "Parklets" were placed where curving roads met, providing points of interest and helping to slow traffic.[31] "Quiet refinement" was the intended effect: planted borders free from gaudy bedding plants, open lawns stretching to the street, a scene of restraint rather than pretense. The firm designed scrolled wooden brackets to identify its pedestrian pathway and rusticated fieldstone entrances to serve as gateways to the community. Besides being beautiful, Crestwood felt secluded and safe.

Signage at the pedestrian walk at Crestwood Way, c. 1925, J. C. Nichols Company Scrapbooks, SHMO-KC.

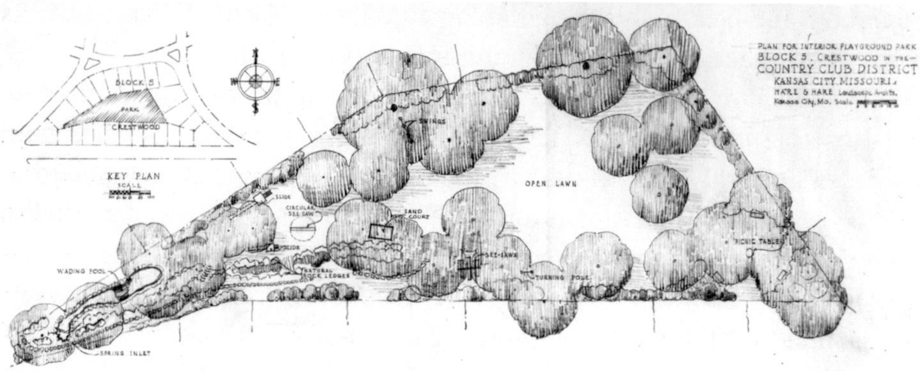

One of several plans for Crestwood interior parks, c. 1925. SHSMO-KC.

Interior parks, intended exclusively for use by a given block's homeowners, added to this sense of seclusion. These were accessible from an owner's back door and lay beyond the backyards, or in Nichols's words, the "garden side" of the property.[32] On Block 5, a "Happy Woods" for children included a sand court, wading pool, swings, and slides, all arranged around an open lawn edged by a spring with rock ledges. Picnic tables were placed beneath the trees. All was hidden from street view by plantings along the perimeter. Banks of flowering shrubs—weigela, viburnum, and weeping forsythia—created a garden view from the rear of the residences that lined this protected and private park.[33]

Social events and projects to build community spirit included "lawn beautiful" contests, house-to-house caroling during the holiday season, flower shows, and model boat races in a neighborhood reflecting pool. Educational pamphlets encouraging bird watching were distributed to residents, and the developers held contests for student-built birdhouses and a census to determine the number and species in the district. The naturalist Ernest Harold Baynes was invited to lecture about the importance of "wild bird guests."[34] The improvement of nesting grounds was discussed, and Nichols refrained from mowing vacant company property one spring to allow meadowlarks adequate time to nest.[35] Hare & Hare provided homeowners with a list of the plants that appealed to area birds. It included elder- and mulberry, Siberian dogwood, and serviceberry, one of the first trees to bloom each spring in Missouri.

As Crestwood was taking shape, so too was the neighborhood of Sunset Hill to the west, another Hare & Hare–Nichols collaboration and the developer's most prestigious undertaking to date. In 1920, Nichols and his family moved to Sunset Hill, to a property previously owned by Charles S. Keith, manager of Central Coal and Coke Company. Along with their new house, named "Ridgewood," they inherited a maturing landscape designed by Hare & Hare. The three-acre grounds of the Georgian Revival–style residence had a formal garden accented with an unusual mix of specimen trees that included Carolina silverbell and dwarf catalpa. Dense hedges of snowberry, viburnum, and hydrangea served as borders, and from its drive—lined on the west side with spiraea and on the east with lilacs—one could catch glimpses of the sweeping lawn. Just as Nichols, and Keith before him, chose to live on Santa Fe Road at the crest of Ward Parkway, Tom Pendergast and other members of Kansas City's elite chose the neighborhood as well. Grounds of many estates on the street were designed by Hare & Hare, and the result was a consistency of design—"harmony" as Herbert referred to it—throughout the neighborhood.

One of the firm's most informal naturalistic designs in Sunset Hill was created for Charles C. and Josephine Peters, two very private individuals who called their Henry Hoit–designed home "Westvue." Hare & Hare's preliminary plan transformed the former pasture adjacent to the Kansas border into a wooded haven. Walnut, hickory, and oak trees, with an understory of redbuds, were planted to screen the perimeter of the four-acre estate. Beyond open lawn lay a small lake with water lilies and lotus which could be viewed from the terrace. A walkway skirting the edge of the lawn in a dramatic arc transitioned to stepping stones leading to the wild garden.

J. C. Nichols home on Santa Fe Road, 1920. NCS.

Northwest of the house, and through an archway, was the formal flower garden which occupied much of Mrs. Peters's time. Hare & Hare superintended the Peterses' landscaping for nearly a decade, directing planting, making adjustments to color and varieties, and approving nursery bills.

Clients of Hare & Hare, including the Hyde and Irving families, had houses that lined Ward Parkway and the blocks that extended from it. Ben C. Hyde was a telephone executive and Princeton alumnus who had hired the local architectural firm of Shepard, Farrar & Wiser to design his res-

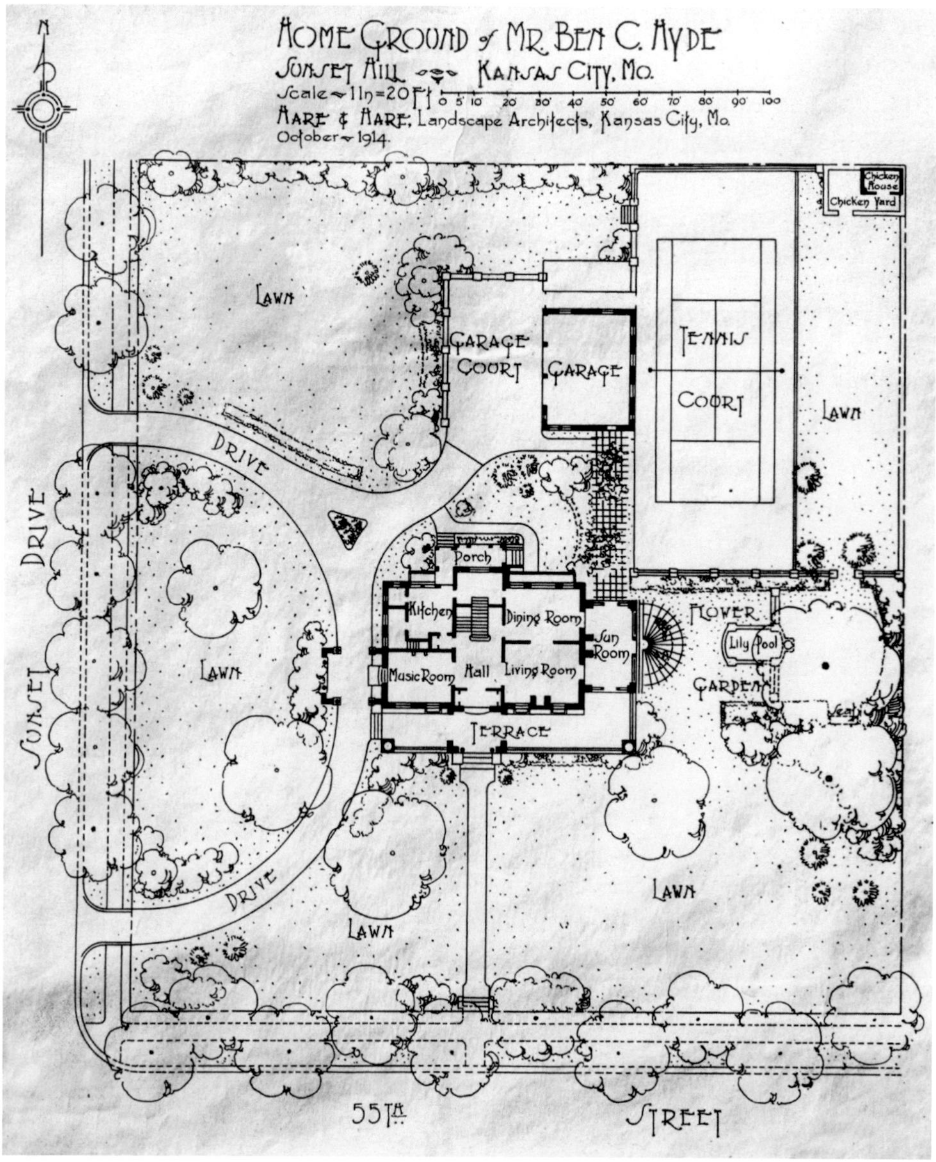

Plan for the Ben C. Hyde residence, with a view of the proposed garden and lily pool, 1914. SHSMO-KC.

Hyde grounds on completion, c. 1920. SHSMO-KC.

idence. The architects oriented the house to emphasize the rear of the property, turning its back on the street so it faced the garden. Views from the living room through the sunroom and the pergola revealed the landscaped grounds and lily pool. Herbert's drawings on linen and vellum illustrate the improvements the firm proposed. The end result was praised by neighbor J. C. Nichols as "splendid."[36]

Grounds for the nearby Junius Irving house were certainly designed with Mrs. Irving in mind. She was a plantswoman, and the property, a Shepard, Farrar & Wiser design, featured a greenhouse for her many exotic plants. Her collection included orchids, an "Australian air plant," and *Schizanthus*, a colorful member of the nightshade family that may have won her the local garden club's "most interesting flowering plant" award in 1922. Hare & Hare's plant list for the grounds—heavy on shrubs and roses—suggested Mrs. Irving's fondness for a cottage garden effect and a palette of pink and purple. The plan, which indicated viewsheds to and from the house, included notes on cultivation of the soil and the procedure for planting spring bulbs "in groups of 10 among the herbaceous perennial plants."[37]

The Irving project is also representative of the firm's interest in tailoring the plan to the owner by including "living lawns," tea gardens, or play yards. In this case, toward the rear of the property they designed a

Herbert Hare's drawing of the Junius Irving residence, Sunset Hill, 1915. SHSMO-KC.

service area—a "clothes yard"—surrounded by beds of annuals with an entrance flanked by catalpa trees. As was customary with commissions such as these, Hare & Hare provided a preliminary site plan showing the house in relation to drives, walks, terraces, and gardens. This was accompanied by another plan specifying plant location and a separate list, typed on long narrow sheets of vellum, citing botanical and common names, with the number of specimens required. The firm often concluded with a presentation drawing, which helped the client visualize the end result, and such was the case for the Irvings. Herbert broke with company policy by identifying himself—"S. H. H. Del."—as the delineator of the charming illustration of the proposed site.

Twenty years later, Mrs. Irving called on the firm to add more than three hundred lilac, spiraea, quince, and viburnum to the grounds of her Sunset Hill home. At about this time many of her plants, including the Kaiserkroon tulips Herbert had suggested, were the subject of numerous autochromes taken by the local photographer Frank C. Lauder, who documented Kansas City gardens and estates. Among these were images of the house and gardens of Mack B. Nelson, a top executive of the Long-Bell Lumber Company, who had one of the largest Hare & Hare–designed landscapes along the street. The company Nelson presided over would soon hire the firm for one of its most important commissions to date.

According to Nichols, "no self-respecting Missourian" wanted to live west of State Line Road before the development of Mission Hills, Kansas.[38]

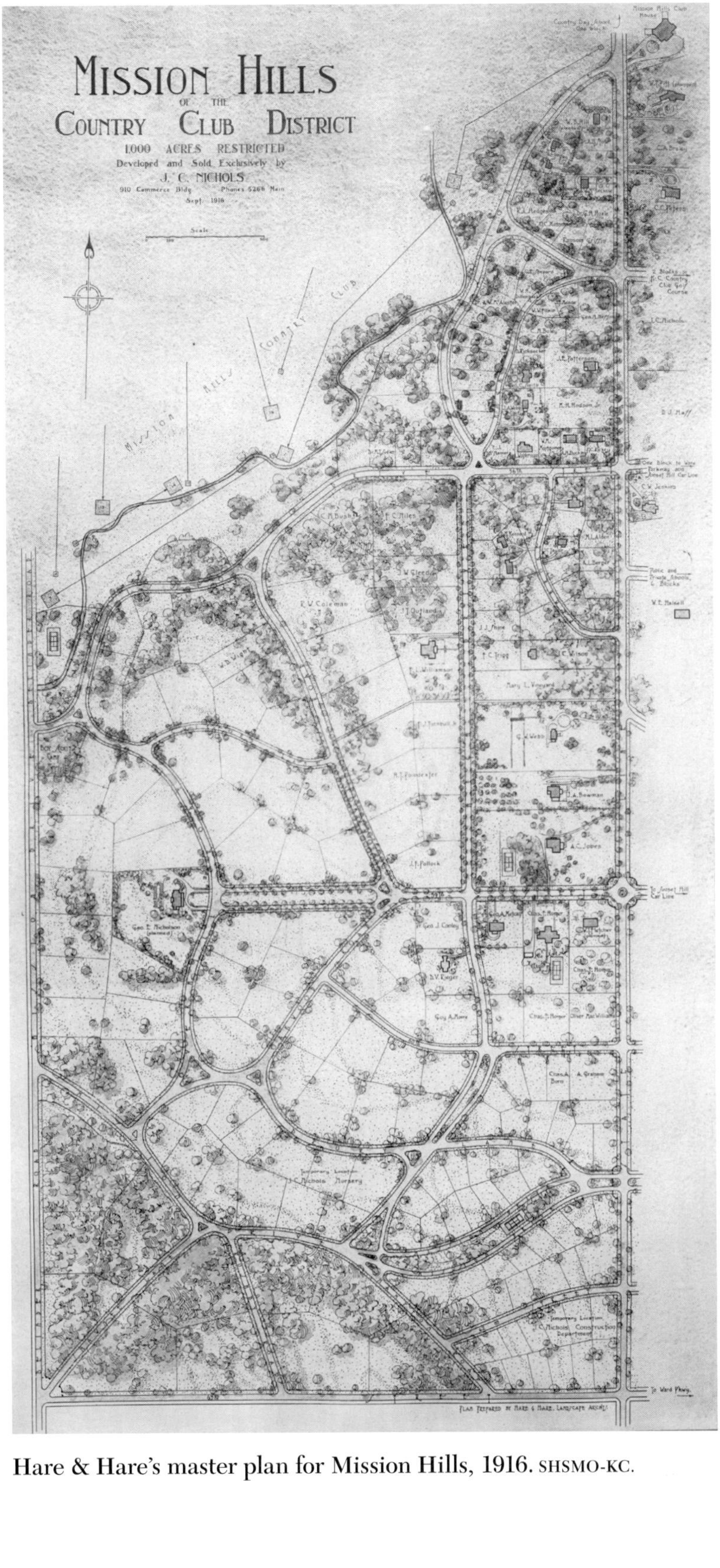

Hare & Hare's master plan for Mission Hills, 1916. SHSMO-KC.

Transformed by Hare & Hare's plan—praised as beautiful, thoughtful, and original—Mission Hills was perhaps the finest neighborhood executed for Nichols.[39] Beginning in 1915 and through the 1920s, more than two hundred finished drawings (not including those for privately commissioned residences) were executed. The ink on vellum paper master plan, which stretches to over six feet in height, is itself visually impressive and conveys the firm's comprehensive approach to the project. Weathervanes, bridges, and precise notes on how works of art should be positioned ("statues to be turned toward the stairs") are among the detailed drawings. Bridle paths and foot trails, campfire sites, and two picturesque water features—Lake Hiwassee and Lake Willow—were created by damming arms of Brush Creek. Plans for the larger picture include countless residential grounds and the parklike spaces that link houses, "grouped for architectural harmony."[40]

In early April 1924, Herbert and Aurel sailed to Europe for a nearly five-month tour of England and the Continent. They were back on American soil by mid-August, returning "poorer but wiser," according to Herbert. Their trip was not only for pleasure. Armed with topographical maps of Mission Hills and a line of credit from the Nichols Company, Herbert was charged with finding suitable artwork for furnishing his landscapes (ultimately $500,000 would be spent throughout the District). Paris, Amsterdam, Berlin, and Venice were among the places they visited and where he bought fountains, garden seats, and sundials. Herbert's sketchbook includes studies of garden ornaments and cross sections of

Mr. and Mrs. John E. Horn estate, Mission Hills, drawn by H. Gordon Whiffen and D. D. Obert, 1932. SHSMO-KC.

Zurich's main street, the Bahnhofstrasse, and the Tapis Vert garden at Versailles, based on his "paced measurements."[41]

The intersection of Mission Drive, Overhill Road, and Ensley Lane was one location in Mission Hills which Herbert sought to adorn with European art. Preliminary drawings, executed before the trip, suggest a formal design was under consideration, and Herbert found works suitable for the site in Rome and Venice. In the spring of 1925, Hare & Hare installed a

A picturesque creek along Pembroke Lane in Mission Hills. Photo by Frances Benjamin Johnston, 1924. Frances Benjamin Johnston Collection, LC.

Lake Hiwassee, autochrome by Frank Lauder, 1932. MVSC.

long narrow reflecting pool anchored at one end with a Carrara marble fountain of swans supporting an urn. To each side were garden seats, and two sculptures representing the seasons were placed at the ends of flagstone paths. This formal space was backed by a screen of twelve-foot-tall salmon-pink Verona marble columns with twisted shafts topped with white marble capitals. Beyond the columns a series of native stone steps lead to a semicircular terrace and, behind it, a wall of evergreens. Up the hillside, overlooking this formal space and precisely on axis with the fountain, two fine Edward Buehler Delk–designed residences complete the setting.[42] Considered a distinctive landmark, the Verona columns appear on the official city seal.

Aside from the numerous and ongoing Mission Hills commissions, Hare & Hare had been at work with Nichols, architect Delk, and a team of other professionals planning Kansas City's Country Club Plaza shopping center, which would become a model of national importance.[43] At once cut-

Herbert Hare feeding pigeons in the Piazza San Marco, Venice, 1924.
SHSMO-KC.

The wedge of land now referred to as Verona Columns Park, Mission Hills, c. 1930.
SHSMO-KC.

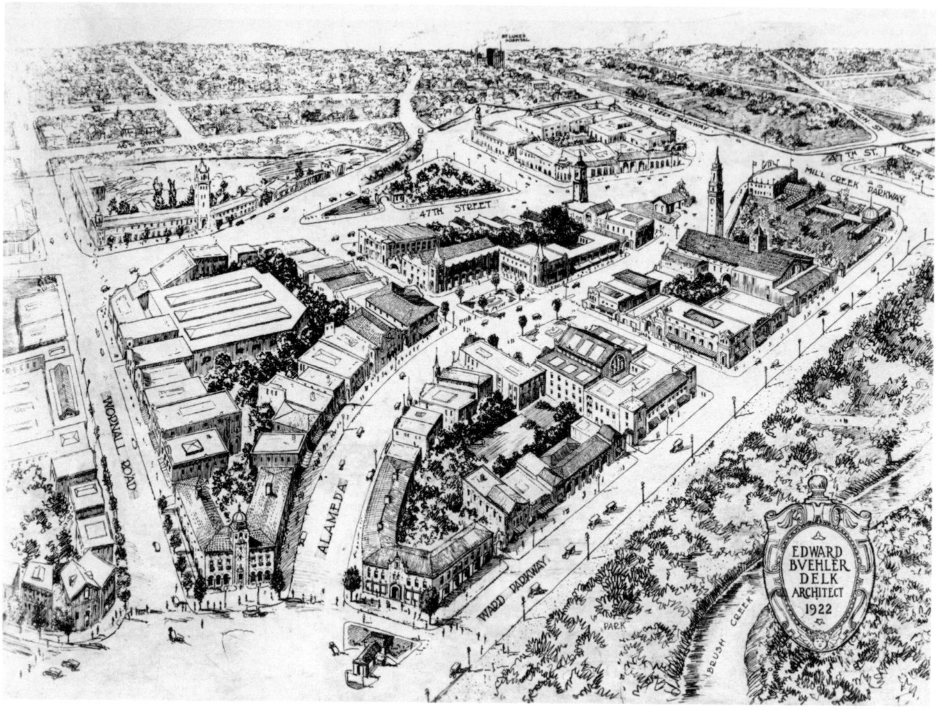

Plan for the Plaza, drawn by Edward Buehler Delk, 1922. SHSMO-KC.

Wilbur Dunn, director of Kansas City Parks, at Brush Creek near Country Club Plaza, 1932. MVSC.

ting-edge and traditional, "the Plaza" was designed to attract an automobile clientele from across the region with architecture inspired by Spanish Colonial Revival models.[44] In keeping with the adjacent neighborhoods of the Country Club District, its blocks were ornamented with a particularly rich collection of fountains and sculpture. Herbert's input is evident in the plan, which retained the scale and ambience of a small-town commercial center.[45] Among the firm's many drawings are traffic patterns and road

Fountain at 47th Street and J. C. Nichols Parkway, Country Club Plaza, c. 1970. MVSC.

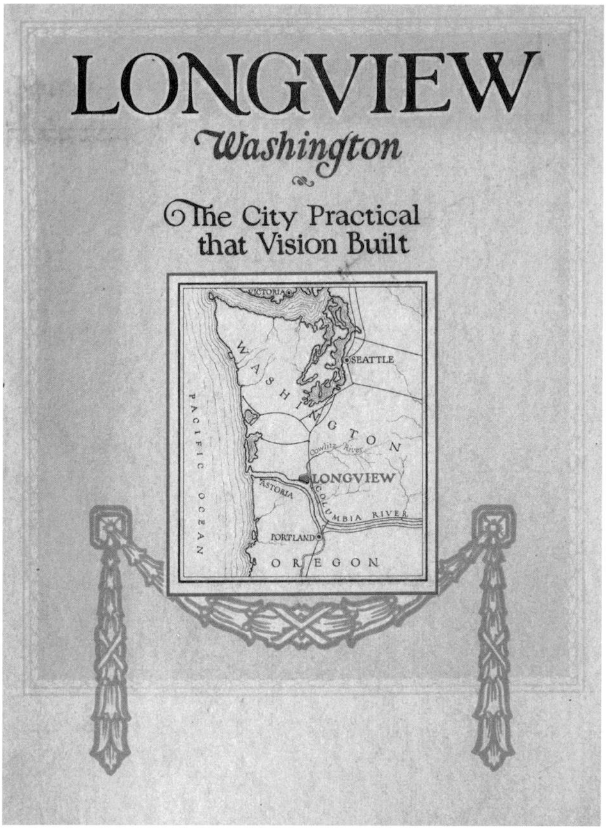

One of numerous booklets promoting Longview as the "City Practical," c. 1928. SHSMO-KC.

revisions but also designs for ornamental street signs and an arched bridge to span Brush Creek. After two years of the firm's involvement, the project plans for the Plaza shopping center were announced to the public. That spring, Herbert's focus shifted from Kansas City to the Pacific Northwest.

The firm's opportunity to engage in large-scale planning would come from fellow Kansas Citian R. A. Long. The businessman had contacted his acquaintance of nearly two decades, J. C. Nichols, for advice on relocating his company's operations to Washington state. Nichols, in turn, recommended Herbert Hare. Long's initial objective was to build an industrial site for logging activities located at a key transportation point. The end result was Herbert's comprehensive master plan for the city of Longview, Washington, which would be promoted as "The City Practical that Vision Built."

In the late 1890s, Robert Alexander Long, of the Long-Bell Lumber Company of Kansas City, owned sawmills and thousands of timber-covered acres in Louisiana, Mississippi, and east Texas. Long had built the company since his arrival in Missouri and, by 1902, had expanded its holdings to include coal mines, logging railroads, and fifty lumberyards. At that time over 850 employees lived in his mill towns, which included Bonami, Ludington, and Woodworth in Louisiana. The company owner prided himself on the fact that Long-Bell towns were communities, with paved streets, churches, and schools, rather than ramshackle labor camps or boomtowns. Their more orderly nature came, in part, from the strict forbidding of saloons.[46]

"Mr. Long," as everyone called him (including Ella, his wife of fifty-two years), was an important figure in Kansas City, with a personal worth of more than $30 million in 1920. A philanthropist and civic leader, he was a benefactor of his local church, the Independence Boulevard Christian Church, and the National City Christian Church, in Washington, D.C. Years later Herbert Hare would describe Long as "an idealist, as well as a shrewd business man."[47] An official of the Loyal Legion of Loggers and Lumbermen once remarked on his surprise on meeting Long for the first time. Rather than a cold and calculating "money-grabber," fixated on dividends and productivity, he found Long to be a generous businessman who wanted a "happy and contented labor force working for him."[48]

For all of Long-Bell's success as one of the largest producers of lumber in the United States, the company was at a crossroads in 1918. With its southern timber stands nearly exhausted, Long, then sixty-eight, faced a difficult decision. Long-Bell could settle its accounts and go out of business or relocate its logging operations and start anew. That May, Long polled his management team and executives, which included his close friend Mack B. Nelson, J. D. Tennant, and Wesley Vandercook.[49] Although these men had been with the firm for decades, they were considerably younger and had families and many productive years ahead of them. Their consensus was to go forward, and Long, who was well into middle age but described as having "the vigor of early manhood," was still energetic and prepared for a challenge.[50] Within a year, the decision was made to go West, and in July 1919, Long and his party visited Cowlitz County, Washington. They spent a week horseback riding through old-growth forests of Douglas fir—taller than any trees they had known in the South.[51]

If Long-Bell was to relocate and invest in the task of starting over in the Pacific Northwest, it would need the ideal location for its milling operations, one with access to transportation by rail and by water, and one that provided room for a mill town to house its workers and their families.[52] The process of determining where to locate lumber operations took more than three years, but after an in-depth study of the region, the Cowlitz County site was chosen.[53]

The purchase consisted of an entire valley in the southwest part of Washington—nearly fourteen thousand acres—approximately halfway between Tacoma and Portland, Oregon, adjacent to Kelso. To the east were the Cascade Mountains—including the snow-covered Mount St. Helens volcano that rose above them—and almost one million acres of National Forest. The proposed site was at the confluence of the Columbia and Cowlitz Rivers, on a wedge of land very much like that at the juncture of the Missouri and Kaw Rivers where Kansas City had begun. The valley was marshy—even swampy—and at times of high water, with the melt of heavy snows, it became a watery fen. Even in drier weather, naturally formed drainage canals, called sloughs, meandered through the valley. Fowler's Slough, which was once a channel of the Cowlitz, curved around the west side of the site, and to the west was Mount Solo. The valley was a scramble of undergrowth—"the worse piece of land I ever saw as far as brush was concerned," according to Vandercook—with stands of oak, ash, and cottonwood trees.

Wesley Vandercook, chief engineer for the company, knew that with proper diking and drainage systems to control flooding, the site was ideally suited for Long-Bell's new project. Since the early 1890s the Columbia River, which empties into the Pacific, had been dredged—deepening the waterway to thirty feet. To the east, the river cut a sea-level passage through the mountains. From the site's location, goods could be shipped westward, by water, to international markets and eastward, by rail, across the country. That the project involved constructing what would become the world's largest saw mills—with rail lines, a deep-water port, and housing for workers and their families—did not faze Long.

J. C. Nichols, Long, and company executives visited the Cowlitz site in March 1922. Nichols's expertise in land use and growth enabled him to help Long envision building an industrial city, one based on a comprehensive plan that allowed for growth that would attract quality workers with its residential and business districts, schools, parks, and churches. A thirty-two-page planning report submitted by Nichols, which provided the broad strokes for the central thousand-acre tract that would become Longview, was completed that spring. Nichols had chosen two others to work with him in preparing it: Letcher Lambuth, a Seattle real estate developer and lawyer, and thirty-four-year-old Herbert Hare. George Kessler, who had previously worked with both Nichols and Long, provided advisory assistance and commented on zoning and deed restrictions.[54]

In May and June 1922, Hare and Lambuth set out on a tour of industrial cities to gather information related to planning. Most of these were new towns, or suburbs, founded in the first decades of the twentieth century by industrial giants such as U.S. Steel, Firestone, Eastman Kodak, and the Aluminum Company of America. The tight six-day itinerary of the first trip began when they boarded a Burlington Railroad car at 11:55 p.m. on May 19.[55] Their first two stops were East St. Louis and Granite City, Illinois; next was Gary, Indiana, followed by Firestone Park in Akron, Ohio, then Kingsport and Alcoa, Tennessee. Given the pace, they must have been met at each city by knowledgeable guides who could keep the tour on schedule.[56] They arrived back in Kansas City at 8:05 a.m. the following Friday. A two-day trip in June, which Herbert took on his own, included visits to Morgan Park in Duluth, Minnesota, and Eclipse Park in Beloit, Wisconsin.

Hare and Lambuth's research and observations were compiled in a final report presented to Long-Bell executives. Illustrated with maps, photos, and statistics, it included information for each of the cities they had visited, addressing population, principal industries, wages, and the number of men and women employed. The data, which reflected changes by decade, included the value per acre for residential, business, and industrial districts, and existing transportation systems. Store counts, the "character of housing," and block and lot sizes were also part of the report. East St. Louis and Granite City, both on the Mississippi River, provided information on dikes, levee heights, and drainage. Brief remarks relevant to a given city were provided—that the schools and playgrounds of Gary, Indiana, founded in 1906 to house U.S. Steel workers, were model examples of their type; that the Tennessee town Alcoa, built by the Aluminum Company of America, constituted the first community planning in the state; and that Firestone Park, a "model village," was created in 1917 for company employees. The report also included observations on Eclipse Park, in Beloit, Wisconsin, for the employees of Fairbanks, Morse & Company, and Morgan Park, built by Minnesota Steel and planned by Morell & Nichols between 1913 and 1922, commended for its admirable "community spirit."[57]

Not included in this final report, but recorded in Herbert's notes, were comments from a conversation with the city planner John Nolen, who had recently created a master plan for the industrial town of Kingsport.[58] They discussed the value of an article in the journal of Great Britain's Garden Cities and Town Planning Association (of which Hare ordered a copy immediately) and the town of Welwyn, in Hertfordshire, as a potential model for this country.[59] Looking to England, and the theories and concepts of Ebenezer Howard and Raymond Unwin, was one step in defining what kind of planning best fit this country.[60] Realizing the need to replace the visionary plans and grand gestures of the City Beautiful (later described by

Henry Vincent Hubbard as "an extensive and stylish coat, covering but not curing a multitude of civic ills") had been an early step in that direction.[61] What modern planning should provide, in the words of the architect Cass Gilbert, was "the city useful, the city practical, the city livable, the city sensible."[62] Within five years Longview would promote itself as just such a place.

The "key plan" for Longview had been drafted by September 1922, when Herbert made a trip to the site and recorded his observations in a thirty-nine-page memorandum.[63] The purpose of this visit was to assess the plan "on the ground," and his notes imply a double checking of the likely effectiveness of the proposed street patterns, block sizes, and building sites. Lambuth had decided on the street names and residential numbering system (although these would be changed per Long's request).[64] Hare's notes reveal his sensitivity to how the plan worked with the topography. He recorded viewsheds that connected the town with Mount St. Helens and noted the importance of retaining the "mounds" to the north for park use.

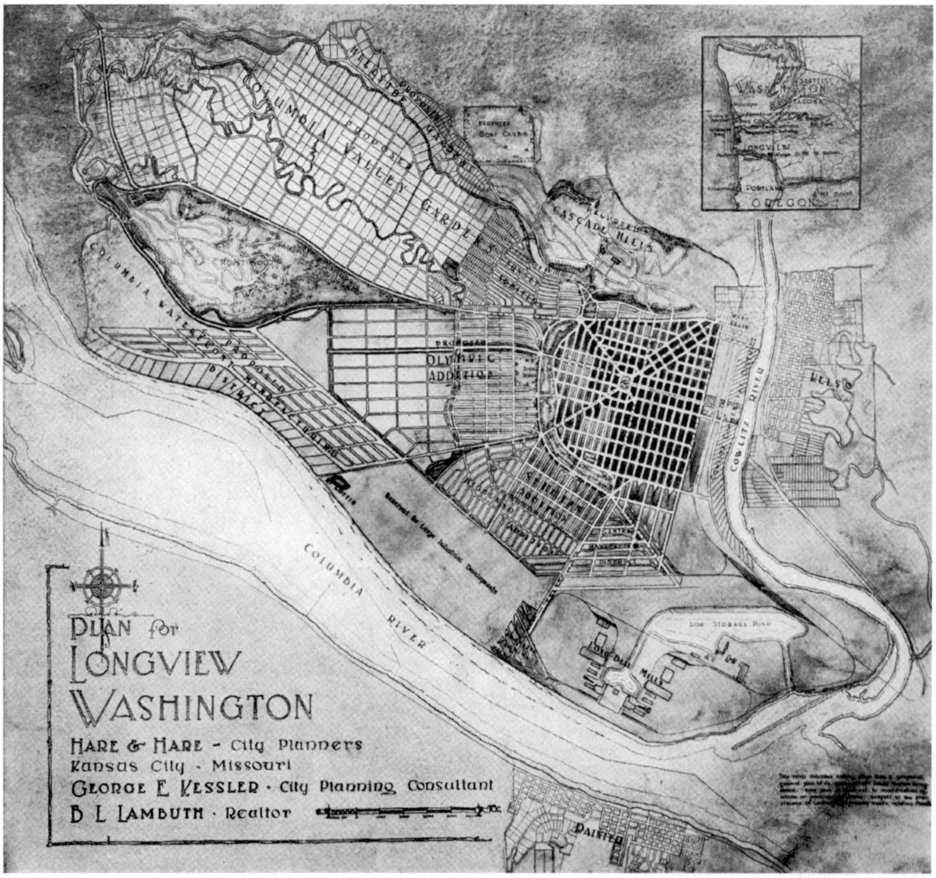

General plan for Longview, 1923. SHSMO-KC.

He also made note of large oak, cherry, and walnut trees to be retained during the process of clearing the land. Fowler's Slough should be remade into a chain of lakes and remain irregular and picturesque. Although minor adjustments were made to the master plan, and some changes "reinstated after discussion," the city's essential organization was fixed.

The city that resulted was based on a series of residential, commercial, and industrial districts or zones. Throughout the plan, undeveloped blocks and open space were reserved to allow for incremental growth.[65] Jefferson Square—six acres of green space encircled by a broad, one-way road—functioned as the civic center that anchored the plan.[66] Curved and arrow-straight walks, whose placement had been determined by Herbert's pedestrian traffic studies, crossed the square and provided accessibility. The pattern they created served as a design element visually connecting the square to the larger network of streets and boulevards, which ranged in width from 50 to 120 feet, with walks beyond. Among these was Broadway, a 120-foot-wide boulevard that linked the civic center and the passenger rail depot, reinforcing the formality that began at Jefferson Square and continued east to the Cowlitz River.

From corners of the civic center, radial streets, or "ways"—Washing-

Plan for the Longview Civic Center, 1923. SHSMO-KC.

A newly planted boulevard adjacent Lake Sacajawea in Longview, c. 1928. SHSMO-KC.

ton, Olympia, and Vandercook—cut diagonal routes through town, and a fourth radial terminated near Commerce Avenue and the business district. An orderly grid of secondary streets linked St. Helens Inn, a group of two-story rooming houses for single (male) mill workers, and the working-class neighborhoods of St. Helens Addition and the Highlands Addition intended to house Longview's African American laborers.[67] Church and school sites were clustered in Longview's southwest quadrant. Small parks, playing fields, and playgrounds, such as one on the west side with a wading pool and sand pile, were woven throughout. A picturesque system of streets, carefully adjusted to the topography, was proposed for hilly sections such as those to the north, past Ocean Beach Highway. Of these, the neighborhood of Columbia Valley Gardens was noted in a promotional ad for its suburban homes and fertile truck farms. Across town to the south was the central manufacturing district—the major plants of Long-Bell Lumber—and a proposed waterfront commercial district that lined the Columbia River.

A key element in the plan, according to Herbert, was Fowler's Slough, whose reedy little ponds would be transformed by dredging and planting. The result was Lake Sacajawea (named by the winner of a citywide contest), over 150 acres of water and park that curled around the west side in a horseshoe shape. Providing beauty and passive recreation—in addition to serving as an equalizing reservoir for storm water runoff—the lake was planted with trees to frame views, bind together the park and surround-

Longview's Lake Sacajawea, c. 1928. SHSMO-KC.

ing neighborhoods, and provide long vistas from the streets. Kessler and Missouri (later renamed Nichols) Boulevards—"the most important scenic roadways in the plan"—would, with time, become shaded by a canopy of American elms. But such plantings were not limited to the lake and its parkways. Blocks and blocks of streets were planted with thousands of hawthorn, mountain ash, horse chestnut, sycamore, and oak trees, the shade of which can still be experienced today.

R. A. Long's vision of an industrial city culminated in the official dedication of Longview, which took place on July 12, 1923. The governor, senators, state representatives, and well-wishers from Portland, Seattle, and Tacoma were among the ten thousand people in attendance. A party of fifty, which included Ella Long and Herbert and Aurel Hare, came from Kansas City. Besides concerts, games, and fireworks, there were tours of the St. Helens neighborhood and the Long-Bell docks, and a steamer trip provided inspection of the dikes. Paving crews continued their work on the street surrounding Jefferson Square as the festivities took place. These were centered around the newly completed Hotel Monticello, six stories of brick and terra-cotta designed by the Kansas City architect F. E. McIlvain. Its lobby, richly paneled in Honduran mahogany, was encircled by *Conquerors of the Trail,* a frieze of murals by the local artist Joe Knowles. For the event Hare & Hare planted the hotel grounds with hundreds of roses, pots of lobelias, and blooming annuals in shades of purple, pink, and salmon. The roof was transformed into a flower garden.[68]

To ensure that his new city offered community and cultural facilities, Long personally funded many of the first important buildings as gifts.[69] One of these was the public library, on the north side of Jefferson Square, an impressive execution of Georgian Revival style designed by Archibald N. Torbitt.[70] Its reading rooms were presided over by portraits of R. A. and Ella Long painted by the Welsh artist Margaret Lindsay Williams, whose usual subjects were British royalty. William B. Ittner, the St. Louis architect known nationally for his inventive school planning, was hired to design the Classical Revival high school that bears Long's name.[71] Acreage for the hospital—and the funding for ornamental flower beds, 26 trees, and 620 shrubs on the grounds—was another of Long's donations. Hare & Hare planned and planted all of these projects—the public library, school, and hospital grounds—just as they did every landscape-related feature in the city.

Although Long respected Herbert's horticultural and planning expertise, the founder of Longview did not hesitate to express his opinion on such matters. Herbert remained gracious through these tests and did his best to accommodate the wishes of his client. When Long requested that the public gardens replicate the colorful and exuberant effects at his Missouri farmstead (44,986 feet of petunias, Joseph's coat [*Alternanthera*], and coleus in the beds alone), Herbert tactfully explained that the Northwest climate dictated the use of different plants, although he assured Long that equally pleasing results could be secured.[72] Over several years, Herbert negotiated with Long over his plan for the placement and spacing of trees along Longview's streets and boulevards. The dense canopy they would ultimately create worried Long, who insisted that the Northwest needed *more* sunshine and *less* shade. In the end, and against Herbert's wishes, the number of trees planted was reduced by one-third.

Herbert must have found his client trying at times, but Long's determination to oversee every detail should perhaps be excused. He was, as the historian Lenore K. Bradley has pointed out, "like a father whose youngest child was born late in life. He could not do enough."[73] To him, Longview, within two years a city of ten thousand, was both a business endeavor and a source of pride. And Long was equally proud of the job done by Herbert Hare; upon the city's completion Long commended him for his "fine mark."[74]

Herbert Hare's numerous articles on Longview appeared in journals in the United States, the Netherlands, and England during the 1920s and 1930s.[75] "In accordance to . . . [his] promise," he sent a booklet on the subject to the garden city planner Raymond Unwin, with whom he'd discussed the project in Amsterdam at the International Town Planning Conference in 1924.[76] The following year, Herbert attended the group's meeting in New York City, where his Longview photographs and the firm's plans were exhibited. Two decades later, in an article for *The American City*, he would consider Longview's planning in light of the advances that had been made and find that it remained "fundamentally sound in its major provisions."[77]

Herbert Hare at Burnett Park, Fort Worth, 1950. *Fort Worth Star-Telegram* Collection, Special Collections, University of Texas at Arlington Libraries.

FIVE

Texas and a Return to Tulsa

Hare & Hare's commissions across the state included all aspects of planning—from parks and universities to levee systems and subdivisions—and encompassed "practically every detail" in approximately thirty Texas cities.[1] In Fort Worth, Hare & Hare served as the city's consultant for nearly forty years, and in 1950, the *Fort Worth Star-Telegram* described Herbert's "imprint" on the city's physical appearance as greater than that of any other person.[2] In neighboring Dallas he accepted the park board's request to become "a second Kessler" for the city and addressed, in particular, the need for connecting parkways, neighborhood parks, and playgrounds.[3] In Houston in 1923 and 1924 the firm became consultant to both the city's park board and its planning commission, and Herbert served as the city's consultant for thirty-seven years.

Fort Worth, in north central Texas, overlooks the confluence of the Clear and West Forks of the Trinity River. Established as a military outpost, it grew into a livestock center; cotton and oil added to the economic base. In 1907, when Sid Hare was at work on the city's first modern burial park—Mount Olivet Cemetery—the saloons and gambling houses of its "Hell's Half Acre" district still flourished. As early as 1888, the landscape architect Nathan Barrett, co-planner of the Pullman suburb south of Chicago, had drawn plans for residential neighborhoods and parks north of the city limit near the stockyards.[4] Individuals and organizations—in particular the City Federation of Women's Clubs—worked, with little public backing or funds, to improve existing park spaces, but it was not until the Fort Worth Park League was established in 1908 that a comprehensive plan seemed feasible. That same year, acting on advice from American Civic Association president J. Horace McFarland, the group contacted George Kessler. His reports and final plan laid out the basis for a park and boulevard system and suggested establishing a permanent park commission. His recommendations were implemented in a piecemeal fashion, and growth over the next fifteen years—a near doubling of population and increase of land annexed into the city—created a need to rethink these earlier plans.

Hare & Hare became consultants to Fort Worth in 1925. The "profound impact" of the firm's nearly forty-year tenure can be credited, in part, to comprehensive park system plans it drafted, the first of these in 1930 and the second in 1957.[5] Kessler's earlier proposal—parks that utilized the city's waterways and boulevards that linked them—was expanded to a network of nearly sixty parks, large and small. Parkway treatments along creeks and rivers addressed use and aesthetics but also flood preven-

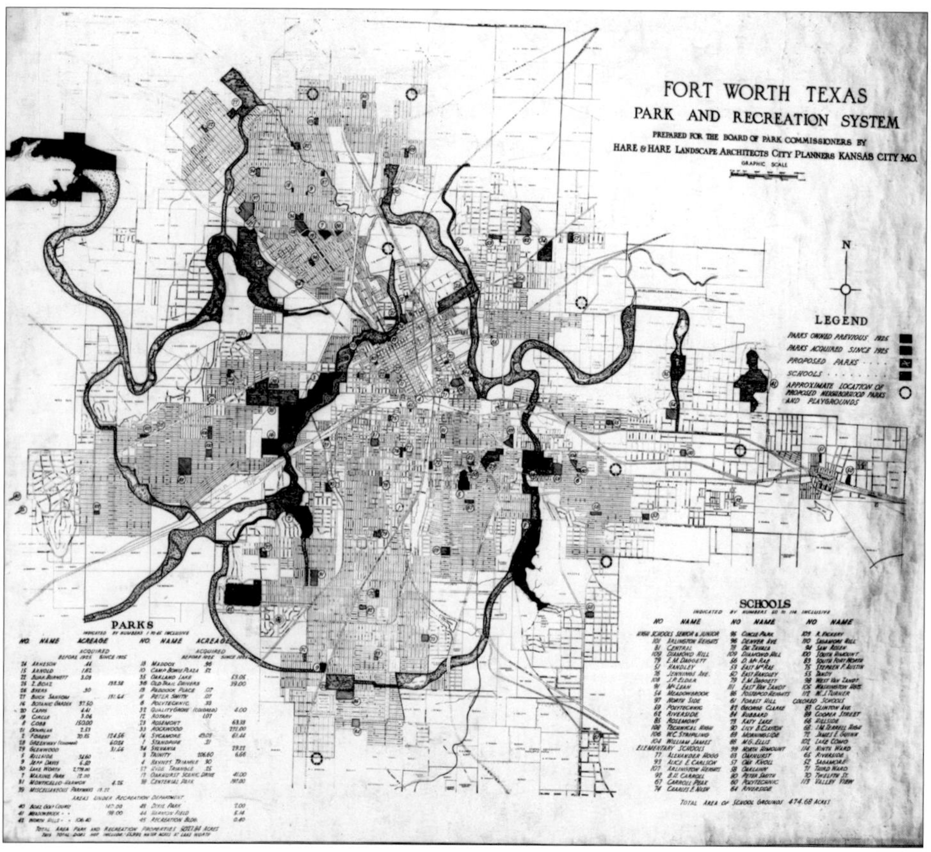

One of numerous plans prepared for the Fort Worth Board of Park Commissioners, c. 1930. SHSMO-KC.

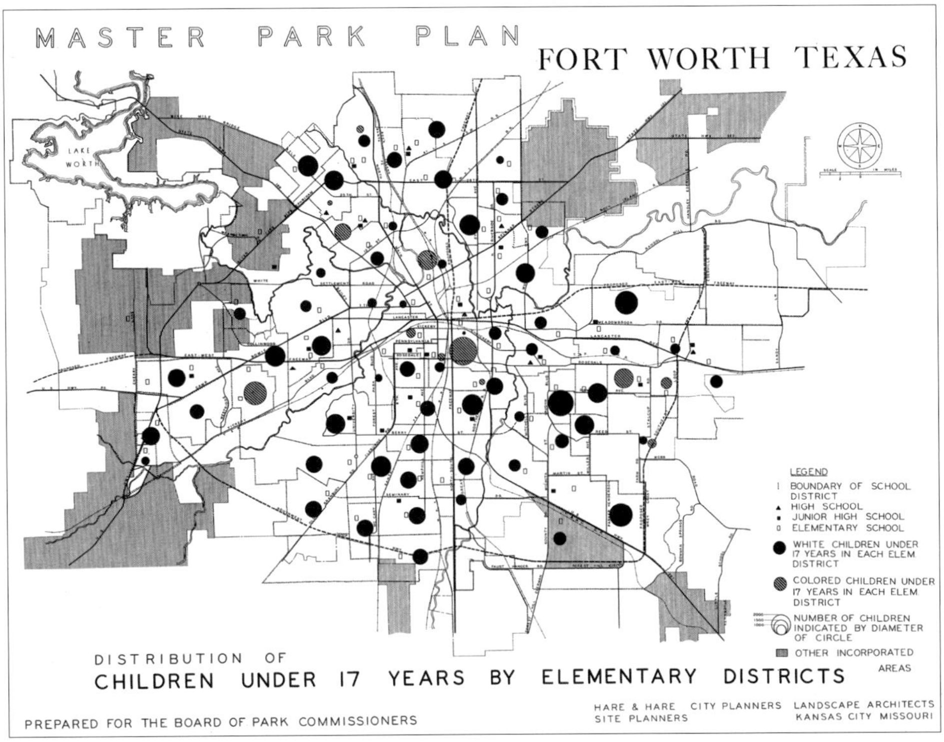

The distribution of children by district from Hare & Hare's Fort Worth schools report, c. 1930. SHSMO-KC.

tion. Public acquisition and control of both sides of principal watercourses ensured protection of the corridors and their associated views. Closing existing gaps in the system with plantings and scenic drives resulted in a city virtually enclosed by green space. The need for more neighborhood playgrounds and for suitable "intensive and organized play" space was also addressed. In 1941, Hare & Hare's typed list of drawings and maps produced for Fort Worth parks was twenty-two pages long (and the firm would serve the city another twenty years).

Major projects included the city's Forest Park Zoo, where Hare & Hare worked off and on for decades. In the 125 zoo-related plans are 78 vellum drawings executed with the same attention to detail as the firm's finest presentation drawings. Herbert seemed to enjoy the commission: at the top of several letters to the Kansas City office he inscribed the date and the words "Monkey Island," implying, in a tongue-in-cheek way, that they were being sent from the island itself. Expansion of the zoo, like many Fort Worth projects, was made possible by Depression-era federal work-relief funding. The park department readily received these funds "because it was the only city department with a well-defined plan"—that provided by Hare

& Hare.[6] Another long-term project on which the firm partnered with the park department was a public school grounds development program which improved fifty-four schools over a twenty-year period. In some instances the program simply "corrected deficiencies" by improving landscaping and

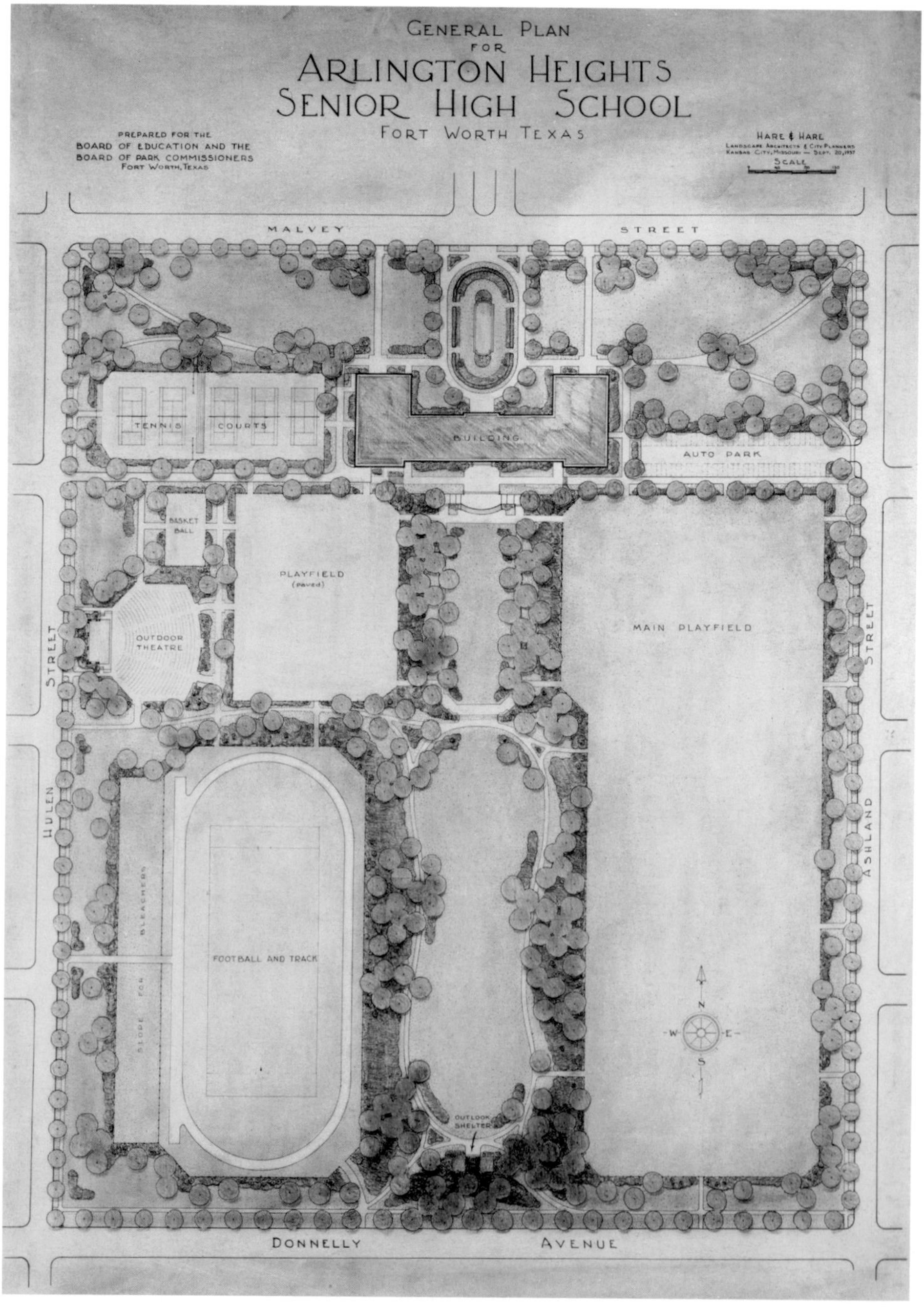

Plan for Arlington Heights Senior High School, from the Fort Worth public school grounds improvement project, 1937. SHSMO-KC.

providing terraces and water fountains. In others, as at Arlington Heights High School (1936), Hare & Hare designed a parklike campus with a reflecting pool, informal walks, and wooded areas surrounding ball fields and sports facilities. The firm's lovely drawing of the school grounds appears to be the work of D. D. Obert, who would later become Fort Worth's second city forester in 1939.[7]

The Municipal Rose Garden (located in the city's Botanic Garden) resulted from the successful give-and-take of Herbert, the Tarrant County

"Rose Gardens in Trinity Park, Fort Worth," 1933. City of Fort Worth, Fort Worth Botanic Garden.

Relief workers at the Rose Garden, 1933. City of Fort Worth, Fort Worth Botanic Garden.

Rose Society, and city forester Raymond C. Morrison.[8] Its design incorporated a formal arrangement, Italian in inspiration, to be viewed from a pavilion of local Palo Pinto sandstone. An eight-hundred-foot vista extended the garden to the river, and a trellised walk, set on a north-south axis, created a long promenade for strolling which quickly earned the name "Peacock Alley." Construction began in early 1933 and employed approximately 750 laborers provided by the Reconstruction Finance Corporation's Relief Committee. Although the men earned a wage of only two dollars per day, they donated money to help purchase roses for the garden they then helped build. The following spring nearly six thousand rose bushes filled its beds.

Three of Hare & Hare's most important clients, E. E. Bewley, Amon G. Carter, and Morris E. Berney, had residences in the exclusive west section of River Crest, which had been planned in 1911 on the bluff high above the West Fork of Trinity River. The firm improved the grounds of Carter's and Berney's houses, which had been built in the early years of the subdivision, but it was involved with the Bewley project from its construction in 1927. Bewley and his wife chose the Houstonian John Staub as their architect, and the "Anglo-Texan country house" he designed broke the pattern set by its neighbors by capitalizing on the view.[9] Set on twenty acres, the house straddled a ridge and faced the low broad plain—and the river—to the north. Construction photographs show little more than a landscape of scrub, dirt, and rock before Hare & Hare's involvement. The firm's plans

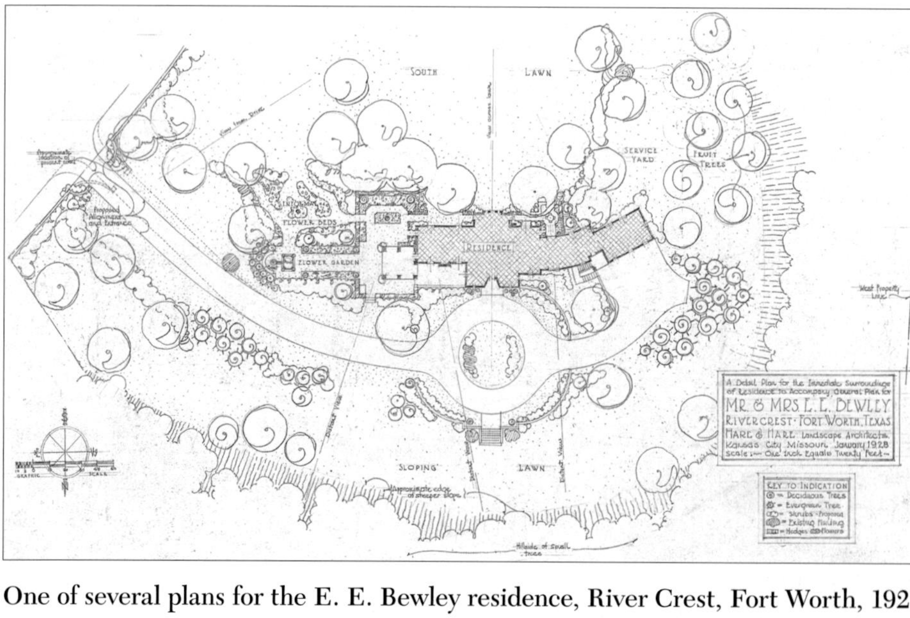

One of several plans for the E. E. Bewley residence, River Crest, Fort Worth, 1928. SHSMO-KC.

include a sloping lawn that dropped from a circular motor court to a grass terrace at midpoint to the wooded hillside below. Notations—"the bottom of the valley" and "the top of the bank"—give a sense of the house's relationship to the larger landscape. The "distant views" toward the river and across the open south lawn are also indicated as defining elements of the plan.

The Bewleys' neighbor Amon Carter had helped build Fort Worth by persuading the oil and aviation industries to locate there. He contributed to the city's education and culture by fiercely promoting (and funding) Texas Christian University and founding a museum of American art to which he donated his collection of Western works by Frederic Remington and Charles Russell.[10] For close to a decade, Hare & Hare "edited" Carter's grounds, removing a wall and small trees to open up a viewshed to the edge of the property and taking out trees of the wrong character (e.g., the parasol-shaped varnish tree, *Firmiana simplex*). Existing specimens were moved to more appropriate locations, and thickets and a grouping of flowering peach trees were kept. Plans for a cutting garden, with a complex tapestry-like pattern, called for more than six thousand tulips and a good number of lilies, followed by two thousand perennials. Two hundred and fifty Chatillon roses, backed by hedges, framed the far end.

Morris Berney, president of the park board for twenty years, lived in a house designed by the Chicago architect David Adler and his associate Henry Dangler. Among Hare & Hare's plans and drawings for the River Crest property were nine vellum plans, a charming fleur-de-lys fountain, and a plant list. One plan indicates how the house is set on the crest of its site and the lawn drops down to a pergola, with a small pool and flower garden below. Two presentation drawings (by D. D. Obert) illustrate alternate views of the garden from the house and from the lawn. Because horticulture was a hobby of Berney's—he was personally involved in planting trees and flowers at city parks when he was on the board—these plans leave many decisions to him, with certain plants and garden features to be "selected by owner." Herbert's firm consulted on Berney's garden from 1930 to 1950, nearly the same span of years the two worked together on the Fort Worth park system. That partnership resulted in improvements to recreational areas, such as those at the 3,700-acre Lake Worth, and in the creation of numerous neighborhood parks, like the one named for Berney in the Hare & Hare–planned subdivision of Ridglea.[11]

Dallas, Fort Worth's north-central Texas neighbor, was a small step ahead when it came to early park planning. The first park board was established in 1905, and by 1923, the city would have 3,500 acres in two dozen

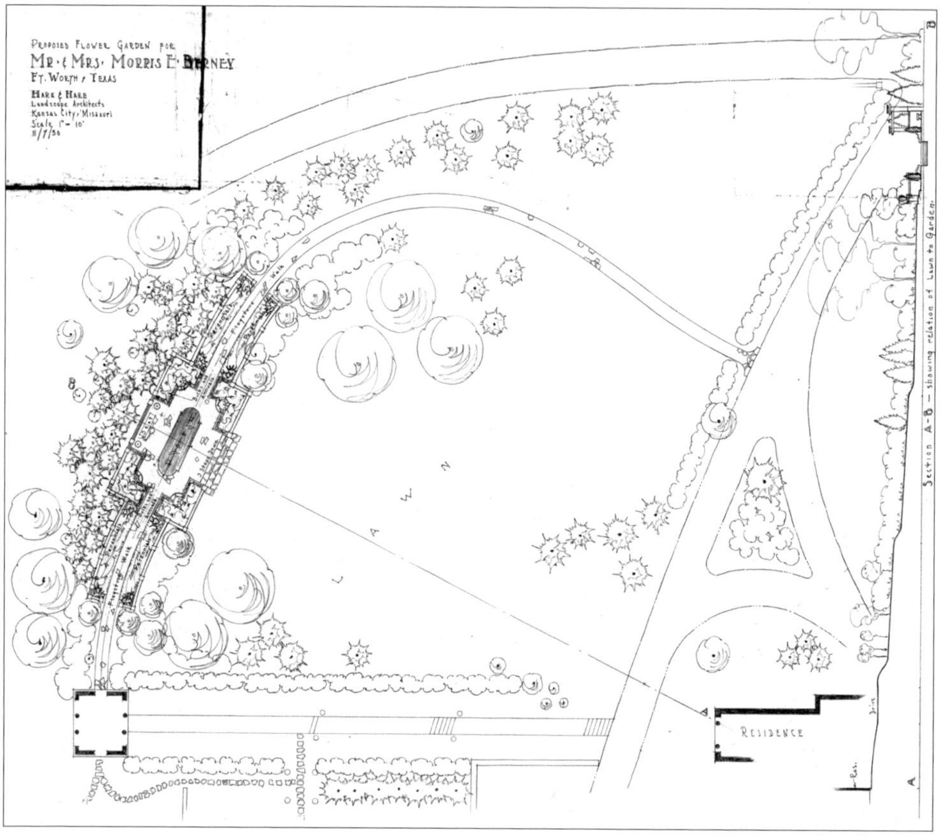

"Proposed Flower Garden for Mr. and Mrs. Morris E. Berney," with elevation drawing showing relation of lawn to garden, 1930. SHSMO-KC.

parks.[12] Dallas hired George Kessler as a consultant in 1909, but few of the comprehensive recommendations in his forty-page report, published three years later, were implemented. (His plans for Turtle Creek Parkway, downtown street alignments, and the straightening and leveeing of Trinity River were the exceptions.) One civic leader who fought to counter haphazard growth during these years was George B. Dealey, the unofficial "father of planning in Dallas."[13] He would remain active, and exert influence as the manager of the *Dallas Morning News,* in the following decades.

Hare & Hare first took on work in Dallas in the early 1920s. The developer Hugh Prather had taken J. C. Nichols's advice in 1923 and employed the firm for his Highland Park West neighborhood and its "shopping village"—a variation of Kansas City's Country Club District.[14] Sid oversaw plans for the Greenway Parks neighborhood off Mockingbird Lane, a few doors down from Highland Park, whose two-acre estate lots, ample green space, and bridle paths were only partially complete. Herbert worked to build relationships, as in the summer of 1924, when he met with city officials and interested parties about the newly formed Kessler Plan Association, whose goal was to implement the unfinished recommendations from 1912.[15] From this meeting on, Hare & Hare would earn the approval of an increasing number of individuals in charge of the city's decision making. Association members would credit Fort Worth's "slow gain" on Dallas to Herbert and his plans (which that city had implemented "religiously").[16] When, in 1931, the organization acknowledged the need for the best consultant to oversee its mission—the "scientific development" of every part of greater Dallas—it contacted Hare & Hare.

In the midst of the Depression, Dallas won out over Houston and San Antonio as the location of the Texas Centennial Exposition, an "empire on parade" celebrating the state's history and progress. It would require a $25 million conversion of Fair Park (the state fairgrounds) and the transformation of nearly three hundred acres in a mere seventeen months. Hugh Prather and Fort Worth's Morris Berney were among the individuals who recommended Hare & Hare for the job, as did the board of directors of the Kessler Plan Association. In a letter to Cullen Thomas, a member of the planning commission, the association laid out its reasoning. Herbert, it said, "knows Texas, her history, her people, her institutions and most important of all he knows our soil, our climate, our plants and he knows how to group plants and buildings in a way that will be at once beautiful and will at the same time tell the story of Texas. If you can find a better landscape architect, get him. The Texas Centennial is entitled to the best."[17]

By early 1935, the master planning team had been hired. It included the local architect George Dahl, Paul Cret as consulting architect, the local firm of Myers, Noyes & Forrest as project engineers, and Hare & Hare as landscape architects. Herbert and Don Bush contributed considerable time traveling to Dallas several times a month; D. D. Obert served as the firm's resident landscape architect overseeing every aspect on the ground, writing weekly progress reports, and keeping the Kansas City office informed. Within a month, a preliminary layout of the grounds had been completed; general plans for landscaping and plant lists were to follow, as were sketches and studies of specific "unit areas."

Eventually, 124 buildings and attractions, many of which were located along three main axes that converged at the center of the park, would occupy the landscaped grounds. The "Esplanade of State" and its eight-hundred-foot-long reflecting basin, enlivened with fountains and cascades, constituted another primary axis. The southeast quadrant included an irregular-shaped lake anchoring a grouping of cultural buildings, which contrasted with the esplanade's formality. Two hundred mature trees,

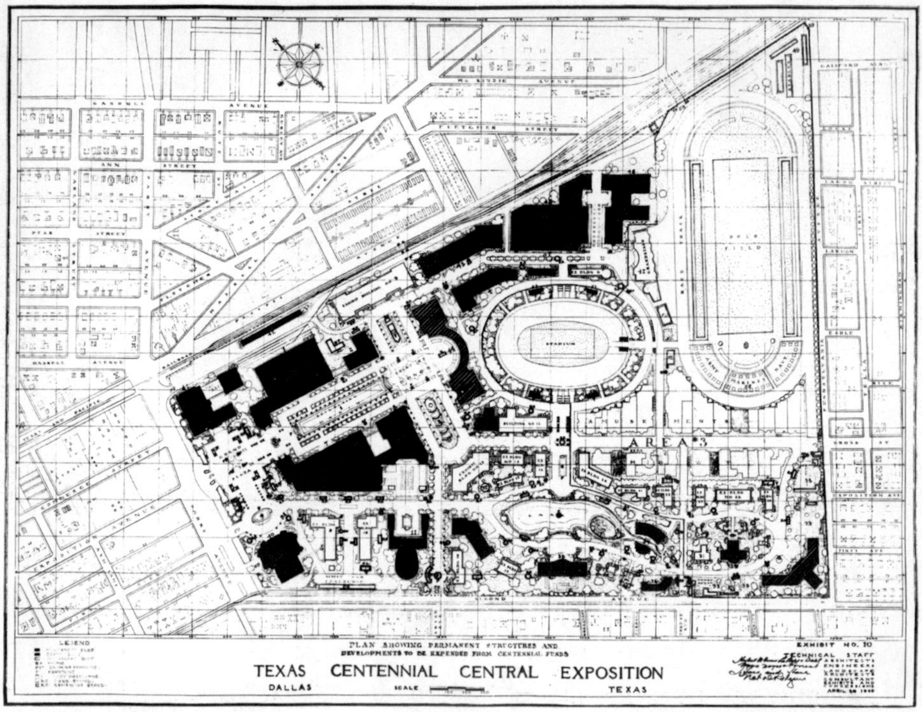

Hare & Hare's plan for the Texas Centennial Exposition, Dallas, 1935. SHSMO-KC.

including palms, live oaks (*Quercus virginiana*), and cedar elms (*Ulmus crassifolia*), were brought in to shade the grounds. Plant estimates for the main concourses alone totaled just under $90,000. Fifty carloads of nursery stock, and plants representing the east, west, and south portions of the state—pines, cactus, and citrus—added color and defined vistas.

The concerted effort to complete the exposition grounds by deadline resulted in the firm's spending 50 percent more time on the project than the contract stipulated. The city park department, which had been involved with planting throughout the project, executed the finishing touches on opening day. Ultimately, only Texans—the architect George Dahl and Ray Foley, the director of works—were credited on the Texas Centennial master plan, a circumstance Herbert worked to correct. In letters to Dahl and the event's general manager, William Webb, he asked that the title be changed to include the firm's name in order to give "fair recognition" of its services; but no revised plans were ever issued by the exposition's publicity department.[18]

In 1939, Hare & Hare was hired as the city's park consultants. Its charge was to prepare a master plan and to design new parks and improve existing ones. The firm would draft two comprehensive reports, completed

Esplanade Fountain at Fair Park, Dallas. Photo by Carol M. Highsmith, 2014. Carol M. Highsmith Archive, LC.

in 1942; the first provided a long-term plan for a parkway and boulevard system in the metropolitan district, and the second addressed parks, playgrounds, and playfields "within the corporate limits of Dallas."[19] Conceived to serve all sections of the community and its "various social and racial groups," the reports detailed, for example, that playgrounds and neighborhood parks should be a maximum distance of two miles apart and no less than ten acres in size. Although the current system met the day's standard of "one acre [of park land] per one hundred population," Hare & Hare advised the purchase of additional land so that the system could grow to accommodate an estimated population of 700,000 by 1970; recommendations included adding 500 to 600 acres in playgrounds, playfields, and neighborhood parks, 4,000 to 5,000 acres in parkways, and 2,500 to 3,000 acres in "reservations"—large natural areas with minimum access.[20]

Dallas did not hire Hare & Hare as its city planners (a decision that may reveal the continued influence of George Dealey, who identified the firm with "park work" only). Instead, the St. Louisian Harland Bartholomew was commissioned to conceive an updated city plan in 1943.[21] The resulting set of reports, *A Master Plan for Greater Dallas,* was five hundred pages in length and organized in fourteen volumes.[22] Its section dealing with parks, parkways, and schools (*Report Number Seven*) incorporated Hare & Hare's 1942 reports, although Herbert is credited only with providing maps to be used as a starting point for further planning. Bartholomew's plan did have some impact, but in less than a decade it

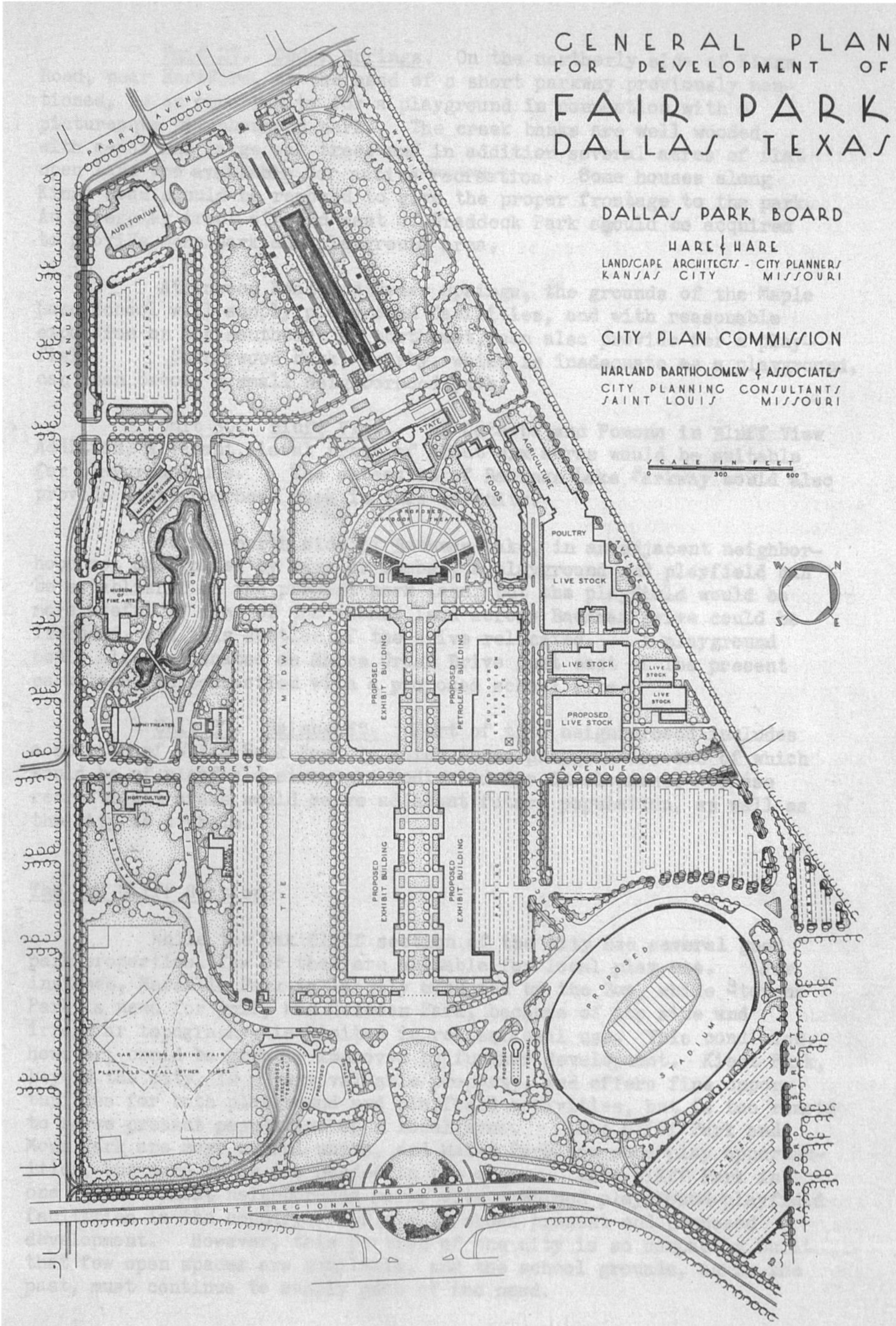

Fair Park, site of the Texas Centennial Exposition, after its redevelopment by Hare & Hare and Harland Bartholomew & Associates, 1944. SHSMO-KC.

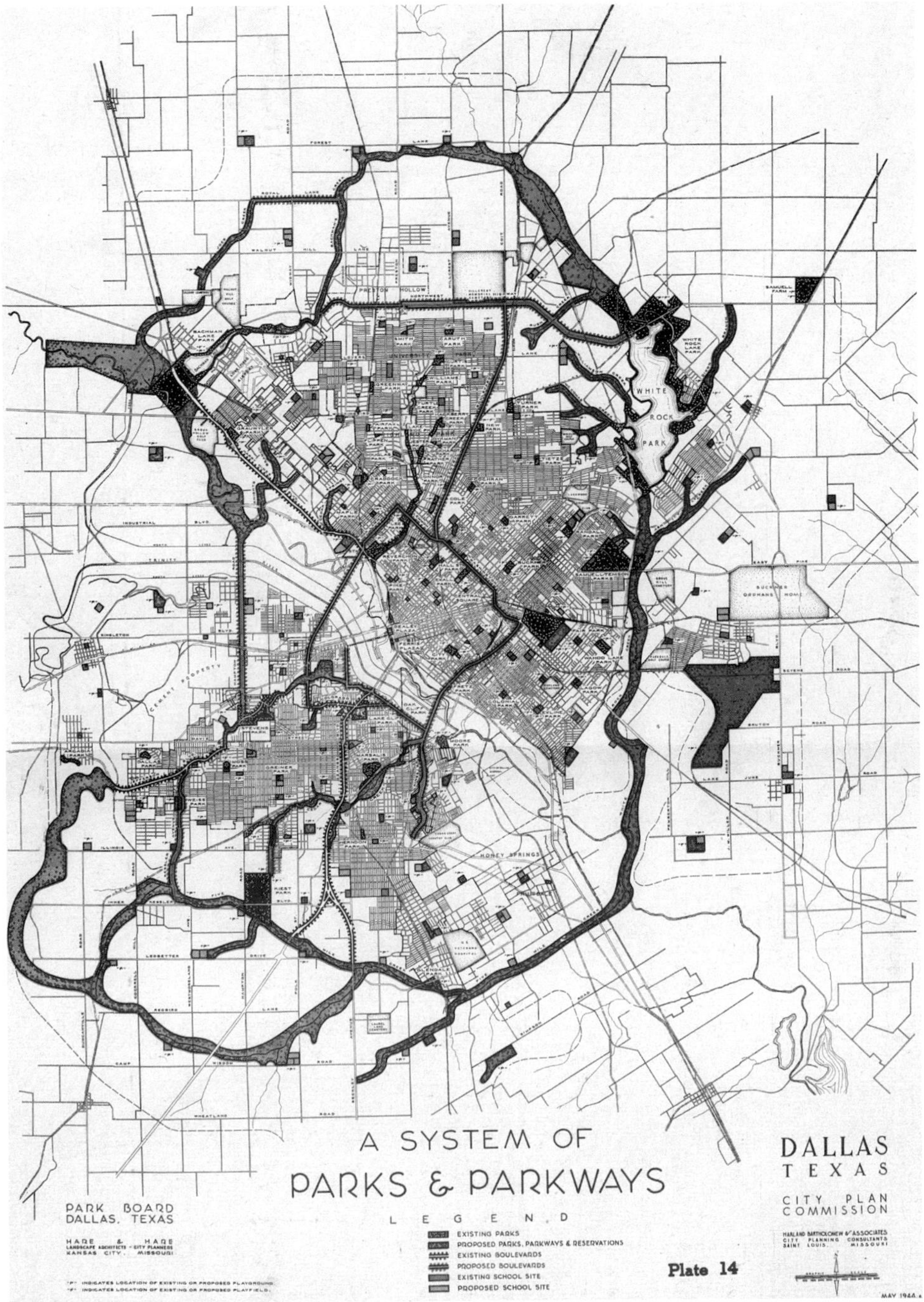

"A System of Parks & Parkways" from Harland Bartholomew & Associates and Hare & Hare, *A Master Plan for Dallas, Texas; Report Number Seven, A System of Parks and Schools*, 1944. SHSMO-KC.

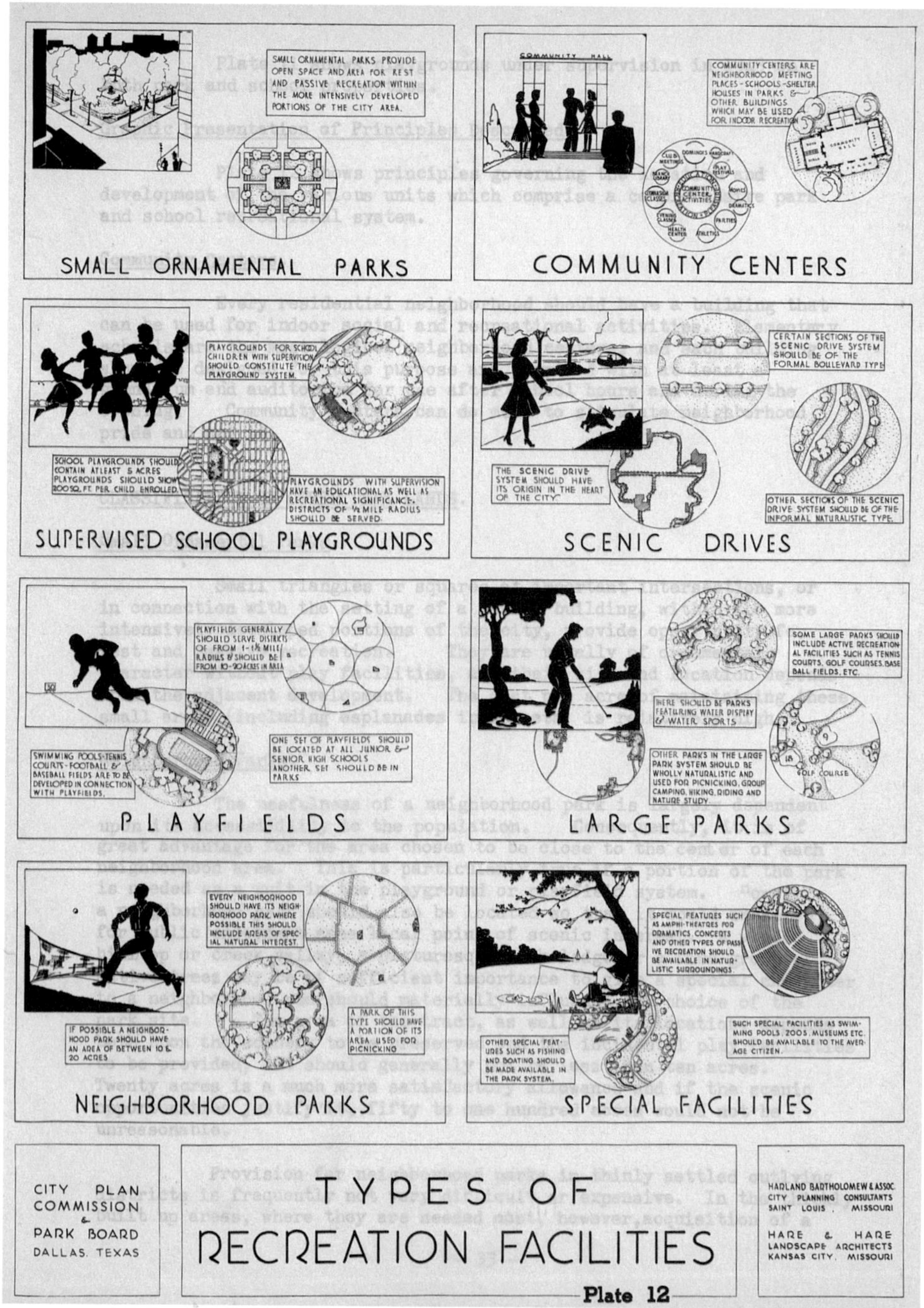

"Types of Recreation Facilities" from *Report Number Seven, A System of Parks and Schools*. SHSMO-KC.

was gathering dust in the basement of city hall.[23] Hare & Hare continued to work on Dallas park projects through 1956, but its plans soon met the same fate. Rediscovered in 2002 during research for a new strategic plan, the firm's documents illustrate the creative process that Herbert and the park department engaged in: working sketches appear to be "the product of free dialogue and open discussion" between the landscape architect and city staff.[24]

Early Houston was a lot like Kansas City. Both were founded in the 1830s at a junction of two waterways suited to transportation and trade. In Houston these were the Buffalo and White Oak Bayous. Most bayous were meandering, slow-moving streams characterized by log jams, sand bars, and a water volume that fluctuated greatly with the seasons. But Buffalo Bayou was an exception. Emptying into Galveston Bay and the Gulf of Mexico, it was deep and wide compared with most, with a more constant water level. The New York land speculators Augustus C. and John K. Allen had invested in 6,642 acres adjacent to this bayou to found the "Town of Houston," so named for Sam Houston, the soon-to-be president of the Lone Star

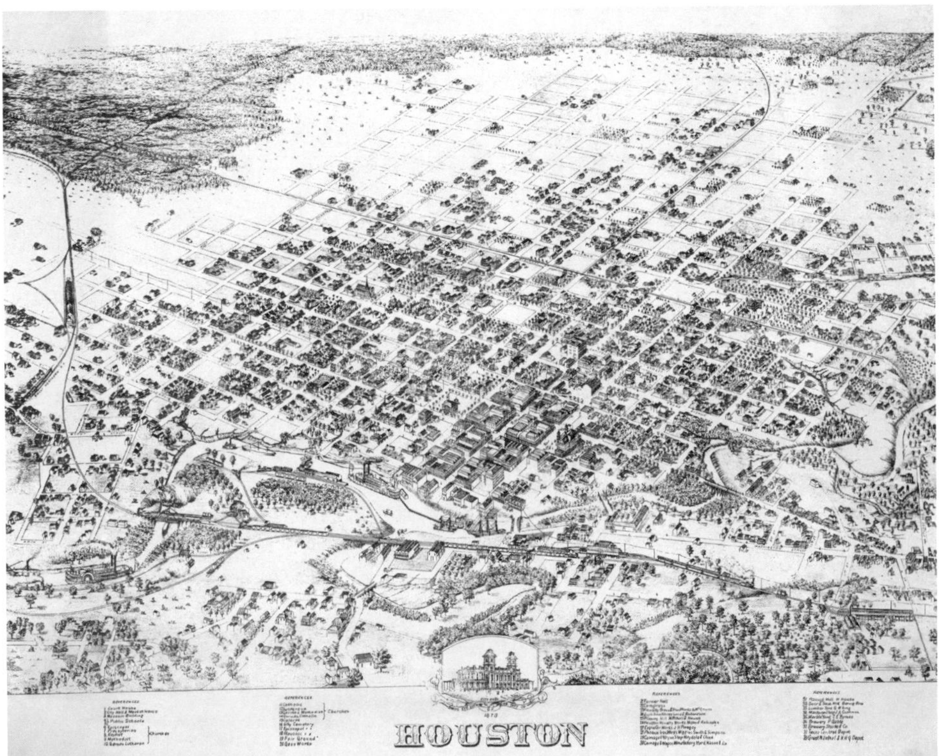

Bird's-eye view of Houston, Texas, 1873. HMRC.

Republic. The site they chose, in their words, would forever "command the trade of the largest and richest portion of Texas."[25]

The gridiron plan that the Allens platted spread out from Buffalo Bayou onto the flat coastal plain. It included two public squares, corner lots for a school and a church, and broad streets "commensurate with the great city they envisioned."[26] Their advertisement promoted the site's abundance of spring water, timber—live oaks and magnolia trees—and southeasterly breezes that blew from the Gulf.[27] Despite these advantages, early residents struggled with many of the same conditions as their Kansas City counterparts. Gullies and ravines cut through town, streets were paths of dust or mud (their solution was to pave them with crushed oyster shells), and livestock roamed commercial blocks. The landing—the economic heart of the city—was quickly becoming choked with boats and cargo.

Between 1850 and 1890, Houston's population rose from just under 2,400 citizens to over 27,000. The following decade it nearly doubled. As a means to attract residents and businesses, it employed the same boosterism used by the Missouri city fathers: nature, so it seemed, had marked this place as the ideal site for progress, with the potential to become a "great commercial emporium."[28] Initially, the town built an economy based on lumber and cotton, its biggest cash crop, and on the varied trade that flowed through. After the 1901 discovery of oil at Spindletop, in fields eighty miles

Boats on Buffalo Bayou, 1895. HMRC.

to the east, the petroleum industry drove its economy. When the dredging and widening of the Houston Ship Channel was completed thirteen years later, the town at the head of Buffalo Bayou became the country's newest deepwater port accessible to ocean-going vessels.

Houston's push for parks began in earnest in 1910, under mayor Horace Baldwin Rice's leadership, with his appointment of a three-member board of park commissioners. Community leaders envisioned a system of parks and boulevards that circled the city and linked its major bayous. Arthur Coleman Comey, a Harvard-trained landscape architect and city planner from Cambridge, Massachusetts, was hired to assess how Houston might attain its goal. His comprehensive 1913 report placed parks within the larger context of city planning and included several recommendations echoing Mayor Rice's aims: the need for the city's bayous and creek valleys to serve as the backbone of the system, with parks lining these waterways, and the preservation of a large tract of land in its natural state for public use.[29] Comey's plans garnered public support but, in a city that would come to be known for its aversion to planning, his ambitious proposals failed to be adopted as policy.[30]

Public-spirited citizens, rather than city politicians, were the driving force behind parks and planning in Houston. George H. Hermann, who spent a lifetime in the cattle, real estate, and oil businesses and served on the first park board, was one such citizen. His 1914 bequests included

Oil drilling rigs near Houston, 1917. HMRC.

Main Street from Texas Avenue, 1910. HMRC.

a 285-acre swath of pine forest along Brays Bayou adjacent to the newly founded Rice Institute on the city's south side, to be used for park purposes, and a square block downtown, which would carry his name, to be retained as "breathing space." Before his death, Hermann and city engineer John W. Maxcy (who laid out the city's first park in 1899) worked together on a plan for the acreage. Clarence L. Brock, superintendent of city parks (from 1912 until 1943), would oversee the beginnings of improvements to Hermann Park.[31]

George Kessler, hired as Houston's landscape consultant in 1915, was ultimately commissioned to design Hermann Park's master plan. Herbert A. Kipp, a drainage expert who had become the city engineer that year, drew many of the working plans and oversaw initial improvements. Aside from the park plan, of which only a drawing of the entrance quadrant survives, Kessler's legacy includes the dramatic improvement of Main Street, which ran along its western edge, from an unpaved road into a boulevard lined with double rows of live oaks. Echoing the axial avenues of Rice Institute's campus (designed by Boston's Cram, Goodhue & Ferguson), Kessler's boulevard imposed "a new sense of rhythm, measure, and pro-

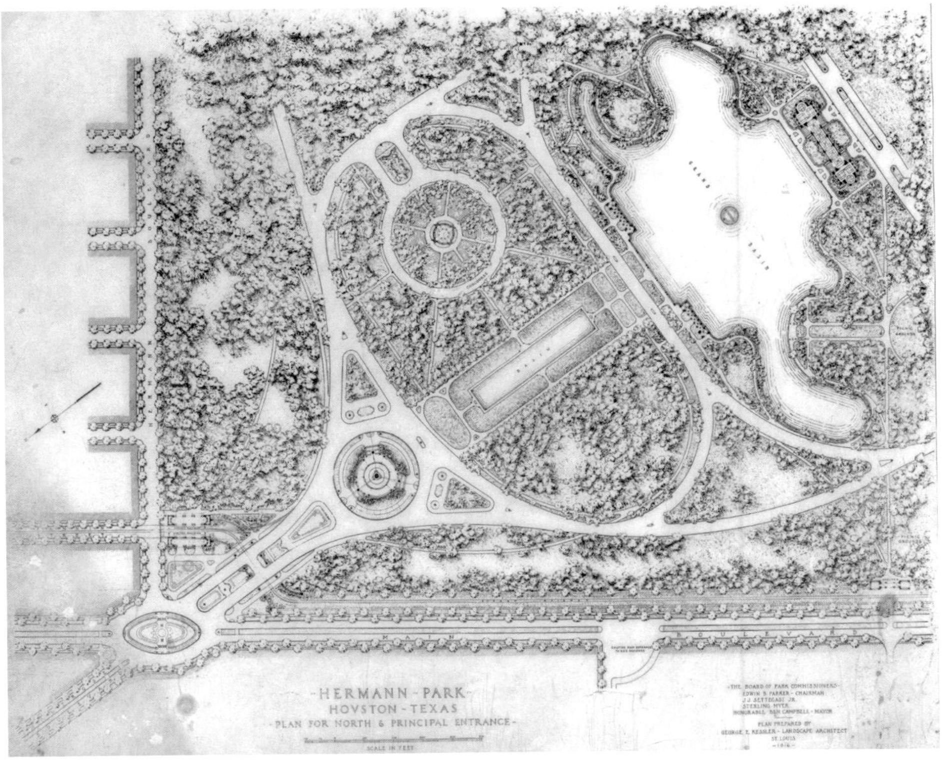

George Kessler's "Principal Entrance" to Hermann Park, 1916. City of Houston Parks Department Collection, HMRC.

portion" to what was still open countryside.[32] After 1917, a lack of funding and World War I curtailed further development of Hermann Park, leaving only the entrance and a few of its drives completed.

In 1910, the Houston investment agent and insurance man Harvey T. D. Wilson wrote to Sid Hare requesting his assistance in designing a residential subdivision on the city's east side across Brays Bayou from the new country club.[33] Unlike other Houston neighborhoods, it would represent a break from tradition in terms of planning. The earlier, elite neighborhoods of Westmoreland (1902) and Courtlandt Place (1907) looked more to the past than the future.[34] These neighborhoods were platted in a grid that meshed with the city's, and their boulevards (with limited access) were lined with grand houses uniformly set back on deep lots. Ornamental gateways and deed restrictions were means by which they identified and retained their special place within the city and beyond the reach of most homeowners. Wilson's project, on the other hand, would be a suburban neighborhood removed from the city. Sid's plan for what eventually became known as

Forest Hill was the first in Houston's history to treat the bayou that curled around the edge of the property as a scenic feature.

Wilson was versed in gardens and design, and aside from his primary businesses he owned a local nursery. On the property he and his brother had inherited (a full city block) he planted roses, long rows of flowers shaded by oaks, and filled star-shaped and round beds with tropical specimens like giant elephant ears (*Colocasia*).[35] It was most likely Wilson who contributed the aesthetic sensibilities and forward thinking to the new project. He

The neighborhood, or "residential park," of Forest Hill, Houston, 1910–1911. SHSMO-KC.

and his two partners envisioned "a boulevard loop" with the club and their suburban subdivision as its principal points.[36] Along that route, the tangled layers of the bayou's native bald cypress (*Taxodium distichum*) grew and oaks hung with Spanish moss. Beneath, shrubby undergrowth of cherry laurel, hawthorn, and dwarf palm (*Sabal minor*) would be lit with seasonal color from blossoms and berries.

Within a few weeks of Wilson's letter, on his return from platting Mission Burial Park in San Antonio, Sid stopped in Houston to walk the ground and meet with Wilson. Two preliminary plans were drawn (with alternatives for the bayou crossing) and plan "B" was accepted. "Your work pleases us very much," the investors wrote, noting their intention to carry out Sid's ideas in their entirety.[37] Ready to advertise, they pushed Sid, via telegram, to have detailed plans back to Houston within days—in time for publication in that Sunday's paper. Although he was unable to meet that deadline, Sid platted the property, provided a working blueprint, and prepared watercolor and planting plans suggesting the locations for trees and shrubs.[38] Two things he left to the developers were the naming of streets (a lesson he may have learned working across town with Bellaire's investor, who favored generic names rather than those with any relationship to Texas) and the number of pines to be thinned across the property.

After this early progress, a series of setbacks began to slow things down. Tracts of needed land could not be purchased. Wilson decided to keep his thirty-acre share on the property's northeast side as his private estate, retaining for himself what would have been prime lots lining Brays Bayou.[39] (He later asked Sid to improve it as a "residential park" and to find a suitable individual to oversee progress.) With Wilson backing away from the commitment, Sid began working directly with his ex-partners, two members of the Vaundun Company (a conflation of the partners' last names). Soon payments began to fail, plans were returned as undeliverable, and a reorganization of the company was prompted when one partner left Houston "under a heavy cloud."[40] The subdivision, Vaundun Place, was renamed Forest Hill.

As it neared completion, the streetcar suburb of Forest Hill would be pronounced a success, "the best about Houston." Its beautiful drives and other features, according to Edward Teas, placed it in the "front rank" of the city's suburban neighborhoods.[41] Its plan was the first with streets that deviated from the grid of downtown. They instead radiated out from the bayou in a series of arcs creating a fanlike shape as they moved eastward. Sid's plantings then tied Forest Hill into a visual whole. By 1912, architect-designed houses, such as those by the local architect W. A. Cooke and the Dallas firm of Lang & Witchell, were built along its streets.[42] In the 1920s, as Forest Hill was becoming a middle-class neighborhood of modest houses anchoring the increasingly industrial East End, Houston's most dramatic growth was taking place on the opposite side of the city.

Clarence L. Brock, Houston's superintendent of parks, telegrammed the Hare & Hare office in late July of 1923, when Herbert was on the West Coast, in Longview, and then Hollywood, on business.[43] Stating that the Houston park board needed plans for its new zoo in Hermann Park, Brock suggested that acceptance of the commission might mean a contract for future park development. Within three weeks Herbert had visited Houston, made an initial assessment of its needs, and submitted to the board a draft proposal for the zoo. He recommended that systemwide planning, rather than a piecemeal approach, might be "more in the nature of the services" the city needed.[44]

Although Herbert wanted the office to remain small enough that he could oversee project details, by the mid-1920s, with the increasing number of commissions and Sid less active, this desire became impossible.[45] Accepting work across Texas (where he would spend one week a month and eventually open a branch office) meant he was increasingly away from the drafting table and served as the public face of the firm, traveling from project to project. Increasingly, Donald Bush and Ralph Reinhardt were entrusted with the running of the Kansas City office, and additional employees, among them draftsmen H. E. Platt, C. W. Bennett, and S. Kleeberg, were hired to manage the growing workload.

An important addition to the staff was Eda Augusta Sutermeister, a 1900 graduate of the Missouri Botanical Garden's horticulture program, and the only woman in the office aside from clerical help. She had worked for George Kessler until his death in 1923, and then joined Hare & Hare, helping Herbert to finish up several Kessler projects. She quickly proved herself more than capable—she was paid at the same rate as Donald Bush—handling aspects of the Longview project, Mount Olivet Cemetery in Fort Worth, and multiple Texas commissions. When planning Houston's zoo, park superintendent Brock chose to work with her rather than Sid.[46] With Herbert called away on business and out of the country one summer, Sutermeister filled in as his equal. She traveled to Houston, in Herbert's words, "in lieu" of him.[47] She would stay with the firm until her death from pneumonia on April 13, 1929. Her death certificate cited no profession.

A preliminary study for Hermann Park's "Zoological Gardens" had been conceived by September 1923, and the plan evolved the following spring. Brock dealt directly with Sutermeister, sending her updates describing day-to-day activities such as the building of pheasant cages and the feeding of animals. Having received his authorization to finalize zoo plans, she executed the revised version signing her work—"E. A. S."—in the lower left corner.[48] It consisted of an informal arrangement of cages and habitats, all labeled, that fit within the zoo's oval footprint. Anchoring the central space were structures for housing primates, birds, and elephants. Outside were triangular parks for deer and bison. Set along the same line of sight, one mirroring the other, were a proposed natural history museum and an aquarium. All of this was arranged around the zoo's most formal space—a series of three reflecting pools lined with rows of live oaks—a spine that linked the zoo to the rest of Hermann Park. Hare & Hare's handling of this space—water, hardscape, plantings—gave form to a landscape often perceived as too flat, even monotonous. The sum effect, according to the architectural historian Stephen Fox, remains "compelling."[49]

The zoo was the first of numerous projects at Hermann Park. Over the next five years Hare & Hare implemented features of Kessler's 1916 plan which became important elements of the park's primary north-south axis. The firm located the equestrian statue of Sam Houston atop a triumphal arch inside the main entrance, completed the long reflecting pool, and

Hermann Park Zoo Concourse. Photo by Gerald Moorhead, c. 1990. Gerald Moorhead Collection, Houston.

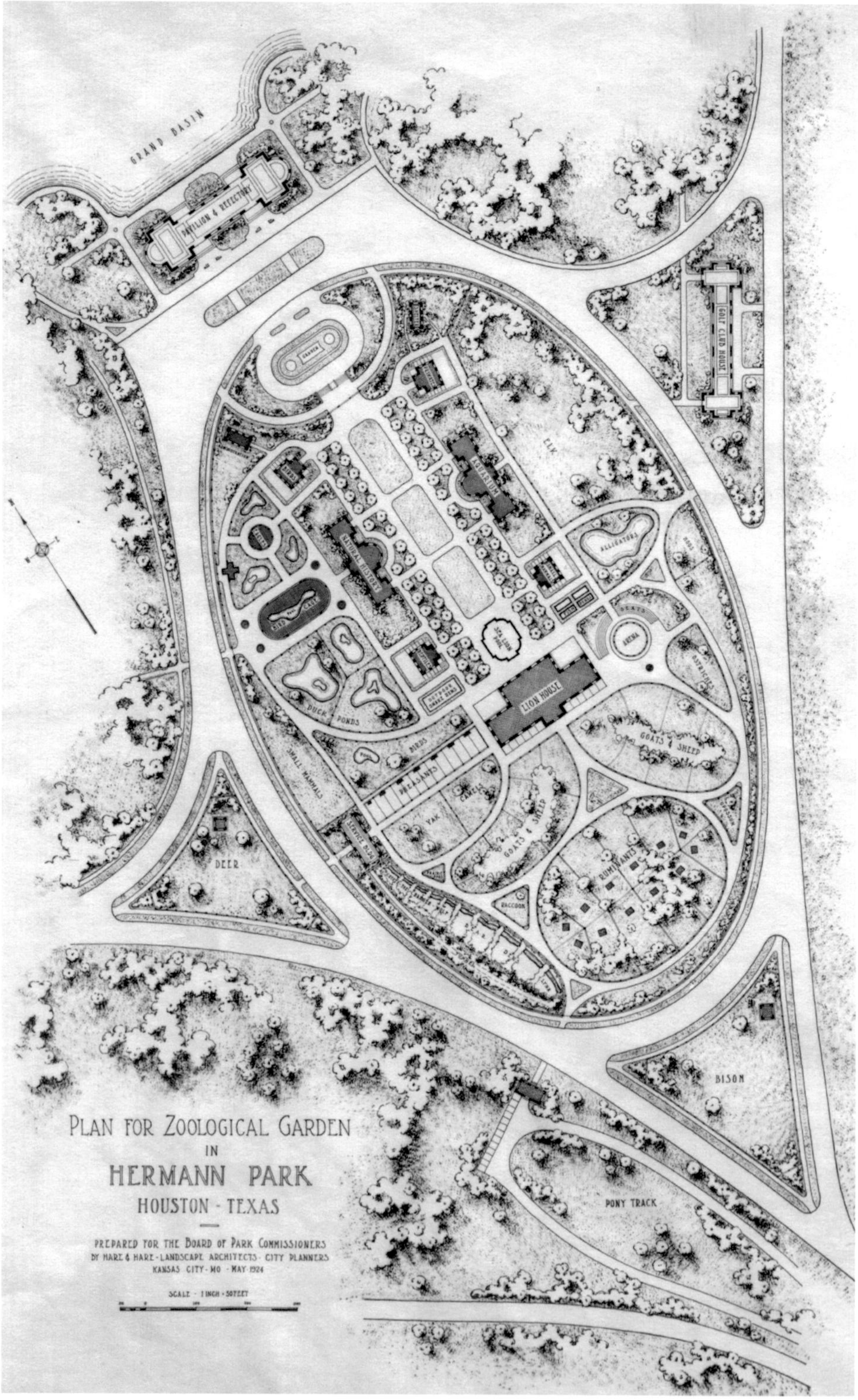

"Plan for Zoological Garden in Hermann Park, Houston," drawn by Eda Sutermeister, May 1924. SHSMO-KC.

began the Grand Basin, all elements in the entrance sequence one experienced before reaching the zoo. General plans for a botanical garden were conceived "about 1925," and plans for a rose garden there (for which Sutermeister determined the color scheme) were drawn four years later. A conservatory planned for the site was never realized. Instead, a center for the Houston Federation of Garden Clubs, with proposed formal gardens, was constructed in its place. In 1930, the firm drafted a new comprehensive plan documenting the park to date and proposing new features with an eye to the future. The plan acknowledged Kessler—the title block includes his name above the firm's and the notation "based on the original"—but its revisions and extensions make the park truly the work of both. The result balanced Kessler's grand gesture—a visionary design rooted in the City Beautiful movement—and Hare & Hare's sound planning driven by use and changing needs.

Hermann Park's multiple additions were overseen by Hare & Hare for more than twenty-five years. Among the firm's later contributions were a 1940 redevelopment of the Miller Memorial Outdoor Theatre (built in the park in 1922) and a major expansion of the zoo (1948–50).[50] This final project, which included screened parking for one thousand cars and sloped seating for ten thousand people, is but one example of how aesthetics were

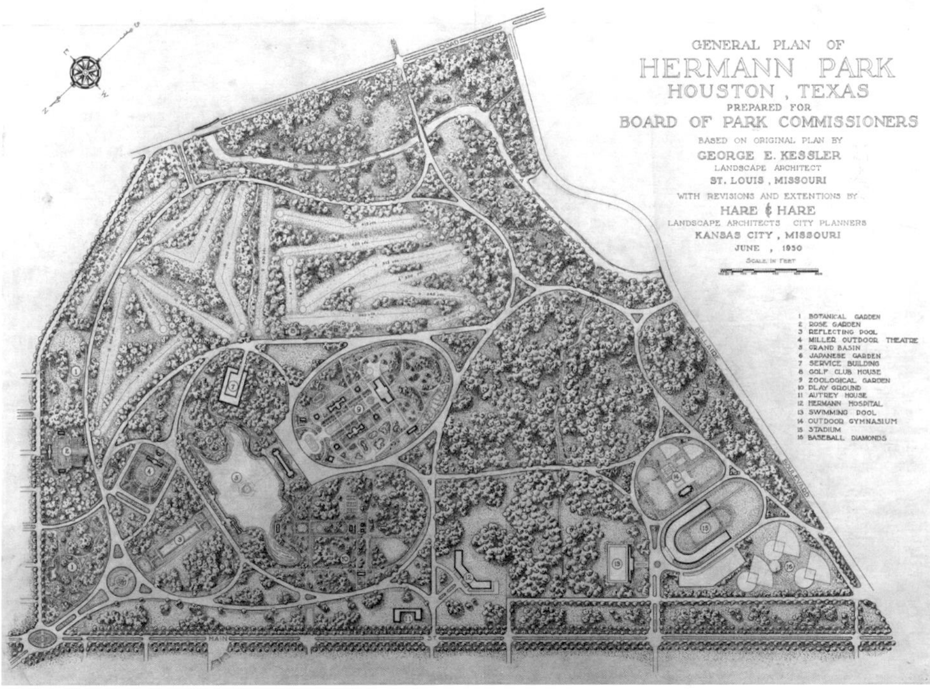

"General Plan of Hermann Park, Houston," 1930. HMRC.

Aerial view of Hermann Park Esplanade, c. 1928. HMRC.

Aerial view of Sunken Garden at Hermann Park, 1928. HMRC.

balanced with the changing demands of use. But the firm met many demands, especially those that would have eaten away at the park's wooded acres, with resistance. It served as a steward for Hermann Park, becoming vocal when inappropriate uses, such as the construction of a public school stadium, a second golf course (the first one pre-dated their involvement), and acreage for the Houston Conservatory of Music, were proposed by citizens and organizations.

On June 2, 1924, the board chairman of the Houston Park Commission wrote to Herbert, who was traveling abroad. Herbert Godwin's letter, addressed to Mr. Hare "somewhere in Europe," started off on a personal note. He talked of the importance of visiting parks and major cities, insisting that Herbert be sure to spend ample time in the "delightful" small gardens of Italy, France, and England.[51] Godwin's interest in gardening had been revived earlier that spring by the formation of the city's first garden club. His letter included a request. On Herbert's return, would he please design Godwin a garden inspired by those he'd seen in Europe, something "really charming," that Godwin could add to gradually?

In the remainder of the letter Godwin provided an update on the commission's recent progress, which included the purchase of 1,503 acres along the upper reaches of Buffalo Bayou west of the city. This property represented Houston's opportunity to add a heavily forested expanse of landscape to its park system. The acquisition—to be used "for park purposes only"—was made possible by the generous terms offered by its philanthropic owners, brothers and sister Will, Mike, and Ima Hogg, who were insistent that conservation of the land be an ongoing priority.[52] It would be named Memorial Park, a reference to its previous use as an army base where thousands of soldiers trained for World War I.[53] Temporary barracks and training facilities had been removed and cleared areas were allowed to

Memorial Park and Houston skyline, c. 2015. MIR for Nelson Byrd Woltz Landscape Architects.

regenerate. Slowly the entire acreage returned to its characteristically lush landscape of native woods, meadow, and wetlands.

For this "suburban forest reservation" along the north bank of Buffalo Bayou, the firm proposed trails, bridle paths, and scenic drives weaving through stands of pine, oak, and native holly. A minimum number of shelters and the site for a "great natural amphitheater," were included, along with an eighteen-hole golf course.[54] The only suggestion of formality was an arrow-straight drive at the proposed eastern entrance, which terminated in a focal point—a monument or gateway—before transitioning into roads that bisected the park and looped around its center. Recreation spaces—the golf course and an open "play area"—were confined to the park's northeast quadrant; the south and west quadrants remained wild and picturesque.

Herbert pledged that nature would be preserved in this public reservation. To protect the character of the place, he suggested that rules be imposed—to forbid the picking of wildflowers, for example—reminiscent of the firm's suggestions for Point Defiance Park in Tacoma. His insistence that "nothing of an artificial nature" be added was challenged in 1940, when several organizations (with ample backing) proposed a "frontier museum" adjacent to the bayou. In a *Houston Chronicle* interview Herbert insisted that a "replica of a Wild West town of early Texas days" might convey an unfortunate "sideshow or carnival atmosphere."[55] In a letter to the mayor and city council, Herbert spoke of the park's wild character as an irreplaceable asset. Granting such demands for new uses and preserving the park's integrity—its beauty as a place for passive recreation—was an impossibility, and he advised them to approach such matters with caution.[56] In upholding the park's interests, Herbert was following the lead of its outspoken (and tenacious) advocate, Miss Ima Hogg; subsequent stewards have likewise voiced opposition to inappropriate additions, including that it become the site of the Astrodome.

A decade after Hare & Hare's initial (1927–28) plans for Memorial Park, Superintendent Brock announced an addition that was a good fit. An arboretum and bird sanctuary was proposed by the board on two hundred acres at the park's southwest edge, to be accessed by gravel paths and roadways paved with shell, which would serve as an "outdoor museum." For the arboretum the firm envisioned a collection of plants and trees, both native and exotic, appropriately labeled for educational purposes. Greenhouses and a conservatory to house specimens "under glass," set among ornate beds and grass panels surrounding a two-hundred-foot-long pool for the display of water lilies and other aquatics, were proposed. Today's taste would consider the

Along Buffalo Bayou

A TYPICAL EXAMPLE OF THE FINE NATURAL SCENERY ALONG THE BAYOUS, WHICH SHOULD BE PRESERVED IN PARK LANDS

Hare & Hare photograph of Buffalo Bayou from *Report of the City Planning Commission, Houston, Texas,* 1929. SHSMO-KC.

conservatory and its grounds too formal for the arboretum's natural setting, but the firm's visually rich drawing (dated January 1940) is a work of art.[57] The project, based on Hare & Hare's plans (but without the conservatory) was finally carried out in the 1960s, in part through the efforts of the biologist and conservationist Robert Vines. Like the rest of Memorial Park, the arboretum remains a respite from the surrounding metropolis.

Buffalo Drive, 1955. HMRC.

Another long-standing objective that Hare & Hare helped Houston achieve was the incorporation of the city's bayous into the emerging park system. The firm's design for Buffalo Bayou Parkway linked Memorial Park (and the new River Oaks neighborhood to the south) to the proposed Civic Center two and one-half miles away. The recommendation was to acquire both sides of the bayou (typically a span of five hundred to eight hundred feet) which would allow room for wide drives and green space to skirt the watercourse. Confident that a well-planned parkway would become the model, Herbert assured the park board that the improvement of other bayou corridors would follow.[58] The end result would be the preservation of these meandering waterways—the one exceptional feature of the coastal Texas topography—as Houston's principal scenic asset. Ultimately, the firm's bayou work went beyond beauty and use to include conservation and maintenance. In 1935, following the worst flood in the city's history, Hare & Hare suggested effective precautions to control flooding and help prevent future occurrences.[59]

In the 1920s, Will Hogg, eldest sibling in the family committed to bettering Houston, was the city's most vocal and determined advocate of park and city planning.[60] He believed a beautiful city made better citizens, and that a well-designed suburban neighborhood with "homes to last for all time" could serve as a model for all of Houston. When Will, his brother Mike, and business partner Hugh Potter conceived River Oaks, they made "no little plans."[61] What Potter called their "distinguished experiment" began with two hundred acres and would increase in size to more than a thousand acres spreading south of Buffalo Bayou over two-and-a-half square miles. Herbert was instructed to lay out this property—farmland and pasture at the intersection of forest and prairie—so as to retain a parklike isolation and "quietude."[62] River Oaks proved to be a lesson in the aesthetic and commercial value of good planning.[63] Fifty years after its inception, the architectural critic Ada Louise Huxtable condemned 1970s Houston but noted River Oaks' exceptional planning.[64]

Hogg and Potter's first step in envisioning River Oaks was to hire Hare & Hare in the spring of 1924.[65] Days after forming a corporation to oversee the development, they traveled to Kansas City to meet with J. C. Nichols and Herbert. After lunch they were given a tour of the Country Club District, no doubt driving down Ward Parkway and across the state line to where the Hare firm was at work on Mission Hills. In Houston a reception was held to kick off the project (the mayor and city commissioners were in attendance), and the city's *Post-Dispatch* described Herbert as the new "expert" in charge. Over the following months Potter and Nichols traveled back and forth between Houston and Kansas City, and Will Hogg stopped in Missouri on a trip back from Los Angeles to spend time "loafing" and discussing the project.[66] The Houston developers, gleaning ideas from Baltimore and California, went also to Highland Park in Dallas (where Hare & Hare was at work on the west addition of that suburb for Flippen-Prather Realty). But it was the Kansas City model they emulated.[67]

The firm produced a range of work for River Oaks, from topographic studies to a master plan. They proposed street signs (which wove the letters

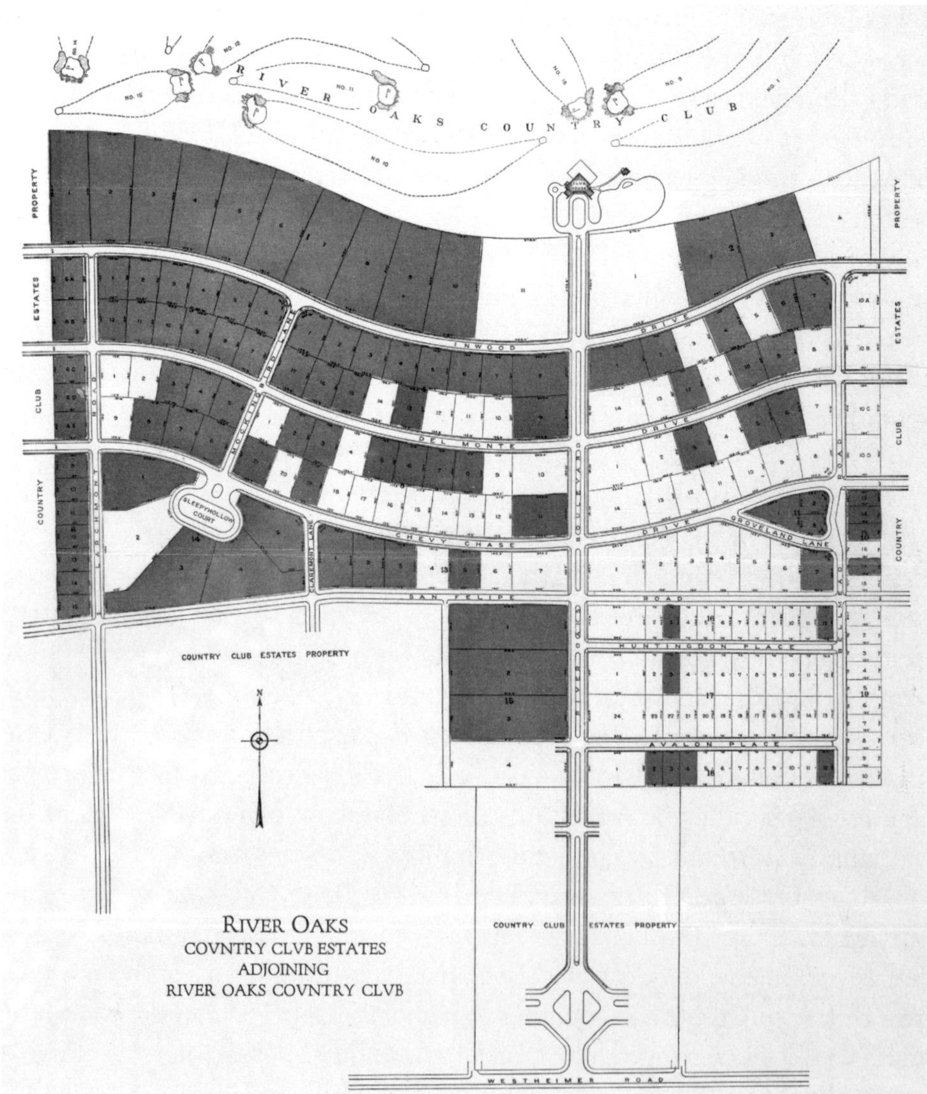

River Oaks plat map, 1930. HMRC.

"R" and "O" into a monogram), walks, and entrances. Plans were drawn for nine-hole golf courses, for a boulevard to be planted with live oaks every fifty feet, and for the one-hundred-foot-wide Buffalo and Kirby Drives, which included broad esplanades. Portions of these, like much of River Oaks, would be planted by the Edward Teas Nursery. Hare & Hare's proposals incorporated at least one subdivision plat that had already been drawn by Herbert A. Kipp (who became the company's chief civil engineer) a few months before the firm was hired. Herbert graciously acknowledged the skill and artistry of Kipp's plat map and made few changes.[68]

The "over one thousand acres restricted" that comprised River Oaks was meant to appeal to a range of (white) property owners and include everything from modest bungalows to large estates.[69] On its south side were sections for homeowners of moderate means, while more exclusive lots lined the bayou (one of these was Homewoods, a secluded "retreat" where Miss Hogg's home, Bayou Bend, was constructed on a fourteen-acre lot).[70] Sites for shopping, school, and churches, as well parks and playgrounds, were conveniently located. Deed restrictions and building codes secured the owners' investments. The Hare & Hare–designed Buffalo Bayou Parkway, only a twelve-minute drive from downtown Houston, made travel efficient and pleasurable. By the early 1930s, River Oaks had achieved the combination of "rural quiet and urban convenience" its developers had intended.

In the same years River Oaks was being transformed from a "gully to a garden" (as one advertisement in the *Houston Gargoyle* put it), Herbert Hare was also at work on more comprehensive planning and weighing the city's needs in light of future growth. Partnering with the city engineer, Lewis Ryon Jr., he coauthored the 1929 *Report of the City Planning Commission, Houston, Texas*.[71] Five years in the making, the report's two objectives were to correct past mistakes and to guide future growth by addressing urgent and far-ranging needs. According to Herbert, who believed that city plans were never finished, that they must be "watched constantly, [and] changed often," flexibility was the key.[72] The foreword, signed by the authors, described in elegant language the art and science of planning in a comprehensive way. It identified order, convenience, and beauty as watchwords and closed by stating the document's intent: "to plan with vision, but not be visionary." Although the report represented the culmination of Will Hogg's years as the planning commission chairman and incorporated goals he had worked toward, Herbert's influence is evident.[73] The report laid out in clear

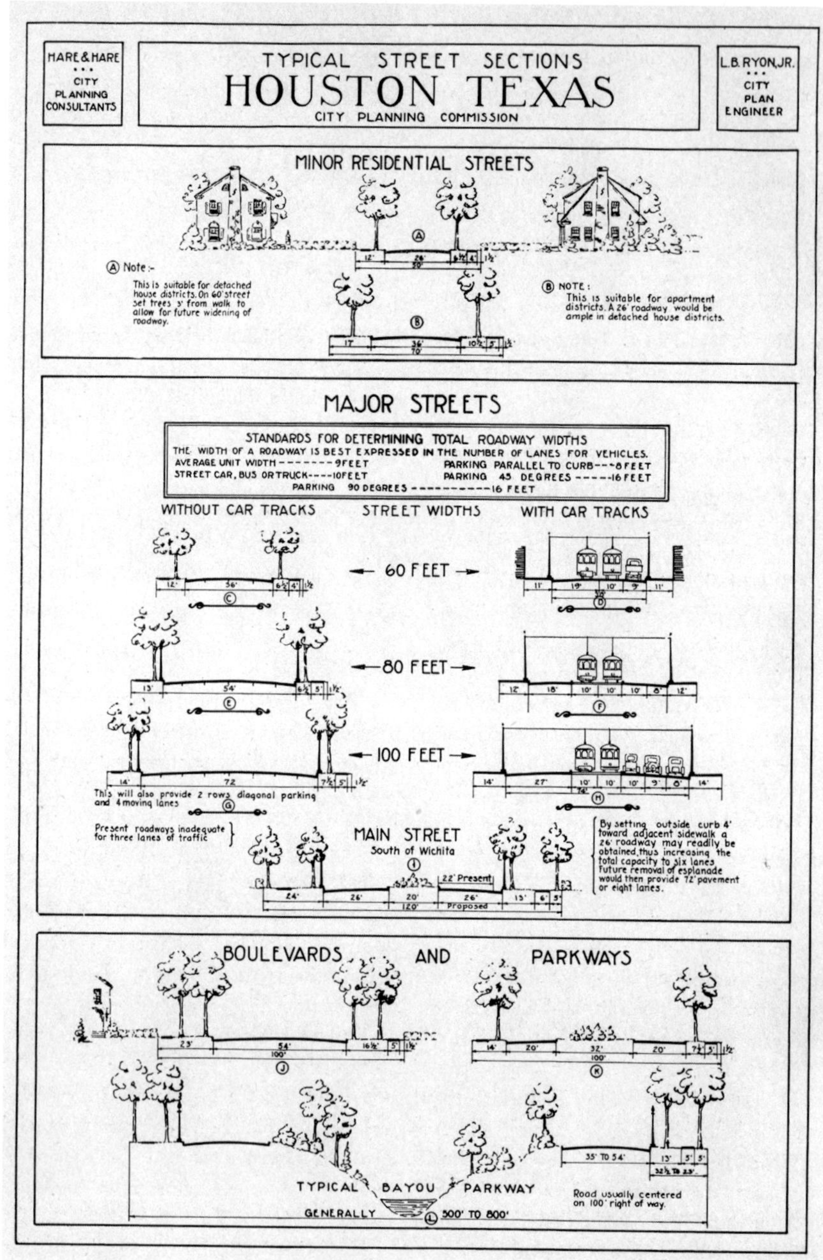

Street, boulevard, and bayou parkway sections proposed in *Report of the City Planning Commission, Houston, Texas*, 1929. SHSMO-KC.

and logical terms how to proceed, but its implementation—the decision to build "a great city or merely a great population"—lay with the people of Houston and their officials.

The 136-page report addressed the development of a major street plan, bayou beautification and flood control, parks, zoning, and a civic center, illustrating these improvements with drawings and photographs. Among its goals was the addition of arterial streets to improve traffic patterns throughout the city. It recommended that the city's more than 2,600 acres in parks (up from 170 acres in 1910) increase in relation to population and growth, and therefore double by 1950, with the addition of twenty parks. The proposed Civic Center, a grouping of high-style buildings arranged around Hermann Park, would draw residents, anchor cultural institutions, and serve as the axis for the comprehensive plan. As if Herbert anticipated criticism from practical-minded opponents, he justified this last project. "Beauty," he wrote, "need not be incompatible with use and convenience . . . [it] in itself has a tangible commercial value." The thorniest subject the report addressed was zoning. Although Herbert explained that zoning meant protection, not regulation, and was a tool to ensure orderly growth, the subject would be a deal breaker for years to come. Critics of a 1946 push for zoning would label it un-American and liken it to communism and Nazi Germany.[74]

Will Hogg had assured Herbert that Houston's civic-minded residents were ready to accept professional guidance, "the sooner the better." But perhaps they had been put off by the 1929 report's somewhat lofty presentation, which began with a quote from the British art critic John Ruskin and included illustrations of Florence's Arno Bridge and the Place de la Concorde in Paris as examples to emulate. And even years later, planning and zoning—which had become standard nationwide—were still consid-

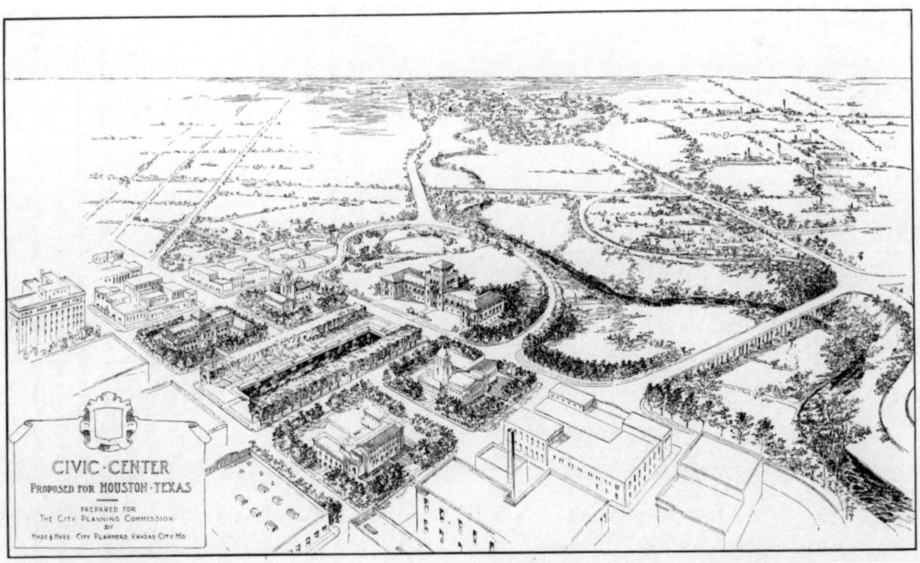

Hare & Hare's proposed Civic Center anchored by the Ideson Building, Houston's main library, 1929. SHSMO-KC.

ered suspect. Opponents, particularly anti-zoning adversaries, insisted their city would not be the work of "slide-rule experts armed with omniscient egotism and a pocket full of silly statistics."[75] Even now, after recent shifts in attitudes toward unregulated development, Houston remains the only major American city with no official zoning policy.[76]

That many of the firm's plans for Houston were implemented over time should be credited to Ralph Ellifrit, a Hare & Hare employee who became the director of the city's newly established planning department in 1940.[77] Already familiar with numerous Houston projects, which he oversaw from the firm's branch office at 2017 West Grey Street, Ellifrit provided continuity in the decades that followed. With Herbert he worked to revise the 1929 city plan and Houston's Civic Center; as director he helped conceive the freeway system and oversaw the acquisition of one hundred new parks. His westward addition of Brays Bayou Parkway extended Hare & Hare's 1926 contribution that linked MacGregor and Hermann Parks. Holding the position of director for twenty-three years, Ellifrit accomplished much in a period when public-spirited planning was "simply disregarded."[78]

Early trips to Houston often included a stop to check on projects in Tulsa, Oklahoma, the first of which had been for clients in the oil business. An important commission for another such client began in 1926 when oil man Waite Phillips and his wife Genevieve began construction of the Tulsa residence they would name Villa Philbrook. Sited on twenty-three acres, the seventy-two-room Italian Renaissance–style residence was the work of the architect Edward Buehler Delk, whose design made reference to historical precedents ranging from Palladio to Bernini. Hare & Hare's design of the grounds drew on Italian models such as Villa Lante, fifty miles north of Rome, but it borrowed freely from other sources. Both Delk and Hare & Hare had been recommended to Phillips by J. C. Nichols.[79] Twelve years later, when the philanthropic family made the decision to donate the property to the city, Herbert Hare would return to assist in planning for its new use as a public art museum and botanical garden.

Waite Phillips, the son of Lewis Franklin Phillips and Lucinda Josephine Faucett Phillips, was the seventh of ten children and the identical-twin brother of Wiate. The twins were born in January 1883 on the family farm near Conway, Iowa, where their parents had settled, raising dairy cows, hogs, poultry, bees, and crops.[80] Waite began his career as a bookkeeper for the Hawkeye Coal Company, in Knoxville, Iowa, where he met his future wife, Genevieve Elliot, the daughter of a local banker.

When he was twenty-three years old, Waite worked for his older brothers as a field superintendent in the Bartlesville oil business and later began managing oil production and pipelines, ultimately forming his own company. Waite and Genevieve married in 1909 and moved to Tulsa nine years later. In 1925, Waite sold his company to a New York investment firm for $25 million. He then turned his attention to developing downtown Tulsa, and to building Villa Philmonte on the 300,000-acre family ranch in Cimarron, New Mexico, and Villa Philbrook, the estate where he, Genevieve, and their two children, Helen Jane and Elliot, lived.

The land on which the couple built was purchased in two allotments, totaling just over sixty-four acres, beginning in 1920. Although it was described as "merely a farm," the acreage (then two miles south of Tulsa's downtown) included a high ridge, open spaces edged by forested groves, and Crow Creek, which ran along its edge. Delk worked with Hare & Hare in siting the house high on the property so as to take in the breeze (and per Genevieve's request). The design of the villa's primary facade is unassuming—long and low, with spare use of classical ornament—its stucco exterior trimmed with creamy-golden Minnesota limestone used for its similarity to Italian travertine. Inside, the "great hall" is ornamented with mannerist columns, richly colored tapestries, and shallow vaulted ceilings painted with neoclassical motifs. Arches and windows frame views to the garden, linking house and grounds. Through a loggia—a porch and outdoor room—one steps onto a terrace overlooking the most formal of gardens.

As is the case with many fine gardens, Villa Philbrook was a collaborative effort between its owners and their landscape architect. Many plans, which were prepared over a two-year period, reveal a process of sorting and editing to arrive at a style and level of formality that fit this young family. What evolved was a synthesis of sources known by Herbert and inspired by his clients' European travels. Genevieve likely weighed in on matters of aesthetics (as she did when decorating their homes) and Waite on matters related to plants (insisting on magnolias to delight his wife) and expense, impulsively changing the plan as he saw fit.[81] Detailed drawings record the process of refining Philbrook's plan which began in the spring of 1926.[82] A French *parterre de broderie*—a bed planted in embroidery-like scrolled patterns—adjacent to paired greenhouses and an enclosed swimming pool appeared in early plans. More suitable for Louis XIV than the Phillips family, it was not incorporated. Bridle paths and rustic features, such as a campfire ring and cabin in a "wild" corner of the property, were also rejected. Neither was architect Delk's suggestion that they incorporate a stone ornament resembling a stylized sea creature (similar to that found at Villa Lante) implemented.[83]

After much revision, the project's main emphasis became the east garden, which was set on axis with the grand hall of the house.[84]

Many of the plants for Philbrook, such as those recorded on a narrow sheet of vellum five feet in length, noted specimens to be "collected from the native woods" on the property.[85] Among these were dogwood, elder, and serviceberry for planting in the borders, on slopes near the house, and throughout the woods. Another list cited poplars, rose of Sharon (*Hibiscus syriacus*), and sumac to be moved according to the owners' wishes. Tall red cedars (*Juniperus virginiana*), fit for the Oklahoma climate, were chosen to

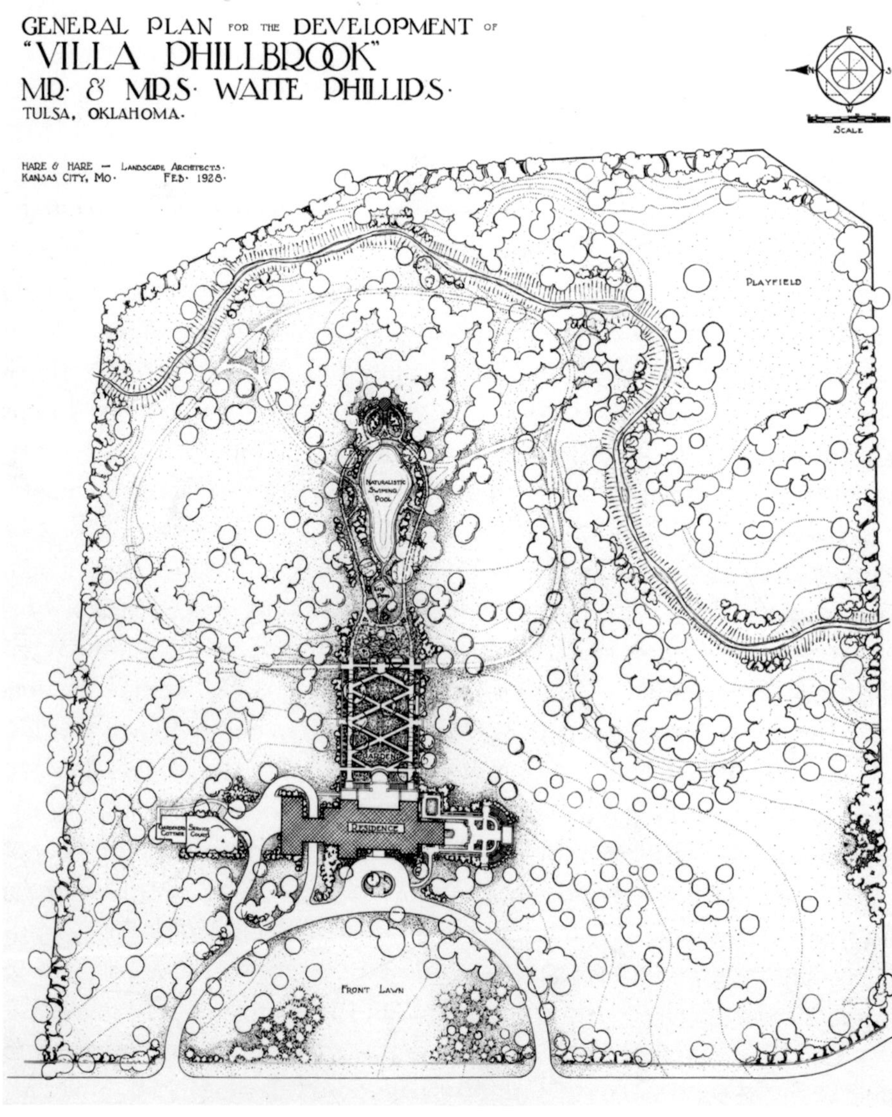

General plan for the Waite and Genevieve Phillips residence, Villa Philbrook, drawn by Hare & Hare draftsman J. T. Roberts, 1928. SHSMO-KC.

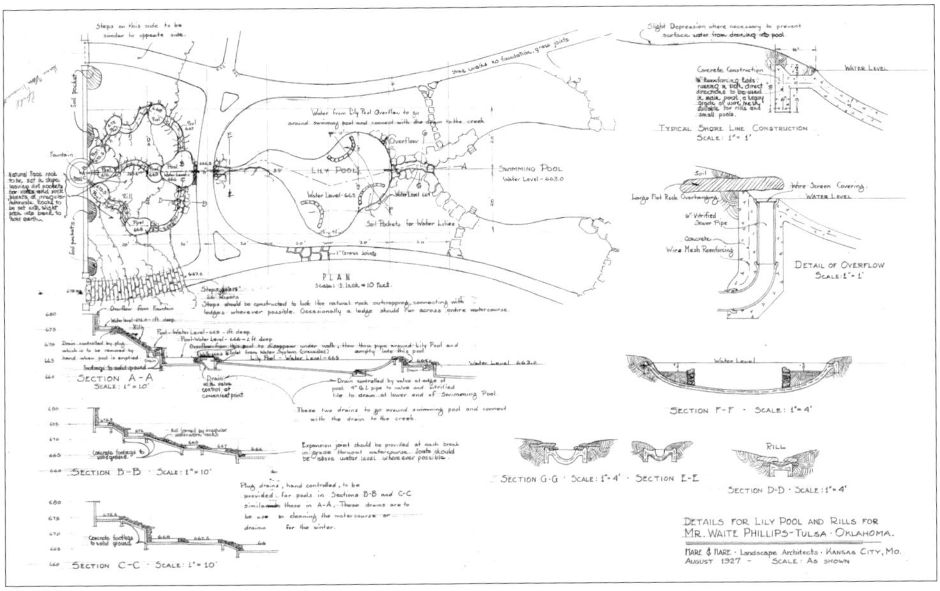

Details and instructions for construction of the lily pool and rills, 1927. SHSMO-KC.

mimic the verticality of Italian cypress. The sloping ramped garden called for beds of English ivy edged with low hedges of Chinese privet (*Ligustrum sinense*) anchored with clipped spheres of bay or boxwood which evoked the Italian preference for a predominantly green palette. Yuccas (a southwestern plant Waite was fond of), planted as specimens along flagstone walks, firmly placed the garden in Tulsa rather than Italy.

Ultimately, the design of Villa Philbrook drew on Renaissance models, in particular Villa Lante, which Herbert had sketched and photographed during his travels. Like so many visitors over the centuries, he acknowledged it as one of the finer sixteenth-century Italian examples, "the flower of them all," where garden and woods came together into a unified whole.[86] Villa Lante displays the defining elements of these prototypes: *compartimenti, prato,* and *bosco*—garden beds, lawn, and forest—enlivened with water and ornamented with classical works of art. The east (main) garden is a series of terraces marked by balustrades and fountains that descend the sloping site. The garden becomes more informal as it drops down the hillside; the strict geometry of a triple-ramped garden nearest the house is followed by a rock garden, then pools, finally yielding to forest. All are linked by a *catena d'acqua,* or water chain, which defines the primary axis and terminates in the gracefully scaled *tempietto* at the base of the hill.[87] The visual link of the temple with the terrace above shaped Herbert's plan from the beginning.

In the fall of 1938, as the Phillipses prepared to move to a penthouse in the Art Deco Philcade building downtown, they donated their residence

Villa Philbrook, view of house from gardens, n.d. Beryl Ford Photograph Collection, Tulsa Historical Society.

to the citizens of Tulsa. The villa would serve as the community's first art museum (the family agreed to remodel the interior at its expense to accommodate this new use), and the grounds, which were initially overseen by the city park board, were to be used "as a botanical garden and for the development, preservation, exhibition and study of trees, shrubs, plants and flowers indigenous to Oklahoma and the southwest."[88] The Philbrook Art Museum (now the Philbrook Museum of Art) officially opened on October 29, 1939. It is no longer outside the city; neighborhoods have grown up around it, but the footprint of the original grounds remains. The additions that have been made to the museum and its landscape are in keeping with Delk and Hare & Hare, whose original design for the east garden is still clear.[89]

By 1925, Sid had become a less visible member of Hare & Hare but still remained engaged in the firm's work. He traveled and met with previous clients, adding to cemeteries—Elmwood in Birmingham and Mount Olivet in Fort Worth—and planning new ones such as Fort Hill Cemetery in Lynchburg, Virginia. Still involved with the AACS, he planned its forty-fifth annual meeting, held in 1931 at the President Hotel in Kansas City.

Villa Philbrook, formal garden from the East Terrace, n.d. Philbrook Museum of Art Archive.

The association's field trips included the city's parks and boulevard system, and a tour of cemeteries featuring Forest Hill and Floral Hills, the last of which was designed by the firm as a "botanical park and burial ground." The group also visited Harecliff, the "mecca of the day's trip."[90]

The focus of Sid's later years was his rustic house and acreage, the "wild-flower preservation zone and bird haven" where he experimented with native plants and rock gardens. He could be found, often in shirt and tie and a fedora, raking leaves or leading tours showing off the giant mulleins sprouting from rock ledges or the *Portulaca thellussouri* he had "discovered wild" near Joplin a decade before. Reportedly, some six thousand visitors had been there in the three and a half years before his death. Many took with them the little booklet he and Mathilda had prepared, with photographs of Harecliff's gardens and its wild landscape on the ridgetop, as a souvenir of the trip.

Sid Hare died unexpectedly of complications associated with heart disease at Harecliff on the evening of October 25, 1938, four months before his seventy-ninth birthday. Two days later he was buried at Forest Hill Cemetery where, in 1896, he had taken the job of superintendent, the position that led to decades of cemetery work. Cards and letters came from the park and planning commissions of Houston, Fort Worth, and the state of Michigan. Landscape architects from across the country sent their condolences; among them were H. O. Whittemore, of the Department of Landscape Design at the University of Michigan, Ann Arbor; Thomas Desmond, of Simsbury, Connecticut; and Saco R. DeBoer, of Denver, who wrote that the profession, and the country, had lost "one of its outstanding men in the work of making our cities more livable."[91] J. C. Nichols and the American Association of Cemetery Superintendents expressed their sympathy. But condolences reflected Sid's wide interests beyond his profession,

Fall cleanup at Harecliff, 1927. Sylvia Mooney.

Sidney Hare and a visitor in the rock garden at Harecliff, 1932. Sylvia Mooney.

One of Hare & Hare's holiday cards sent to friends and associates, 1925. SHSMO-KC.

such as those from Chicago's Union League Club (whose concerns and activity ranged from the 1893 Columbian Exposition to nonpartisan political reform) and from the Audubon Society.

A. D. Taylor, president of the ASLA at the time, sent a telegram on behalf of the organization which acknowledged Sid's "sterling qualities," describing him as "one of the few pioneers in blazing the trail which all professional landscape architects are following today."[92] A personal letter to Herbert followed in which Taylor wrote of the real privilege it had been to know his father, whose friendship of many years he valued.[93] He praised Sid's straightforward manner, "sincerity of purpose," and genuine love for his work. "You have had a rare privilege," Taylor confided, "to share a comradeship these many years with a father whose mental abilities and whose ideals were as great as his." His tone lightened when he described the "original and delightful" Christmas cards he had received from Sid and Mathilda each holiday season.

Lake of the Ozarks Bluffs, Miller County. Photo by Charles Trefts, c. 1935. SHSMO-C.

SIX

Balancing Recreation and Conservation

In January 1941, at an ASLA meeting in Washington, D.C., Herbert began a four-year term as the organization's president after serving as vice president under A. D. Taylor and as treasurer for eight years. In a series of annual reports focusing on the war, he would address the disruption of the organization's normal activities and summarize the diverse contributions that landscape architects had made to the war effort.[1] When the conflict ended, the profession could return, he hoped, to its "primary purpose" of promoting human welfare by improving the environment, whether urban or rural, designed for rich or poor.[2]

Stating that the nation's cities could not continue "to grow on the periphery and decay at the core," Herbert identified blighted urban areas as a postwar priority.[3] The improvement and addition of local parks, parkways, and playgrounds fell within this area of civic improvement. Housing was another pressing need; low-cost inner city and single- and multiple-family options in new neighborhoods were required. The growing demand for interstate highways and airports, though less urgent, also had to be addressed. Landscape architects would be called on for postwar projects that ranged from "smaller domestic problems" to the broader phases of planning for land use and conservation.[4] Within this last category was the continued need for facilities to meet the increasing demand of the nation's leisure-time desires.[5] By the time he gave these ASLA addresses, Herbert had already been at work on several significant recreation/conservation projects in Missouri.

Civilian Conservation Corps, Camp Roaring River, Cassville, 1933. MDNR.

After Theodore Roosevelt's contribution to national parks, meeting the population's recreational needs had continued with President Franklin D. Roosevelt's New Deal programs, in particular the Works Progress Administration (WPA), Civilian Conservation Corps (CCC), and the Federal Emergency Relief Administration (FERA). The first two programs had an unprecedented effect on state parks, and FERA facilitated land purchases for recreational use. Roads, infrastructure, and facilities built by the CCC were the first improvements of their kind at many sites, and at the same time that the agency provided new jobs, it constructed more infrastructure than in the "entire history of the system to that time."[6] But a concern shared by the profession, one that Herbert cautioned about, was the rush to capitalize on New Deal funding; the "new form of federal largesse" had often resulted in park development and land acquisition with little regard for the "big picture."[7] In-depth systematic planning was needed—a blueprint for the future to prevent waste and duplication.[8] Federal and state agencies working together helped achieve this goal.

Herbert Hare was among the planning professionals advocating for state parks and helping to frame the discussion about these outdoor recreational spaces.[9] His first presentation on the subject was made at the sixth National Conference on State Parks meeting in Hot Springs, Arkansas, in 1926, and was later published in Herbert Evison's seminal book *A State Park Anthology*.[10] In it he outlined how the knowledge, ability, and training of landscape architects uniquely qualify them for such planning. In the years that followed, Herbert addressed fundamental points such as protecting landscape while increasing public access, the elements of good design, and the inclusion of historical and archaeological sites.[11] Hare &

Hare applied these practices in Missouri beginning in 1933, first at the privately funded Lake of the Ozarks project and then, through its appointment by the National Planning Board, as consultants for park planning on a statewide level.

Missouri began to purchase land for public use in the early 1920s under the leadership of pro-parks governor Arthur Hyde who helped secure funding for park acquisition. The first six parks, a total of 24,000 acres in the southern portion of the state, were recreational sites known to Missourians for their outstanding natural beauty.[12] Early and important additions to the system resulted from the work of the Daughters of the American Revolution and the Mark Twain Memorial Park Association, citizen groups that secured two historic sites under state ownership: the Arrow Rock Tavern on the Santa Fe Trail and Mark Twain's birthplace in the town of Florida near St. Louis.[13] By the early 1930s, 38,000 acres in the picturesque Ozarks were being used for public hunting and fishing but no development existed for other recreational activities, such as camping and hiking.

Hare & Hare's involvement in comprehensive planning for Missouri's parks began in late spring of 1933 after the completion of Bagnell Dam, a

Fishing the Meramec River, Crawford County, c. 1904. Duncan Photo, State of Missouri Collection, SHSMO.

Lake of the Ozarks. Photo by Gerald R. Massie, c. 1945. MSA.

private project launched by the Union Electric Light and Power Company of St. Louis (now Ameren). The dam's impoundment of the Osage, Niangua, Gravois, and Grand Glaize Rivers created the Lake of the Ozarks, with over 55,000 surface acres and an irregular shoreline of 1,150 miles, which provided new opportunities for park recreation.[14] The lake curled in a serpentine shape through four counties and a rugged terrain of rock- and gravel-filled soil, scrub oak, and red cedar. Remote and thinly populated, the land had never been of agricultural value (except in the upper reaches to the north); but once the hydroelectric project was complete, its value for recreation became clear. Union Electric Light and Power owned the majority of the shoreline surrounding the lake. To jump-start development in the area, the company hoped to receive funding from the National Industrial Recovery Act, which authorized billions of dollars for the construction of public works.[15]

Louis H. Egan, president of Union Electric's land and development division, hired the team of Harland Bartholomew and Herbert Hare to investigate recreation-related opportunities at the new lake. The resulting report would be the first of the two planners' many joint efforts. "Suggested State Parks, Park Ways and Highways in the Lake of the Ozarks Region" was preliminary in nature (twenty-five pages in length including two maps) but proposed specific ways in which the company and state could work together to set aside land for parks and onshore acquisition and protection.[16] The report outlined the requirements for "public recreation and scenic enjoyment" in the form of camping, boating, and "pleasure driving," giving equal merit to these three forms of recreation and noting that each warranted special design, control, and expenditure. In its first few pages, the team called for a farsighted policy to safeguard the waterway and its shoreline.

Hare and Bartholomew identified the three best park sites for the Lake of the Ozarks based on their scenic beauty, recreational potential, and accessibility.[17] The first site was on the east side where Glaize Creek joins the main channel of the Osage; another was to the southwest at the junction of the Niangua and Little Niangua Rivers; and the third was farther west at what the report referred to as the "great bend" near a little town named Proctor. Recreation facilities would be confined to these three areas, leaving miles of the main channel and its shoreline free of development. Throughout the report, Hare and Bartholomew identified features of the landscape worthy of protection—dolomite and limestone cliffs (one stretch named "the Palisades" years earlier by steamboat pilots); slices of high bluff at Hurricane Deck and Lover's Leap; tiny Drum Rock island; and Onyx Cave, where one can boat into darkness "amid the cooing of pigeons."[18]

The proposed Glaize Creek location was chosen for its cave-riddled bluffs, gently sloping shores with occasional sandy beaches, and narrow coves known for good fishing. Its recommended size—8,500 acres of water and land combined—was ample enough for a "resort center" with a hotel, campgrounds, boat docks, and picnic areas. The rugged topography, and even better fishing, of the Niangua made it another outstanding choice.[19] The smaller 4,600-acre site would house less-intrusive facilities—campsite, trails, and secluded spots for nature study. The potential park at Proctor was 5,000 acres chosen for its expansive views, gentle sloping ground, and land that could accommodate more dense development, such as a resort hotel with a casino and golf course, which might be built in the future.

Key to Hare and Bartholomew's plan was protection of the "delightfully unspoiled naturalistic effect" of the lake's wooded slopes and rugged bluffs. At present, a person could ride the waves, take in "intimate" and expansive vistas, and feel "far removed from the city and the works of man."[20] Hare and Bartholomew realized that controlling development on shoreline property was the only way to maintain these views and the associated experience. After identifying shoreline protection as an essential component of their plan, they suggested that the state acquire land along both sides of the lake, from the bluffs near the Glaize Arm on the east to the Proctor park on the west side and up the Niangua. Anticipating a reluctant response from Union Electric (which likely planned to sell these many acres to private investors), the planners described this "rather bold" recommendation as "absolutely indispensable" to the project's success.

Last, Hare and Bartholomew's Lake of the Ozarks report laid out a plan for scenic drives and what it described as "parkway approaches." One hundred fifty miles of drives (and occasional side road observation points) would link the three parks and create a circuit around the lake for pleasure driving and taking in views of the surrounding hills, valleys, and water. The approaches (190 miles total) would be wide parkways, free of commercial traffic, linking Kansas City and St. Louis to the lake. In each direction these routes would follow river valleys, with an occasional climb to higher elevations, to produce changing vistas and "lend added charm to the route." Equally important, they provided much-needed access to this remote area as only two highways had been constructed, both on the east side. Four new bridges would enhance accessibility and cut down on travel time for those who preferred not to wind around the edges of the lake.

Hare and Bartholomew's boldest recommendation was not under-

Parkway in Lake of the Ozarks State Park. Photo by Hadley K. Irwin, c. 1945. MDNR.

taken—the entire shoreline was never reserved as public parkland—but one important proposal was realized. Within two years the federal government acquired land along the Glaize Arm, in the location the team had earmarked, and one of the state parks they envisioned began to take shape. Its total acreage nearly equaled the 18,000 acres they deemed necessary to meet the region's growing demand for recreational facilities. With the support of the Land Planning Committee of FERA, the National Park Service developed it as a Recreational Demonstration Area (RDA).[21]

RDAs were a new category of park meant to accommodate organized youth groups such as scout troops and the YMCA, as well as individuals, and provide affordable recreation for people of lower and middle incomes. Visitors could camp in secluded cabin clusters, have meals in CCC-constructed dining halls, hike, and swim.[22] Six group camps, accommodating from twenty to two hundred people, were built at Lake of the Ozarks. Ultimately, the RDA was transferred from federal ownership and is now a state park, the largest in the system at 17,200 acres and, according to the historian Susan Flader, "the public's great good fortune."[23]

Hare & Hare had been at work on the Lake of the Ozarks project for seven months when Missouri responded to the federal directive by establishing state-level planning that addressed every aspect of public welfare. The team of Herbert Hare and Harland Bartholomew was appointed by the National Planning Board as the state's consultants, and Governor Guy Park followed by creating a board of eleven citizens and four state officials to collaborate with the federal program. Through collaboration with other state and federal agencies, including the National Park Service, Hare and Bartholomew began to make progress toward their goal of producing a "flexible general guide for all future development."[24]

The first of many reports produced by Hare and Bartholomew's team, "A State Plan for Missouri" (1934), included data covering matters from land use to taxation and contained maps that provided a visual record of the distribution of park areas in relation to population. The report represented the first such planning ever implemented at the state level in Missouri. Much of its data and many of the Hare and Bartholomew maps were incorporated into all planning documents that followed. The 442-page state plan progress report submitted a year later, subtitled "Facts, Findings and Recommendations," was an exhaustive gathering of information that created a picture of Missouri's people, industry, commerce, and natural resources.[25] The chapter dedicated to parks began with the assertion that recreation qualified as "a higher need" of the people and addressed ways to meet the growing demand for accessible facilities and to correct the geographic inequities of the existing system (too few parks in the north and central portions of the state and in small towns).[26] The report recommended providing the equivalent of one acre of park land per fifty people in cities and one acre per one hundred in rural areas.

Balancing use and protection was once again a key objective of Hare and Bartholomew's work. Guidelines were proposed on how to develop southern Missouri's plentiful streams and springs (among the largest freshwater springs in the country) for suitable recreation yet preserve them in their natural state; to acquire easements along both sides of these waterways as a means of control; and to protect them from industrial and

Swimmers at the Lake of the Ozarks State Park. Photo by Hadley K. Irwin, c. 1950. MDNR.

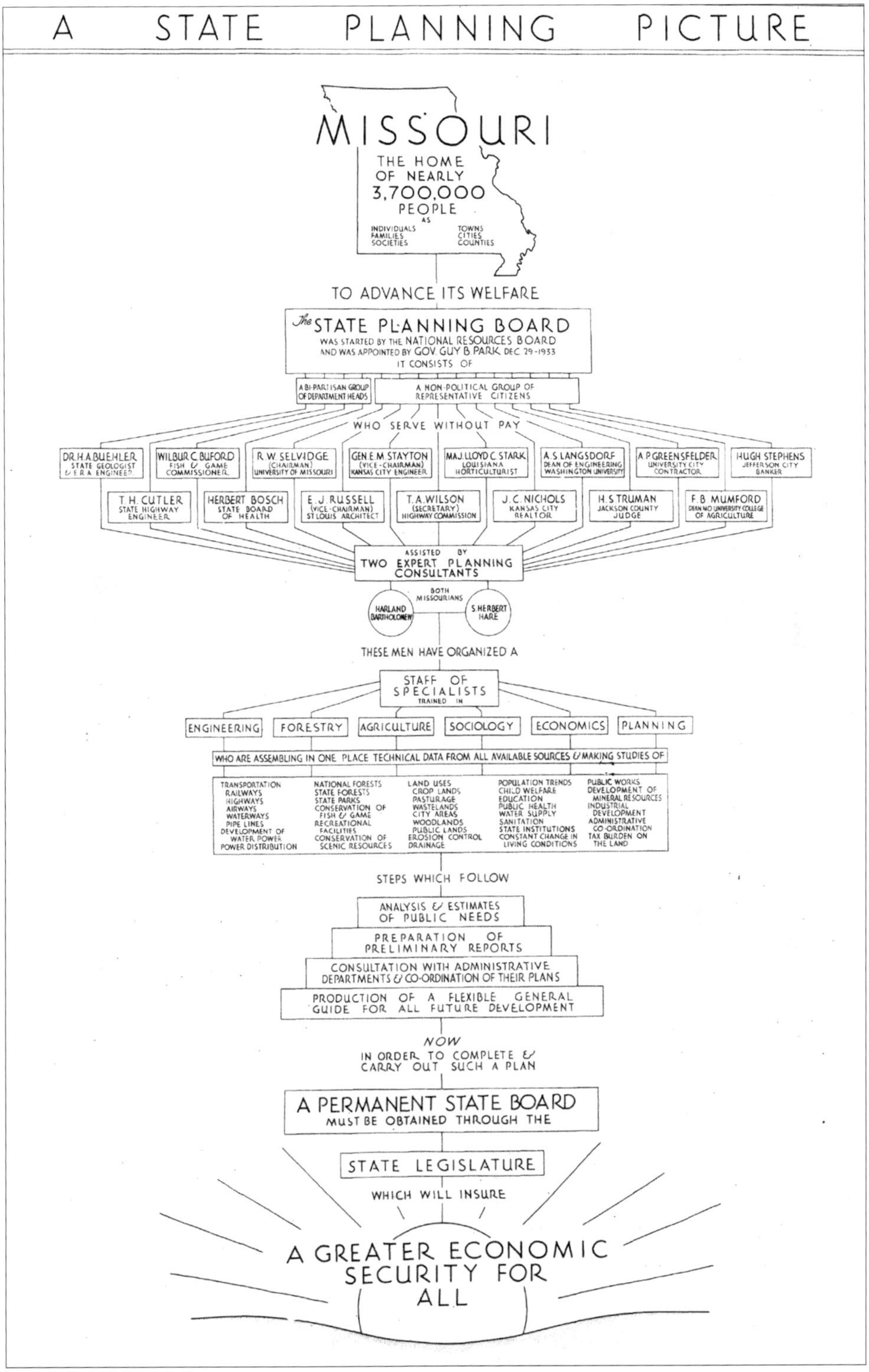

Organizational chart of responsibilities of the Missouri State Planning Board, plate 88 in “A State Plan for Missouri: Facts, Findings, and Recommendations,” 1935. SHSMO-C.

other types of pollution. The report's suggestion to include a group of state parks—Alley Spring, Big Spring, and Round Spring—in a system of "National Monuments" anticipates their ultimate inclusion in the Ozark National Scenic Riverways.[27] Hare and Bartholomew's prescient recommendation to protect recreational streams became a reality in 1964 when the Current River and the Jacks Fork River became the first federally protected natural, free-flowing streams in the nation (and the model for the Wild and Scenic Rivers Act of 1968).[28] The recreational value of national

Boating on Big Spring in the Missouri Ozarks. Photo by Hadley K. Irwin, c. 1965. MDNR.

forests—wilderness areas—as a supplement to the expanding state park system (of which three million acres were in the process of being purchased) was also emphasized.

Hare and Bartholomew also laid out the rationale for a statewide parkway system, the beginnings of which had been conceived in their earlier Lake of the Ozarks plan. With increased use of the automobile, additional highways were needed, but the issue was more than a matter of transportation; "pleasure driving" was considered a recreation in its own right.

Walking the trail along Alley Spring. Photo by Robert E. Brown, c. 1950. MDNR.

The network of roadways they proposed was independent of the highway system, and of commercial traffic, with limited entry and exit points and right-of-ways to guard against commercial encroachment and visual blight such as billboards. Two thousand miles in length, this system would crisscross the state and extend to each corner, connecting state parks, passing through national forests, and running along sections of the Missouri and Mississippi.[29] These "long, narrow parks or forestways," totaling 144,000 acres, would include as many "scenic, scientific and historical points as possible."[30] Although the idea of expanding this system beyond the state line, via the construction of an interstate parkway linking the Lake of the Ozarks and Chicago, was considered within a year, neither that plan nor the larger one was implemented.

By 1940, Hare and Bartholomew had directed and compiled numerous reports that addressed state-level planning. Among these was a separate study of scenic resources and a recreation plan—a blueprint for growth—for state parks, monuments, "roadside zones," parkways, and wayside areas.[31] One component of the study was a 457-page "manual" that included the early history of the system, data and illustrations drawn from earlier reports which formed the basis of research, and updated attendance and use figures. The manual recorded visitors' place of residence, distance trav-

Proposed statewide system of parkways for Missouri, 1935. SHSMO-Columbia.

eled, and time spent at a given park, as well as visitors' comments and requests.[32] This vision for the future reflected the joint recommendations of Missouri's planning board and newly formed park board and presented "in concise form" a guide for development.[33] Laying out what should be done and how, it addressed financing, policy, administering the system, and immediate and ultimate objectives. Eight new recreation areas were proposed for underserved regions of the state. Added to the series of base maps conceived by the consultants were charming illustrations contributed by the National Park Service: a bird's-eye view of a "Typical State Park" and a series of vignettes depicting the range of recreational opportunities in the state, from wildlife areas to waysides.

Between 1938 and 1940, the team also produced a series of large-scale drawings for state parks, twelve of which were executed by Hare & Hare.[34] A complement to the documents the team had produced to guide the system as a whole, these were intended to guide development at individual sites. Many were accompanied by written reports meant to "amplify" their proposals and cover policy and procedure which could not be shown graphically. Among these were plans for some of the earliest acquisitions such as Roaring River, in the state's far southwest corner in Barry County, known for scenic beauty and trout fishing. Numerous suggestions for the Roaring River site included sensitive restoration of landscape recently obliterated by floodwater and a failed dam. Instructions addressed the aesthetic, the practical, and the obvious: after the stream channel was stabilized, a picturesque effect should be sought, and when shaping the broad valley floor campsites and structures should be above flood level. Neither the poorly sited dam (completed only three years before) nor the reservoir it created was rebuilt.

These Hare & Hare plans addressed the realities of a changing world: a greater number of visitors, more automobiles and parking space, and the public expectation that state parks include facilities for active recreation—ball fields, swimming pools, and tennis courts. While meeting recreational needs, these plans continued to balance recreation and conservation. The firm constantly advised its clients to set aside large parcels of land as refuge for wildlife (in one case specifically for prairie chickens); to purchase as much adjacent acreage as possible to buffer the surrounding landscape from park activity; to group new facilities (and move existing ones when necessary) so as not to harm the processes of nature. The protection of distinctive landscape features—cairns, natural bridges, and marshes—was an ongoing priority. Historic sites of merit and evidence of Native habitation should also be preserved and become educational components of a park and recreation program if doing so posed no threat to the natural environment. One such example was the firm's inclusion of the "Old Fort" in the plan for Van Meter State Park, which has since been identified as a Native American earthwork.

The firm's logo on these park plans bears the initials of S. Herbert Hare and Donald Bush, by then a principal of the firm, who had designed, drawn, and revised them. Ben R. Lantz, with the firm only a few years, was included on several as a designer and draftsman, as was Ralph Ellifrit in the year before he left Missouri to oversee the Houston office. With only a few exceptions, these projects remain plans on paper. U.S. engagement in World War II, beginning in December 1941, shifted all energy to the war effort; federal recreation programs and funding ceased. Concurrent changes in political leadership at the state level forced Missouri's park system into a period of "severe constraints, retrenchment, and even crisis."[35] These grave circumstances relegated the Hare & Hare plans for specific parks to a bottom drawer, where they were then forgotten.

The holding pattern that began in the early 1940s persisted in Missouri for more than a decade. Documents in the state park archive suggest that when the period of sudden and rapid expansion of the state park system began in 1955 (twenty-six new parks in the following fifteen

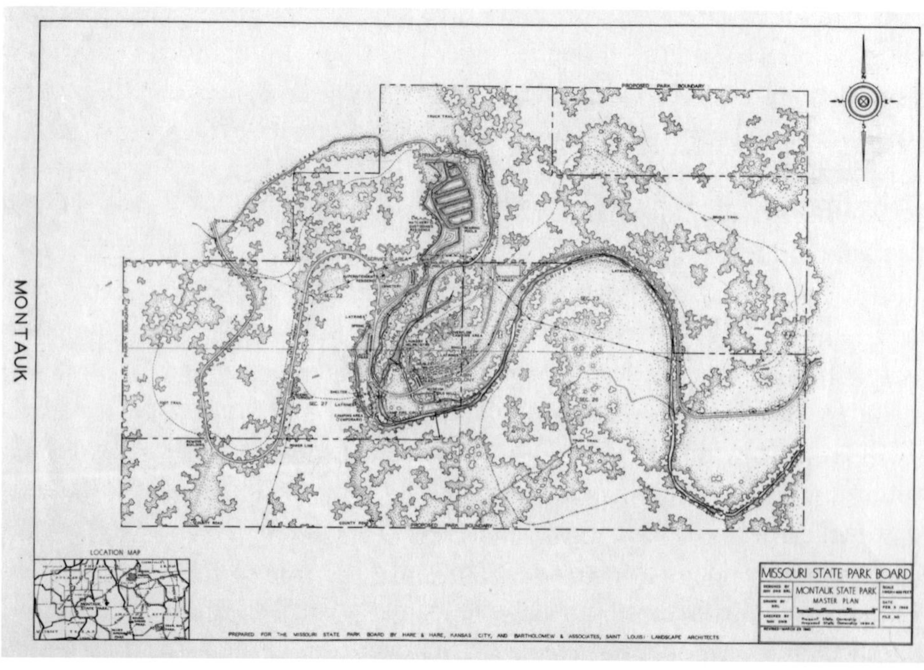

Hare & Hare's Montauk State Park Master Plan, 1940. SHSMO-KC.

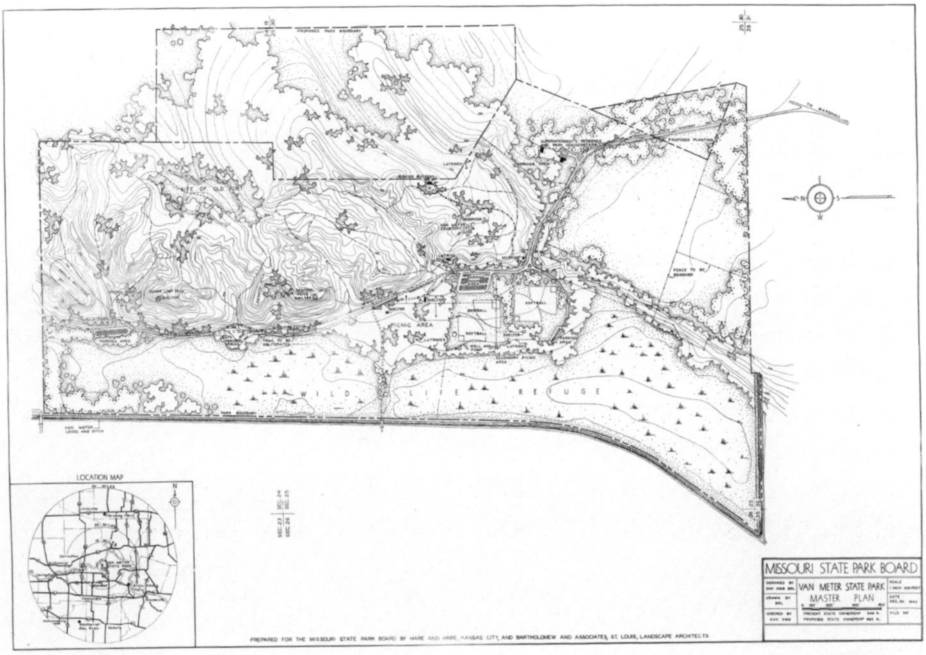

Hare & Hare's Van Meter State Park plan showing the "Old Fort" and land to be set aside as a wildlife refuge, 1940. SHSMO-KC.

years) in-house staff, rather than Hare & Hare, handled the majority of the work. Its "new, original designs" suggest they did not refer back to earlier master plans.[36] Reports and planning for the firm's twelve earlier parks have only recently been "rediscovered" in the Hare & Hare company records. Two reservoir parks on donated leases from the U.S. Army Corps of Engineers—Table Rock Lake and Pomme de Terre (completed in 1958 and 1961)—were the last such projects with Herbert's initials on them.

In a field of growing specialization, senior partner Donald Bush welcomed the variety of opportunities that the firm's commissions brought them. In 1947, for example, there were plans for a campus for the Boys Town of Nebraska and a strikingly modern outdoor living space—a patio—for a family in the Missouri river town of Louisiana; the same year, plans for a Montana Veteran's Administration hospital were executed, as were those for a Key Biscayne development for a family whose patriarch had passed along an appreciation for Florida's subtropical environment. Conservation and conscientious land use were of increasing interest to the firm's clients. Two particular projects bear this out—one outside of

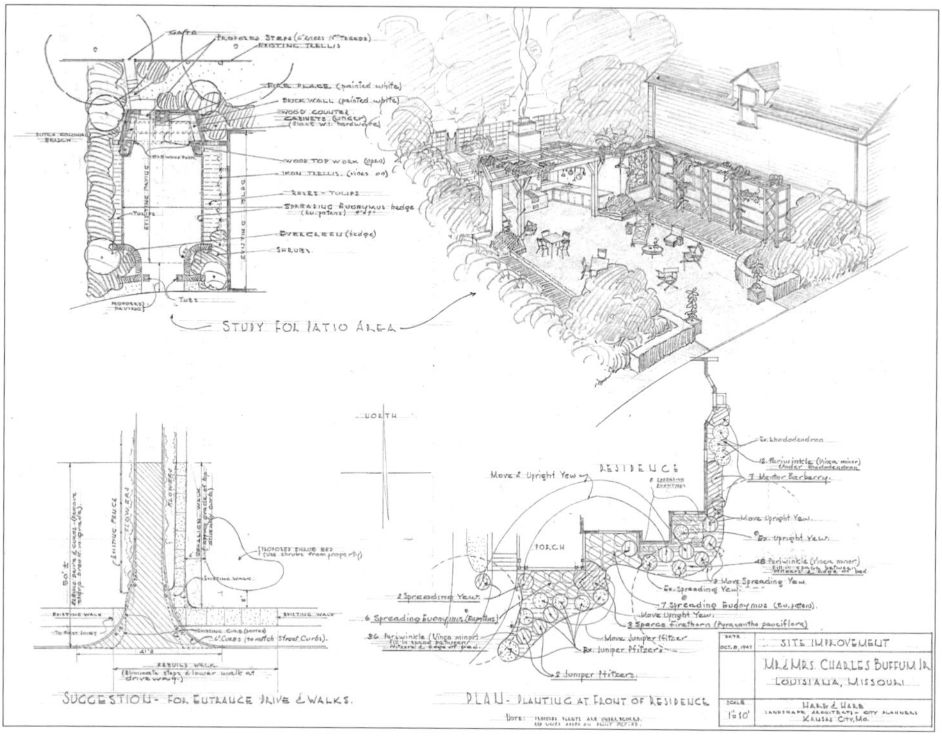

Site improvements at the Charles Buffum Jr. residence, Louisiana, MO, 1947. SHSMO-KC.

St. Paul, Minnesota, and the other in west central Louisiana—close collaborations between the clients and Bush, who personally supervised both.

In the spring of 1949, Louis W. Hill Jr. arrived in Hare & Hare's Kansas City office to talk about his family's interest in developing a "model village" on land it owned just outside of St. Paul.[37] The property he spoke of was North Oaks, one of the many avocations of his grandfather, James J. Hill, the industrialist and builder of the Great Northern Railway. In the nineteenth century North Oaks had been an experimental farm of 4,800 acres known for its innovative techniques in husbandry and agriculture and for extensive conservation practices. James's son Louis, who had spent weekends tromping through the farm's barns and fields as a youth, preferred the life of a gentleman farmer.[38] He saw the property's potential in different terms—as a residential development—and as his personal notes suggest, he had given thought to its planning.[39] Upon his death, Louis Jr. and his family decided to carry out their father's idea of planning a community with "space for living" that combined the best of country and urban life.[40]

"Nature has dealt liberally" with this place, North Oaks' farm superintendent N. E. McKissick wrote in the spring of 1900.[41] Its fresh air was filled with the fragrance of wild rose and mignonette, and its streams with brook trout. The water of its largest lake was said to possess medicinal qualities equal to those found in the thermal springs of Germany. Mosses and ferns were so abundant that the "pen and brain of a Linnaeus" would be needed to record them. In all, it was a home fit "for a Ruskin, an Agassie [*sic*]," and other, less gifted, lovers of nature.[42] Half a century later, the landscape would not be described using such romantic prose, but appreciation for it remained unchanged. And, as McKissick observed, it would require "energy, foresight and shrewdness" to protect it.

Hare & Hare's "Preview" for North Oaks Farms (1949)—its master plan—evolved through discussion with family members and guided the community's paced growth over fifty years.[43] Although the plan proposes locations for stores and schools, and even a golf course and clubhouse, their footprint is dwarfed by thousands of acres of lakes, marshes, and recreation areas that extend beyond to the north and east. As all of Ramsey County is a game preserve, swaths of wilderness and stands of the deciduous conifer tamarack (*Larix laricina*) were retained to feed and shelter wildlife.

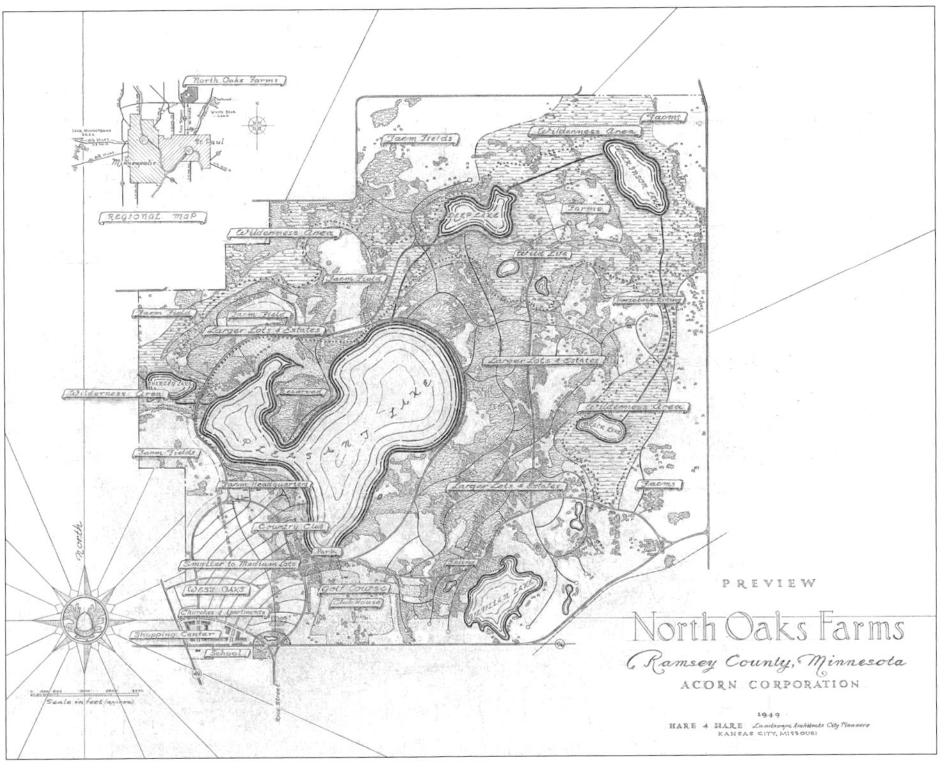

Hare & Hare's North Oaks Farms "Preview," 1949. SHSMO-KC.

Pleasant Lake, the largest of five lakes on the property, anchors the plan. Pockets of residential lots, ranging in size, are woven throughout, and along the streets, birch (*Betula papyrifera*), honey locust (*Gleditsia triacanthos*), and hawthorn would be planted.

The "Preview" was also a presentation piece that allowed the draftsman to convey the project's unique character in visual terms. Tiny horseshoe-shaped marks are used to denote bridle paths, and hatched strokes, suggestive of stylized grass, identify land reserved for wildlife. Attention to detail, apparent in the delineation of "Ramsey County, Minnesota" in graceful script and a compass rose ornamented with an acorn set on oak leaves (rather than a simple arrow) to indicate the cardinal directions, suggests both ability and passion.

The collaboration between Don Bush, Louis Jr., and construction crews involved making decisions in the field; walking the ground (sometimes in snowshoes) often determined exact lot locations and viewsheds. Roads followed the paths of deer trails or were laid out by crews instructed by Bush about "what to look for" and how to follow the land's contours.[44] The less grading the better, and according to Louis Jr., never should roads look "engineered." Bush and Louis Jr. honored Hill's legacy by going out in

North Oaks survey team, early 1950s. Private Collection of the North Oaks Company.

the field, at times on horseback, and sketching ideas that were then sent to Kansas City for review. Only minor changes were said to be made.

But the nearly two hundred plans of North Oaks Farms in the firm's archives, from topographic studies to plant lists, indicate that not all the planning was intuitive. Don Bush supervised North Oaks for twenty-one years, returning regularly.[45] During that time, new roads (including one that bears his name), reforestation, and additional neighborhoods around Pleasant Lake called for Hare & Hare plans. Development was slow and steady, just as the family had envisioned, and wilderness areas (many of which are now protected by conservation easements) remain a defining feature.[46]

The goal at North Oaks was to integrate, yet protect, wilderness as a part of community development. Hodges Gardens, a Louisiana project of the early 1950s, involved land use practices of a different sort which reclaimed the site through reforestation and adaptive reuse. It began with A. J. and Nona Trigg Hodges's purchase of 107,000 acres, a remnant of the piney woods that run in a swath across east Texas into Louisiana. These had been stripped by logging and abandoned, as had the property's quarry operation, where rock for coastal jetties had been mined. Hodges and university specialists experimented with timber management there and the crossbreeding of loblolly and slash pine (*Pinus elliottii*), replanting thousands of acres in seedlings.[47] It was the ideal place, according to the Hodges, to create a picturesque "garden in the forest." A conservatory and greenhouse complex from the New York manufacturing firm of Lord & Burnham (known for its innovative glass houses since 1849) was purchased, and springs were dammed to create a 225-acre lake adjacent to the defunct stone quarry.

When Don Bush first visited Louisiana, he and Hodges hiked across the quarry, an exercise that would be repeated, in one form or another, during Bush's many visits. Of the more than 4,700 acres to be set aside for public use, almost 950 would be dedicated to the garden, and the quarry's 60 acres, its "mounds of stone, hummocks and sugarloafs" a perfect framework for plantings, would be its centerpiece.[48] Together Bush and Hodges envisioned how the irregular and steep terrain—which dropped down as if terraced by nature rather than mined by man—could become a garden. As at North Oaks, major decisions were made on-site under the supervision of Bush and Hodges.[49] A master site plan was never executed. Hodges described the process as following "nature's lead in every step."[50]

Although nature did speak in terms of planning, not all decisions were based on instinct. One can imagine Bush's gentle suggestions for locating walks and terraces, and his proposing where a vista cut through the woods could frame another view. Detailed plans were prepared by the firm for an experimental rose garden of traditional design (a strikingly modern pool and fountain, never executed, was proposed to accompany it). Its double staircase plan, a contemporary variation of the Italian water chains that Herbert loved, illustrates how the steps should be canted at an angle, "just

Waterfall at Hodges Gardens, c. 1970. State Library of Louisiana.

so," in relationship to the lake. Throughout the garden, pools drip, rock-lined rills curl through the woods, and waterfalls spill over ledges—all fed by a reservoir recycling water from the lake.

The Shreveport firm of Walker & Walker designed the garden's visitor center/gift shop (as well as the couple's residence on the lake's "House Island"). Architecturally these, and the Lookout Tower, are examples of midcentury modern design, a surprising choice for a "garden in the forest" and one that distinguishes it from its peers.[51] The end result is an arrangement of formal features within a naturalistic landscape: piney woods as the backdrop for the brilliant color of azaleas or camellias and the apricot scent of sweet olive (*Osmanthus fragrans*).

Although Hodges Gardens opened to the public in 1957, while it was still incomplete, the formal dedication took place three years later. On the first day of May, a group of family, friends, and employees gathered at a patch of land once left bare from clear-cutting. Among those introduced to the crowd were C. B. Byrd, construction supervisor at the site, T. E. Campbell, the garden's director of forestry research and wildlife management, and Walter Chalupnik, the horticulturalist in charge of the greenhouse and propagation. Federation of Garden Clubs presidents from Arkansas, Mississippi, and Louisiana were in attendance, as was Donald Bush.[52]

Drifts of azaleas in pine forest at Hodges Gardens. Photo by Debbie Smith, 2010. National Center for Preservation Technology and Training.

Herbert had felt poorly off and on for a year when, on April 18, 1960, at his home on West 49th Street Terrace, he died from a heart condition just as his father had.[53] He was not quite seventy-two years old. His wife Aurel had died two years before in Brookline, Massachusetts. His sister Nell, the only remaining family member, would arrange for his service at a nearby funeral chapel and request no flowers be sent. Two hundred and twenty-five friends and associates attended the service, officiated by a Christian Science reader who recited selections from the Bible and from Mary Baker Eddy's *Science and Health with Key to the Scriptures* (likely the Hares' 1939 edition, bound in blue morocco). The private burial was at Forest Hill Cemetery.

Nell was remembered in her brother's will. To her he left his home (where he and Aurel had lived only briefly after thirty years in various apartments) and funds adequate to draw on for the remainder of her life.[54] He left a bequest to Huldah Simms, the secretary who had made sure the Hare & Hare office ran smoothly for thirty years. Bequests, with stipulations, were made to two educational institutions: the Kansas City Art Institute for awards to students working in traditional (representational) forms of art rather than "abstract or modern" modes; and the University of Kansas City (now a campus of the University of Missouri) for scholarships, teaching, or a library fund, with the caveat that the bequest not be used in any way relating to medical or pharmaceutical subjects. Gifts were left to his church and other Christian Science institutions—a nursing home and a school. The balance of the estate, upon Nell's death, would go to the Mother Church, the First Church of Christ, Scientist, Boston.

Herbert had drafted his will one year before his death, but planning for the future of Hare & Hare had begun long before that. "Anxious that his firm be perpetuated," and lacking a family member who would carry the firm forward, he had begun taking measures soon after his father's death in 1938. Over two decades, partners had been added "with a stair-step of ages" to ensure continuity. In recent years he had begun to give up his share of the business, allowing partners to take over. As indicated in his will, upon his death any percentage of ownership that remained his would stay with the company. "Most fortunate to the profession," wrote Eldridge Lovelace, whom Herbert had mentored years before, was that "he carefully planned his affairs so that . . . the office could follow in the tradition established by him and his father."[55]

In the spring of 1960 the firm had just finished producing a promo-

The new Hare & Hare team after Herbert's death in 1960. SHSMO-KC.

tional booklet for potential clients. In it was a list of its members, a roster of the architects, engineers, and economic planners with whom the firm had collaborated on successful projects, and selected lists of their work by category (eighteen pages). On the cover were photographs of their sleek offices on West 10th Street, which included all the hallmarks of midcentury modern style. After Herbert's death the team that carried on consisted of partners Donald Bush, H. Gordon Whiffen, Chalmer V. Cooper, Robert Lee Bell, and Richard H. Kellenberg, and E. John Warren, an associate who had recently joined the firm. The eldest was sixty-two and the youngest thirty-three, all midwesterners except one, with a range of backgrounds and strengths to contribute to the firm.

Crestwood Park at 54th and Cherry Streets, 1920. J. C. Nichols Company Records (K0106), SHSMO-KC.

Legacy

The years that span World War I, the Depression, and the Second World War represent a period when the plates shifted in America: its economy and society changed dramatically. The profession of landscape architecture responded in kind; as A. D. Taylor noted, "new occasions teach new duties."[1] Emergency work during wartime and the large government projects of the New Deal employed practitioners on an unprecedented scale. The return to civilian life and reduction in government programs then forced members of the field to adjust to a new set of circumstances. Private commissions had changed. There were fewer requests for estate grounds and upscale subdivisions and a greater need for pedestrian, but essential, public projects. Added to this, leading members of the field—a generation trained in Beaux-Arts classicism—had retired or passed away. Younger practitioners, with different training and sensibilities, filled the void.

That the firm of Hare & Hare was successful, and remained busy, during these unstable years is remarkable on multiple levels. Success lay in its ability to adapt to circumstances by balancing public and private commissions. The firm expanded its practice to meet new demands such as urban redevelopment and low-cost housing, yet continued to attract clients who commissioned country clubs, golf courses, and impressive residential grounds. To stay in business for decades is cause enough for celebration; doing so with such success is another. By 1950, there were other milestones to celebrate. Herbert had completed his tenure as ASLA president, participated in the organization's fiftieth annual meeting (of which he was designated an honorary member of its planning committee) at the Shoreham Hotel in Washington, D.C., and attended the fortieth anniversary celebration of his Harvard class. That June marked Hare & Hare's fortieth year in business.

Sid and Herbert Hare, by their very natures, refused to call attention to themselves, but their work, and that of the firm, continues to speak for them.[2] Countless neighborhoods, such as Nichols Hills in Oklahoma City, Westboro in Topeka, and Yale Park in Salt Lake City, bear the mark of the model, Kansas City's Country Club District. Hare & Hare master plans serve as references for smaller Midwest cities, such as Columbia, Missouri, and Lawrence, Kansas. Parks large and small still bear their imprint and are valued by citizens and city officials alike. At Point Defiance Park, munic-

Lake Sacajawea, Longview, Washington, c. 1928. SHSMO-KC.

A Hare & Hare streetscape in Mission Hills, 2017. Photo by Richard Welnowski.

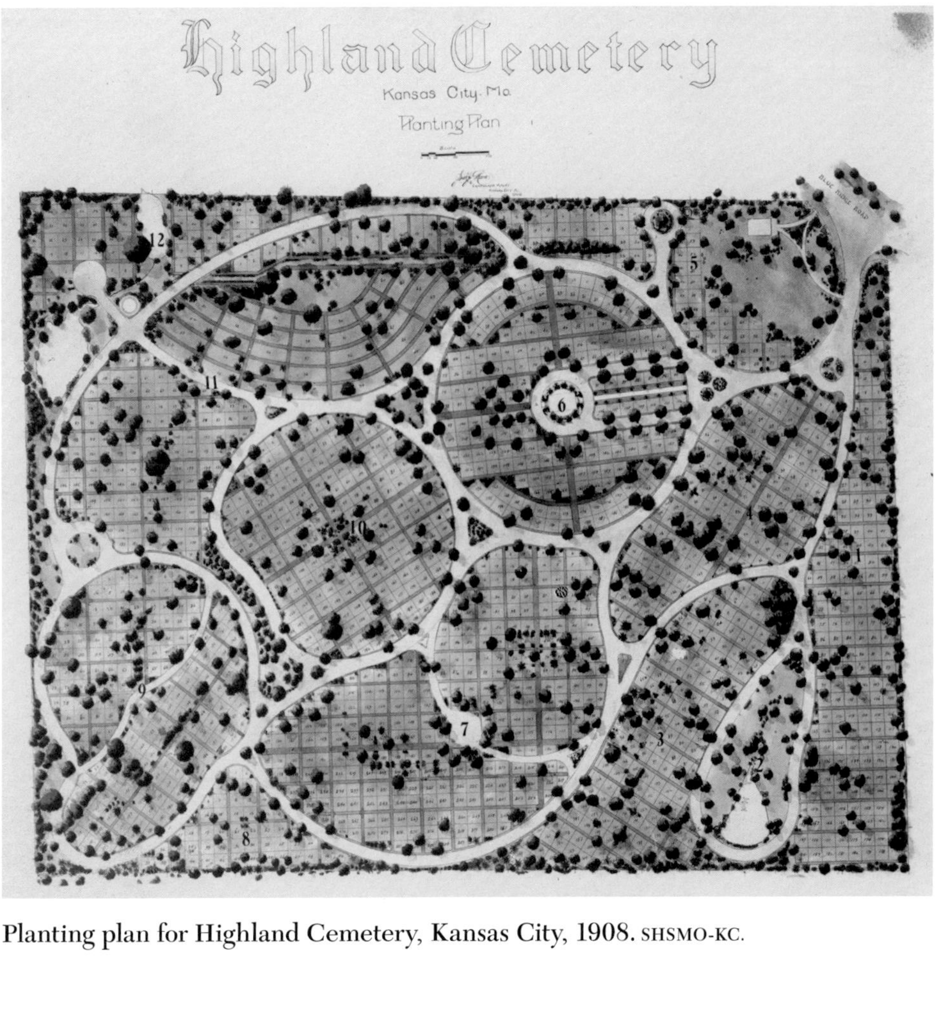

Planting plan for Highland Cemetery, Kansas City, 1908. SHSMO-KC.

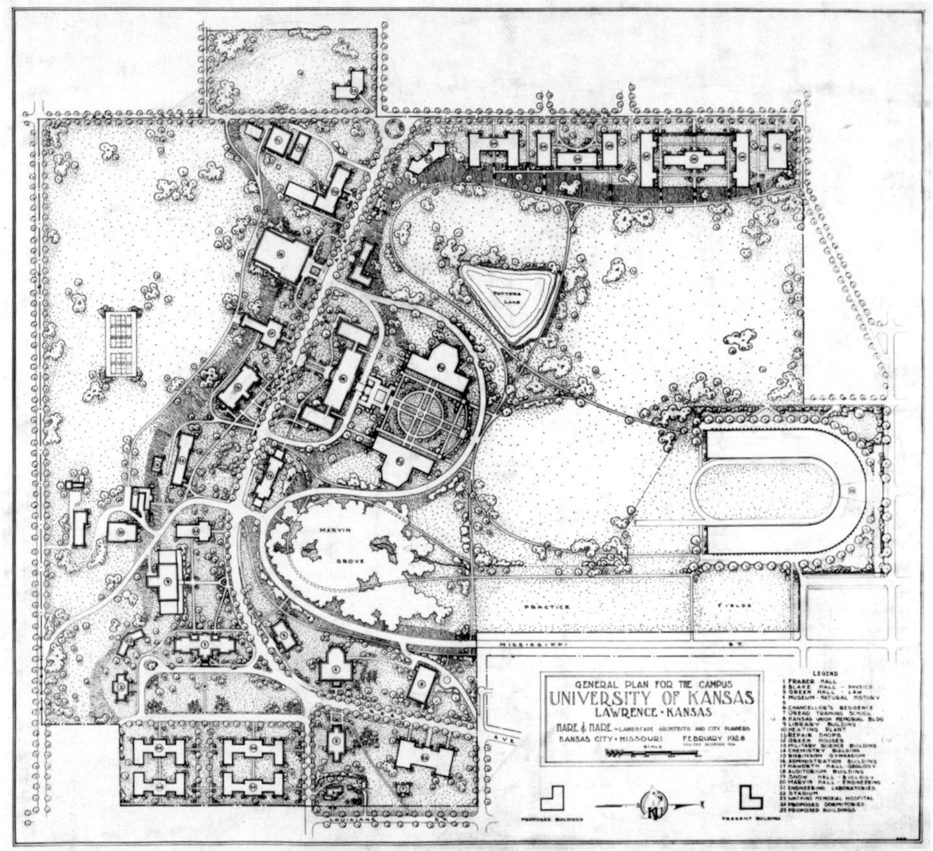

Campus plan for University of Kansas, Lawrence, 1928. SHSMO-KC.

ipal planners, with input from the public, determined that Hare & Hare's 1911 plan continued to meet public needs and that an updated master plan would be devoid of major changes. As part of Dallas's long-range development plan, the city's park and recreation department intends to preserve and showcase its Hare & Hare parks. And the important contribution to the environment and quality of life made by Lake Sacajawea in Longview, Washington, has prompted city officials to commission a preservation plan to guide its stewardship.

Given the vast number of commissions executed by Hare & Hare, this book is but an introduction to their work. Many significant projects, such as those at the University of Kansas, Lawrence (where commissions spanned five decades, from 1916 to 1955), and the Corpus Christi Bay Front master plan (1944–47), are beyond its scope. Among the many projects awaiting further research is Hare & Hare's planning of more than two thousand acres for the Woodlawn Trustees, in the Brandywine Hundred in Wilmington, Delaware (c. 1929–33). Although plans exist in the firm's archives, its name is absent among Woodlawn documents at the Hagley Museum and Library. Another project deserving attention is Kansas City's Highland Cemetery (1909), the country's first (and perhaps only) modern cemetery for African Americans. Local jazz musicians, doctors, and school teachers, who had been "ruled out" of other cemeteries, are buried there. Sid deemed that they deserved "as good as the white man gets" and drafted twelve ink-on-linen plans with large colorful beds of coleus and cannas and a stone cottage for the superintendent's residence which he described as "a beauty."[3] Then there are the "clues" and tantalizing references to projects that, to date, we know nothing about: Sid's mention of work in White Plains, New York; reference to a subdivision in Victoria, British Columbia, for the Canadian developer W. H. Gardner; a project in Hawaii yet to be identified; and an inquiry about subdivision planning by R. E. Whitley (whose father developed West Hollywood). The purpose of Herbert's frequent trips to California has yet to be explained.

This book ends with the death of Herbert Hare in 1960, but the firm's

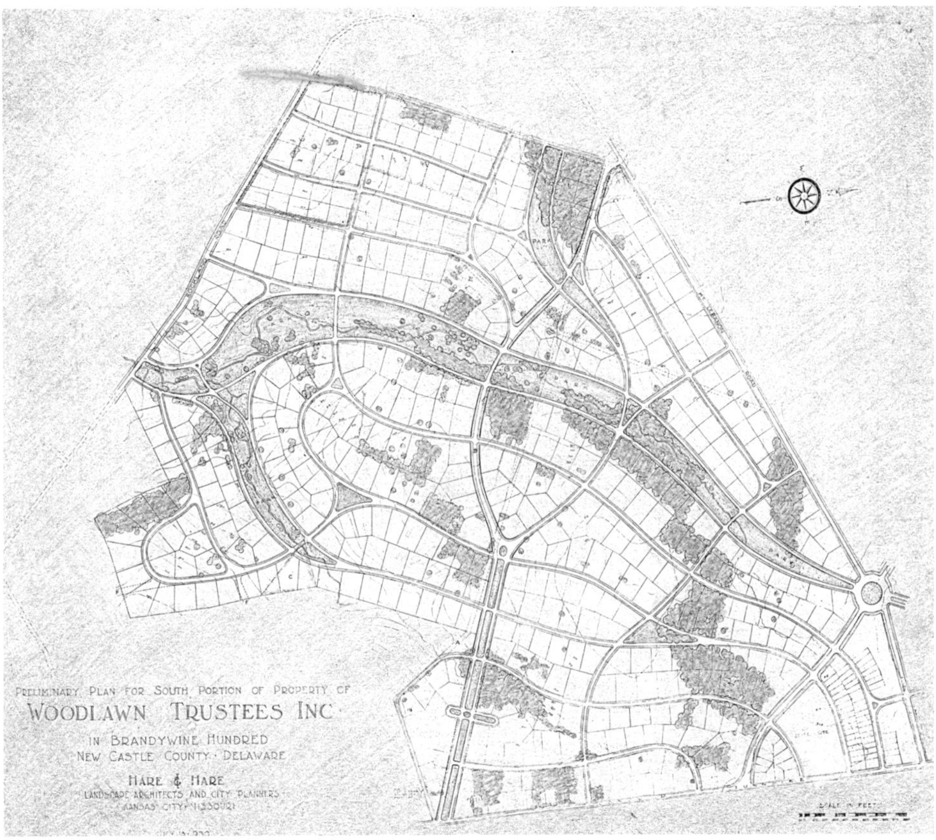

"Preliminary Plan for South Portion of Property of Woodlawn Trustees," 1930. SHSMO-KC.

Herbert Hare in the gardens of Villa Serbelloni on Lake Como, Italy, 1924. SHSMO-KC.

Sid Hare and forsythia at Harecliff, autochrome by Frank Lauder, 1934. MVSC.

history did not. Purchased in 1979 by Kansas Citian Ralph H. Ochsner, it was merged with Ochsner & Associates, planning consultants, the company he had established a decade before. In partnership with Herbert's former employees Chalmer Cooper and Robert Lee Bell, the firm continued under the name of Ochsner Hare & Hare. In 2010, it celebrated the one hundredth anniversary of the founding of the firm. Today Ochsner Hare & Hare is a design studio of Olsson Associates, with whom it merged in 2014. Sidney and Herbert Hare's commitment to "the constructive purpose of making our cities and countryside more convenient, efficient, livable and beautiful" continues.[4]

Archives and Abbreviations

HHCR	Hare & Hare Company Records (K0206), SHSMO-KC
HMRC	Hare & Hare Collection, Houston Metropolitan Research Center, Houston Public Library
JCHS	Sidney Hare Collection, Jackson County Historical Society Archives, Independence, MO
LC	Library of Congress, Prints and Photographs Division
MDNR	Missouri Department of Natural Resources, Division of State Parks Archive
MSA	Missouri State Archives
MVSC	Missouri Valley Special Collections, Kansas City Public Library, Kansas City, MO
NCPTT	National Center for Preservation Technology and Training
NCS	J. C. Nichols Company Scrapbooks, SHSMO-KC
NSC	Nell Stevenson Collection, Jackson County Historical Society, Independence, MO
SHSMO	State Historical Society of Missouri Digital Collections/Photographs
SHSMO-C	State Historical Society of Missouri Research Center–Columbia
SHSMO-KC	State Historical Society of Missouri Research Center–Kansas City

Notes

INTRODUCTION

1. Herbert Hare to Hare & Hare (attention Eda Sutermeister), n.d., folder 23, box 7, HHCR.
2. Herbert Hare to Harry Ford Sinclair, January 5, 1914, box 3, HHCR.
3. James Sturgis Pray, "The Department of Landscape Architecture in Harvard University," *Landscape Journal* 1 (January 1911): 1.
4. Sid J. Hare to W. H. Mullins, July 20, 1912, box 1, HHCR.
5. Richard J. Gentile, "Upper Carboniferous Crinoids: An Extraordinary Collection by Late 19th Century Amateur Paleontologists, Kansas City, Missouri, U.S.A.," *Geological Curator* 7 (November 2003): 375.
6. Unidentified garden club minutes, April 14, 1925. Sylvia Mooney (current owner of Harecliff).
7. Roscoe E. Wright, "Hare Tonic," *Houston Gargoyle,* December 18, 1928.
8. Fellow University of Kansas City trustees honored Herbert upon his death with a resolution that included this quotation. Box 3, Nell Stevenson Collection, Jackson County Historical Society, Independence, MO (NSC).
9. Among these were drypoints, lithographs, and wood engravings by artists who have come to be known for their depictions of Hawaii—John Melville Kelly, Madge Tennent, Alexander Samuel MacLeod, and Huc-Mazelet Luquiens, one of the print club's founders.
10. "Harecliff," *Kansas City Post,* July 4, 1926.
11. These works are in the collection of the Nelson-Atkins Museum of Art, Kansas City.
12. Herbert Hare, "The Setting for a Museum of Fine Arts," *Landscape Architecture* 29 (January 1939): 92–96. The firm's drawing of the museum was the image on one of the many holiday greeting cards sent to friends and clients over the years.
13. "A System of Parks and Boulevards for Joplin, Missouri 1913," p. 31, box 93, HHCR.
14. Staff identified only by initials during this early period include "RWD," "CAW," and "FVS."

15. After Herbert's death, and Huldah's departure, Elizabeth Lemmon, who married staff member H. G. Whiffen, ran the office.
16. "Planning the City: An Interview with Ralph Ellifrit," *Houston Review* 3 (Winter 1981): 205–6. Ellifrit earned his degree in landscape architecture, with an emphasis on city planning, from the University of Illinois in 1932.
17. David G. McComb, *Houston: A History* (Austin: University of Texas Press, 1981), 161.
18. Richard B. Fowler, "Herbert Hare's Turning Point Was a Spiral Curve," *Kansas City Star*, July 5, 1931.
19. Whiffen, who held a bachelor's degree from Pennsylvania State College, left the firm in 1931 but returned in 1937. Cooper attended Iowa State University and remained a partner at Hare &Hare, Inc., until his retirement in 1986. Prior to Herbert's death, the landscape architects Ben R. Lantz, Robert William Dyas, and Robert K. Maiden (listed as a "Graduate Landscape Architect") and the city planner William O. Flint were among those who worked at the firm.
20. This formality was retained by Dan Kiley and Jaquelin Robertson's 1987 design for the Nelson-Atkins south lawn when it became the site of the Henry Moore Sculpture Garden.
21. J. C. Nichols Company Scrapbooks, K0054, vol. 1, 117–18, SHSMO-KC.
22. Edward M. Bassett, "A Zoning Tour," *City Planning* 3 (October 1927): 309.
23. Warren Manning to Sid J. Hare, September 2, 1925. Two other letters written that month (Sid to Manning and Manning to Sid) continue the conversation about the need for, and logistics of, setting aside large amounts of land for parks and reserves. Manning's letter to Sid closes with "I hope I may hear from you again and I shall be glad to be kept in touch with the work you are doing there and also to keep you in touch with work I am doing along similar lines if you are interested." Folder 1.13 (1d), box 67, HHCR.
24. Herbert Hare, "A Year at War," *Landscape Architecture* 33 (April 1943): 81.
25. *Report of the City Planning Commission, Houston, Texas*, 1929, introduction, box 104, HHCR.
26. Herbert Hare lecture notes for University of Kansas, 1914, folder 01.02 (1fi), box 67, HHCR.

1. EARLY KANSAS CITY, SID HARE, AND THE "FIGHT FOR PARKS"

1. Christopher Hare was born in Louisville and his parents were from Maryland and New Jersey. Isadora Hare was born in Kentucky, as were her parents. The couple would go on to have eight children, six of whom lived to adulthood.
2. William Griffith, *The History of Kansas City, Illustrated in Three Decades* (Kansas City: Hudson-Kimberly Publishing, 1900), 106.
3. Carrie Westlake Whitney, *History of Kansas City* (Kansas City: S. J. Clarke Publishing, 1908), 109.
4. George Ehrlich, *Kansas City, Missouri: An Architectural History, 1826–1990* (Columbia: University of Missouri Press, 1992).
5. Sid J. Hare to Joseph Meinrath, March 9, 1926, Sid J. Hare Papers, MVSC.
6. Hare and Butts's findings were presented at the International Committee on the History of Geological Sciences Symposium in Dublin, Ireland, in 1905. See Richard J. Gentile, "Upper Carboniferous Crinoids: An Extraordinary Collection by Late 19th Century Amateur Paleontologists, Kansas City, Missouri, U.S.A.," *Geological Curator* 7 (November 2003): 373–80.

7. Last Will and Testament of Caroline Korphage, filed February 23, 1917, NSC.
8. Jackson County land deed, August 26, 1885, NSC.
9. William H. Wilson, *The City Beautiful Movement in Kansas City* (Columbia: University of Missouri Press, 1964), 20.
10. Janice Lee et al., *A Legacy of Design: An Historical Survey of the Kansas City, Missouri, Parks, and Boulevards System, 1893–1940* (Kansas City Center for Design Education and Research, in cooperation with the Western Historical Manuscript Collection–Kansas City, 1995), xii; Cydney Millstein and Paul Novick, "Kansas City Parks and Boulevards Historic District," National Register of Historic Places Nomination, Listed June 17, 2016, 35.
11. Wilson, *City Beautiful Movement*, 43.
12. Ibid., 33.
13. "Its Plans May Be Dropped," *Kansas City Star*, April 24, 1893.
14. Wilson, *City Beautiful Movement*, 59–60.
15. W. H. Eckman, ed., *Public Parks: A Compilation of Facts and Statistics Gathered from Official and Other Sources . . . Together with a Brief History of Park Undertakings in the United States* (Cleveland, OH: J. B. Savage, 1888).
16. "The Park Board's Report," *Kansas City Star*, August 28, 1893. The Olmsted firm would propose additions to the Kansas City plan that were never implemented.
17. *Report of the Board of Park and Boulevard Commissioners of Kansas City, Missouri, Embracing Recommendations for the Establishment of a Park and Boulevard System for Kansas City. Resolution of October 12, 1893* (Kansas City: Hudson-Kimberly Publishing, 1893), 4.
18. Ibid. and *Report of the Board of Park Commissioners of Kansas City*, 1906.
19. Herbert first worked with Kessler on Fort Worth's Burnett Park in 1920. A mutual respect existed between Kessler and the Hares, and in later years, letters written by Kessler were addressed to "My dear Herbert." After Kessler's death in 1923, the firm carried forward several of his unfinished projects.
20. Walter P. Tracy, *Kansas City and Its One Hundred Foremost Men* (self-published, 1924); Lee et al., *Legacy of Design*, xv; Millstein and Novick, National Register Nomination, 34; Deon Wolfenbarger, "Historic Resources Survey of the 1893 Parks and Boulevard System, Kansas City, Missouri," prepared for the Prairie Gateway Chapter, ASLA, 1989; and William Worley, "Kansas City Architects George Kessler, Henry Wright, and Sid and Herbert Hare," *Kansas History* 20 (Autumn 1997): 192–205.

2. SID HARE AND THE DEVELOPMENT OF THE MODERN CEMETERY

1. "Botany for a Cemetery," unidentified newspaper article, NSC.
2. See A. E. Shirling, *Trees of Forest Hill, Kansas City, Missouri*, c. 1938. There were at least three editions of this guidebook. Sid Hare's copy dates from after 1927. NSC.
3. Sid J. Hare to George Law, December 10, 1904, box 1, HHCR.
4. Shirling, *Trees of Forest Hill.*
5. "Veteran Sid J. Hare Passes On," *AACS Bulletin*, November 1938, 392.
6. O. C. Simonds, who called Strauch "the fountainhead of the modern cemetery," quoted in Christopher Vernon, *Graceland Cemetery: A Design History* (Amherst: University of Massachusetts Press in association with Library of American Landscape History, 2011), 148.
7. Downing quoted in Rudy J. Favretti, *Jacob Weidenmann: Pioneer Landscape Architect* (Hartford, CT: Cedar Hill Cemetery Foundation, 2007), 37.

8. Hotchkiss came to Bellefontaine in 1849 and stayed for forty-six years. His son, Frank Hotchkiss, followed as superintendent for the next twenty.
9. R. J. Haight, *AACS Proceedings of the 36th Annual Convention*, Omaha, Nebraska, 1922.
10. Adolphus Strauch, *Spring Grove Cemetery: Its History and Improvements* (Cincinnati: R. Clarke, 1869).
11. Strauch visited Weidenmann and the two consulted about the project. See Favretti, *Jacob Weidenmann*, 42.
12. In 1888, *The Monumental News* published Jacob Weidenmann's illustrated essay, "Modern Cemeteries," which mentioned the "open lawn system."
13. Also in 1881, the landscape architect H. W. S. Cleveland, who worked at Graceland prior to Simonds's arrival, published *A Few Words on the Arrangement of Rural Cemeteries* (Chicago: George K. Hazlitt).
14. Vernon, *Graceland Cemetery*, 151. Vernon cites Walter Creese's observation that at Graceland, Simonds fused the initial rural cemetery type of Mount Auburn with Strauch's landscape lawn plan at Spring Grove (159).
15. Edward A. Merriam, "The Late Arthur W. Hobert," *Park and Cemetery and Landscape Gardening* 30 (April 1920): 52.
16. "Constitution and Bylaws of the Association of American Cemetery Superintendents," *Proceedings of the Sixth Annual Convention of the Association of the American Cemetery Superintendents* (Chicago: Modern Cemetery Press, 1892), 55.
17. AACS president Fred R. Diering noted how the organization had helped to create an awareness of "system in the office, system in the grounds, system with the employee." See James J. Farrell, *Inventing the American Way of Death, 1830–1920* (Philadelphia: Temple University Press, 1980), 120.
18. O. C. Simonds, *Landscape-Gardening*, reprint of 1920 ed. (Amherst: University of Massachusetts Press in association with Library of American Landscape History, 2000), 301.
19. "The exponent of Art in the Monument Field" is the banner for *The Monumental News*, and the "cemetery as a business . . . how to maintain, develop and beautify at a profit" is that for *The Cemetery Beautiful*.
20. William Stone, superintendent of Pine Grove Cemetery, Lynn, MA, in his presentation "What a Modern Cemetery Should Be," *AACS Proceedings of the 10th Annual Convention*, St. Louis, 1896.
21. Haight was described as "intellectually honest and enthusiastic," always "pounding away for the cause." He would be voted into the Hall of Fame of Cemetery Administration in 1940. Ernest Stevens Leland and Donald W. Smith, *The Pioneers of Cemetery Administration in America* (New York: Sterling Press, 1941), unpaginated.
22. The journal was published as *The Modern Cemetery* from 1891 to 1895, as *Park and Cemetery* from 1895 to 1900, and as *Park and Cemetery and Landscape Gardening* from 1900 to 1931.
23. According to R. J. Haight, topics included "the entire gamut of things pertaining to cemeteries—from bugs, birds and beetles, to reptiles, [and] roads." *AACS Proceedings of the 36th Annual Convention*, Omaha, Nebraska, 1922.
24. Part one of the *Hand Book* began with Hare & Hare's ten chapters dedicated to "Organizing and Developing a Modern Cemetery."
25. Sid J. Hare, "The Influence of Surroundings," *Park and Cemetery* 7 (September 1897): 156–57.
26. Ibid.

27. *Salem Daily News*, March 22, 1889, as cited in *Columbiana County Cemetery Inscriptions* 12 (1984): 1021.
28. J. R. Vernon to Sid J. Hare, October 1, 1900, box 1, HHCR.
29. Sid J. Hare to J. R. Vernon, June 21, 1901, ibid.
30. Sid J. Hare to Salem Cemetery Company, March 4, 1901, ibid.
31. *Rules and Regulations of the Salem Cemetery Association, Grandview Burial Park, Salem, Ohio*, Salem Public Library, n.d.
32. Sid J. Hare to J. R. Vernon, November 26, 1901, box 1, HHCR.
33. W. H. Mullins to Sid J. Hare, December 13, 1901, ibid.
34. J. R. Vernon to Sid J. Hare, March 9, 1901 and February 5, 1913, ibid.
35. Sid J. Hare to J. R. Vernon, February 28, 1913, ibid.
36. "Remodeling an Ancient Cemetery in Costa Rica," *Park and Cemetery and Landscape Gardening* 27 (November 1917): 241.

3. THE FOUNDING OF THE FIRM

1. Richard B. Fowler, "Herbert Hare's Turning Point Was a Spiral Curve," *Kansas City Star*, July 5, 1931.
2. Ibid.
3. Ibid.
4. Sid J. Hare, "The Influence of Surroundings," *Park and Cemetery* 7 (September 1897): 156–57.
5. Howard Evarts Weed's advertisement, adjacent to Sid's in the same issue, is in the same vein: "Let H. E. Weedout All Unsightly Features of Your Cemeteries, Parks and Homegrounds."
6. James Sturgis Pray commented on the Harvard faculty member Benjamin M. Watson as "a widely recognized expert, yet not a specialist." Melanie L. Simo, *The Coalescing of Different Forces and Ideas: A History of Landscape Architecture at Harvard, 1900–1999* (Cambridge: Harvard University Graduate School of Design, 2000), 2.
7. Charles W. Eliot, *Charles Eliot, Landscape Architect*, reprint of 1903 ed. (Amherst: University of Massachusetts Press in association with Library of American Landscape History, 1999), 273.
8. Mariana Griswold Van Rensselaer, "Landscape-Gardeners Needed for America," *Century Illustrated Monthly* 34 (June 1887): 313–14.
9. Frank A. Waugh, *Book of Landscape Gardening*, reprint of 1926 ed. (Amherst: University of Massachusetts Press in association with Library of American Landscape History, 2007), 4–5.
10. In 1914, the ASLA still sought consensus on a "common name for the profession," voting on other options that included "landscape designer," "landscape engineer," "landscapist," and "landscapor," with "landscape architect" receiving the most votes.
11. Sid also joined kindred organizations devoted to the improvement of public landscapes, including the American Park and Outdoor Art Association, which merged with the American League for Civic Improvement in 1904 to become the American Civic Association.
12. Hare, "Influence of Surroundings," 156–57.
13. George Kessler, "The Cemetery," *Park and Cemetery* 18 (September 1908): 408–9.
14. Sid J. Hare to R. J. Haight, January 31, 1907, folder 01.29 (1fii), box 67, HHCR.
15. Sid J. Hare, undated draft of an article on Mount Hope Cemetery, box 1, ibid.

16. The firm returned to Joplin, executing more than thirty public and private projects through the 1950s.
17. Sid J. Hare to R. J. Haight, November 15, 1907, folder 01.29 (1fii), box 67, HHCR.
18. Sid J. Hare, undated draft of an article on Mount Hope, box 1, ibid.
19. As illustrated in Howard Evarts Weed, *Modern Park Cemeteries* (Chicago: R. J. Haight, 1912), 127.
20. "Beautiful Bellaire Brochure," n.d., Houston Area Digital Archives, http://digital.houstonlibrary.org. Images originally from the Bellaire City Library Collection.
21. Sid J. Hare to R. J. Haight, October 19, 1908, folder 01.29 (1fii), box 67, HHCR.
22. Sid J. Hare to Edward Teas, November 7, 1908, box 1, ibid.
23. Sid J. Hare to William Wright Baldwin, November 24, 1908, ibid.
24. Hare to Baldwin, December 15, 1908 (emphasis added), ibid.
25. Plan in RG D 026, key 1461, HMRC.
26. The Teas Nursery remained in the family, and in business, for one hundred years. By 1951, the nursery had planted more than one million trees in the Houston area. After it closed in 2011, the five-acre property became Evelyn's Park, a public park.
27. Fowler, "Herbert Hare's Turning Point."
28. Ibid.
29. Melanie L. Simo, *The Coalescing of Different Forces and Ideas: A History of Landscape Architecture at Harvard, 1900–1999* (Cambridge: Harvard University Graduate School of Design, 2000), 2.
30. Eliot, *Charles Eliot, Landscape Architect.*
31. Report of the President of Harvard College and Reports of Departments (Cambridge: Harvard University, 1910): 52–53, folder 1.10 (1fi), box 67, HHCR; GSD History Collection, Student Affairs—Student Work: An Inventory, Special Collections, Frances Loeb Library; Anthony Alofsin, *The Struggle for Modernism: Architecture, Landscape Architecture, and City Planning at Harvard* (New York: Norton, 2002), 37, 44, 67.
32. Because a bachelor's degree with courses approved by Harvard was required to earn a master's, Hare left without an official degree despite fulfilling the course requirements.
33. See James Sturgis Pray, "Planning the Cantonments," *Landscape Architecture* 8 (October 1917): 1–17.
34. Eldridge Lovelace, "Necrology," *Landscape Architecture* 50 (Summer 1960): 242, 244.
35. Sid J. Hare to R. J. Haight, March 28 and June 11, 1910, folder 01.29 (1fii), box 67, HHCR.
36. The firm's advertisement for Wagner Place in Jefferson City, MO (1912), describes this coalescing of art and nature within a neighborhood, folder 1.5 (1fi), ibid.
37. Undated article in H. C. Flower Job File, box 1, HHCR.
38. Drawings for H. C. Flower, boxes 1 and 1 x 3, ibid.
39. The Ruskinian Gothic residence was designed c. 1880 by the Boston architectural firm of Peabody & Stearns. In 1908, the architect and fellow Christian Scientist Solon S. Beman completed an extensive remodeling of the residence, creating a cozier environment for Eddy while still accommodating her large staff.
40. Dickey, a prolific writer on Christian Science, served on the board of directors of the Mother Church from 1910 until 1925 and coedited Eddy's memoirs.
41. Sid J. Hare to Adam Dickey, June 20, 1910, box 1, HHCR.
42. Sid later described George Hill as "among the leading intelligent park superintendents" he knew, in contrast to others who had "no love for the work and no intelli-

gence to carry out a plan if they had one." Sid J. Hare to George Hill, August 11, 1911, folder 1, box 1, ibid.

43. As described by Frederick Heath, Metropolitan Park District of Tacoma, to Sid J. Hare, November 1, 1910, ibid.
44. Sid J. Hare to George Hill, September 15, 1910, ibid.
45. Frederick Heath, Metropolitan Park District of Tacoma, to Sid J. Hare, November 1, 1910, ibid.
46. *A Preliminary Report for the Improvement of Point Defiance Park, Tacoma, Washington,* folder 5, ibid.

4. KANSAS CITY'S COUNTRY CLUB DISTRICT AND THE "NEW INDUSTRIAL CITY OF THE PACIFIC NORTHWEST"

1. Sid J. Hare to R. J. Haight, March 19, 1913, folder 01.29 (1fii), box 67, HHCR.
2. Sid J. Hare to family, February 9, 1905, box 1, ibid.
3. R. N. Kesterson to Sid J. Hare, May 27, 1908, ibid.
4. Sid J. Hare to R. N. Kesterson, March 2, 1905, ibid.
5. Herbert Hare to Harry Ford Sinclair, January 5, 1914, box 3, ibid.
6. Herbert Hare to Harry Ford Sinclair, January 17, 1914, ibid. Drawings and plant lists for H. F. Sinclair, box 5 x 3, ibid. The plantings were barely mature in 1918 when the Sinclairs moved to a French Chateau–style mansion at 2 East 79th Street in New York City.
7. Joshua Cosden to Herbert Hare, April 11, 1916, box 3, ibid.
8. Sid J. Hare to R. J. Haight, May 2, 1914, folder 1.29 (fii), box 67, ibid.
9. "Harecliff," *Kansas City Post,* July 4, 1926.
10. According to Sid, they were not as attracted to the less verdant southwestern landscape. Sid J. Hare to George Hill, September 16, 1914, folder 3, box 1, HHCR.
11. Sid J. Hare to George Hill, January 31, 1913, folder 2, ibid.
12. Herbert Hare to James Sturgis Pray, September 2, 1910, folder 1.29, box 67, ibid.
13. Eldridge Lovelace, "Sidney Herbert Hare," *Landscape Architecture* 50 (Summer 1960): 242–44.
14. Soon after, Hare & Hare designed a master plan, which built on George Kessler's partially implemented plan of 1904 for the KU campus.
15. Herbert Hare lecture notes for University of Kansas, Kansas City Art Institute, folders 01.02 (1fi) and 01.05 (1fi), box 67, and notes for a presentation titled "Rock Gardenitis," folder 1.11 (2a), box 51, HHCR.
16. Frances Bush, "City's Natural Beauty Inspired Sid Hare," *Kansas City Times,* December, 21, 1977.
17. Sid J. Hare to R. J. Haight. July 22, 1918, folder 1.29, box 67, HHCR.
18. Diary entry as published in "Realty Briefs," *Kansas City Realtor,* February 15, 1943, folder 01.13 (1d), box 67, HHCR.
19. William S. Worley, *J. C. Nichols and the Shaping of Kansas City: Innovation in Planned Residential Communities* (Columbia: University of Missouri Press, 1993), 68.
20. Worley describes Nichols's method of planning the Country Club District as "not so much an innovation as it is a synergistic enterprise: a bringing together the best thinking available at the time" (ibid., 291). Norman T. Newton called the Country Club District "one of the finest residential sections in the United States." Newton, *Design on the Land: The Development of Landscape Architecture* (Cambridge: Belknap Press of Harvard University Press, 1971), 474. Jon A. Peterson refers to the

Country Club District, Roland Park, and Forest Hills Gardens as the three "remarkable suburbs" that "crystallized new interest in high-quality, large-tract, elite suburban design." Peterson, *The Birth of City Planning in the United States, 1840–1917* (Baltimore: Johns Hopkins University Press, 2003), 278.

21. Jessie Clyde Nichols, "Planning for Permanence, NYC, 1948," J. C. Nichols Company Records, K0106, box 108 f. 12, and "Autobiography-Genealogy, 8/23/1880–2/16/1950," K0106, box 321 f. 0, SHSMO-KC.
22. Richard Longstreth, "J. C. Nichols, the Country Club Plaza, and Notions of Modernity," *Harvard Architecture Review* 5 (1986): 123.
23. Bouton also worked with the Olmsted firm on Forest Hills Gardens in Queens, New York, beginning in 1909. His integrity, artistic judgment, vision, competence, and concern for the "well-being of his fellow man" was cited in a pamphlet for the development. Susan Klaus, *A Modern Arcadia: Frederick Law Olmsted Jr. and the Plan for Forest Hills Gardens* (Amherst: University of Massachusetts Press in association with Library of American Landscape History, 2002), 68.
24. George Kessler, under Bouton as general manager, planned the first phase of this East Coast project in 1891. The two had worked simultaneously in Kansas City a few years before—Kessler at the exclusive neighborhood of Hyde Park (financed by the firm of Jarvis & Conklin, who also helped finance Roland Park) and Bouton, who oversaw housing construction, at a similar subdivision called Kenwood. The Olmsted firm was responsible for a second plat of Roland Park in 1897.
25. Nichols's level of personal involvement could be interpreted as a patriarchal iron fist. Worley describes Nichols as a "benevolent despot" (*J. C. Nichols*, 168).
26. In 1917, Nichols raised the question of "selling [to] Jewish People" before a national group of real estate developers, all of whom were adamantly against it. The sale of property to African Americans was not considered worthy of discussion. Worley, *J. C. Nichols*, 149, 151.
27. Longstreth, "J. C. Nichols,," 121.
28. Newton, *Design on the Land*, 474.
29. Sally Schwenk, "Crestwood Historic District," National Register of Historic Places Nomination, Listed November 1998, 43.
30. *Country Club District* [CCD] *Bulletin*, December 1924.
31. The naming of these bits of landscape reflects Nichols's flair for promotion and his practice of creating an image of prestige; labeled as "triangles" on the firm's plans, they became "parklets" and "piazzettas" in company bulletins. Ibid., November 1921.
32. Worley, *J. C. Nichols*, 113. See also Schwenk, "Crestwood Historic District."
33. Two of Crestwood's interior parks were subsequently resubdivided to be included in the adjacent lots. Nonetheless, the land remains undeveloped, providing a common area for the surrounding residents.
34. Works by Ernest Harold Baynes (1868–1925) include *Wild Bird Guests: How to Entertain Them* (1915), which has a chapter on the organization and management of bird clubs and a preface by Theodore Roosevelt.
35. Worley, *J. C. Nichols*, 279.
36. J. C. Nichols to Hare & Hare, November 20, 1914, box 2, HHCR.
37. Junius Irving project, boxes 3 and 5 x 3, ibid.
38. See Worley, *J. C. Nichols*, 82.
39. Nichols to Herbert Hare, December 29, 1916, folder 2, box 2, HHCR. The firm went on to plan the adjacent community of Indian Hills, which met the high bar set by Mission Hills.
40. "Announcing Mission Hills of the Country Club District," *Kansas City Star*, Sep-

tember 17, 1916. Many of these houses were designed by the local architects Edward Buehler Delk and Edward Tanner, another element that contributes to the "harmony" of the neighborhood.

41. Herbert Hare to R. A. Long, August 18, 1924, folder 2, box 6, and Herbert's European drawings, 1924, f. 1.26, box 51, HHCR.
42. *CCD Bulletin*, August 1925.
43. Nichols's team of professionals included Hare & Hare as landscape architects and planners, architects Edward Beuhler Delk and Edward Tanner, and George Kessler as planning adviser. Hare & Hare's participation is documented in the following sources: boxes 5 and 10 x 3, HHCR; *CCD Bulletin*, June 1922; Country Club Plaza Survey (JAASO72-R) on file at the National Register and Survey Section, State Historic Preservation Office, Missouri Department of Natural Resources; and in Robert Pearson and Brad Pearson, *The J. C. Nichols Chronicle: The Authorized Story of the Man, His Company, and His Legacy, 1880–1994* (Lawrence: Country Club Plaza Press, dist. by University Press of Kansas, 1994), 97, 280.
44. For the defining characteristics of the Plaza, see Longstreth, "J. C. Nichols," 124–32.
45. Ibid., 128.
46. Lenore K. Bradley, *Robert Alexander Long: A Lumberman of the Gilded Age* (Durham, NC: Forest History Society, 1989); *From Tree to Trade* (Kansas City, MO: Long-Bell Lumber Company, 1920).
47. Herbert Hare, "Longview's Planning—In Retrospect," *American City*, August 1948, 137.
48. Bradley, *Robert Alexander Long*, 146. Referring to the project that would become Longview, the official went on to say that Long "was going to build a monument to himself and his company here in the West."
49. The team also included Samuel Morris, who would become general manager of Long-Bell's western operations, and Frederick Bannister, who briefly served as president of the company.
50. As cited in Bradley, *Robert Alexander Long*, 43. This description of Long was originally published in a leading trade journal, *American Lumberman*, July 2, 1904, which dedicated nearly the entire issue to Long-Bell.
51. Long-Bell would ultimately buy up nearly 70,000 acres. Many of these were purchased from the largest private timber holder in the world, Weyerhaeuser Timber Company, which had bought 900,000 forested acres from the Northern Pacific Railroad in 1900.
52. For the history of Longview, see John M. McClelland Jr., *R. A. Long's Planned City: The Story of Longview* (Longview, WA: Westmedia, 1998).
53. Wesley Vandercook, chief engineer of the project, spent months gathering data to guide decision making. His findings were compiled in an exhaustive 140-page report that assessed eight potential sites—three in the vicinity of Portland, four near Astoria, and one on the Cowlitz River near the small town of Kelso.
54. "Longview, Washington, A Wonder City in a Wonderland," folder 16, box 6, HHCR, SHSKC-MO.
55. Documents relating to the tour of industrial cities and Longview planning, folder 1, ibid.
56. At Kingsport, for example, they met with J. Fred Johnson, president of the Kingsport Improvement Corporation.
57. Supplementary information on Kingsport and Mariemont, Ohio, another Nolen project, was sent separately as an addendum to the report. The planning of Mariemont overlapped with that of Longview, which began the spring of 1922.

58. Herbert Hare, handwritten notes, folder 1, box 6, HHCR.
59. The form of English garden cities—a town center with radial streets linking neighborhoods and districts on the outskirts reserved for industry, all surrounded by open land—"proved to be a resilient and persistent model." Charles D. Warren, "John Nolen and the New Synthesis in American City Planning," introduction to John Nolen, *New Towns for Old*, reprint of 1927 ed. (Amherst: University of Massachusetts Press in association with Library of American Landscape History, 2005), l.
60. The evolution of this process is discussed in Klaus, *Modern Arcadia*, 31–37.
61. Henry Vincent Hubbard and Theodora Kimball Hubbard, *Our Cities To-Day and To-morrow: A Survey of Planning and Zoning Progress in the United States* (Cambridge: Harvard University Press, 1929), 263.
62. As cited in Peterson, *Birth of City Planning*, 264.
63. Herbert's handwritten notes are titled "Memoranda of Points Discerned and Observed During Visit to Kelso Sept. and Oct. 1922," folder 15, box 6, HHCR. Kelso is the town east of the Cowlitz River where the team's office was located early in the planning process.
64. Long approved only two of the names chosen by Lambuth: "Vandercook" and "Kessler."
65. Reserving space for specific purposes and allowing for incremental growth, a practice implemented by J. C. Nichols in his Missouri and Kansas projects, was discussed by Raymond Unwin at the International Federation for Town and Country Planning and Garden Cities conference in New York, April 1925. Critics of the Longview plan claimed that these spaces suggested a forlorn emptiness rather than forethought. See *International Town Planning Conference, New York, 1925, Report*, 206–7.
66. The Kansas City firm of Hoit, Price & Barnes served as consulting architects for the civic center. The project was originally named Jefferson Square, in honor of Thomas Jefferson and his commissioning of the Corps of Discovery, which reached the Columbia River near Longview. It has since been renamed R. A. Long Square.
67. Longview's plan, which reflects the period's acceptance of racial segregation, includes districts for houses and apartments exclusively for "persons of the white race." The placement of the "better" neighborhoods along Lake Sacajawea and in the wooded hills on the north side is an example not only of segregation but of the "social and topographical hierarchy" characteristic of planning during this period. See Warren, "John Nolen," lxxi.
68. "Vision City Is Dedicated," *Kansas City Star*, July 13, 1923, folder 1, box 6, HHCR; McClelland Jr., *R. A. Long's Planned City*, 58–61.
69. Long made a personal commitment to spend $1 million over five years for civic improvement. By 1926, the Long-Bell Company had invested $6.5 million in Longview.
70. Torbitt, born in Mexico, MO, came to oversee construction of the McIlvain-designed Monticello Hotel. He stayed to design many of Longview's public buildings and residences for Long-Bell executives, with Hare & Hare designing the landscape plans.
71. Plans for the school were published in "Three-Building School Group, Longview, Washington," *American Architect* 132 (August 5, 1927): 141–48. Ittner employed his H-shaped open plan, which included an innovative power plant that made fuel from mill refuse.
72. Hare even agreed to Long's request that he and John Null, the city's new park supervisor, tour Portland, Seattle, and Tacoma to see what plants provided the best display. Null, a former Seattle nurseryman, would serve as Longview's park superintendent for the next forty-nine years.
73. Bradley, *Robert Alexander Long*, 148.

74. R. A. Long to Herbert Hare, January 18, 1928, folder 11, box 6, HHCR.
75. See "The Planning of a New Industrial City," *American City*, November 1923, 501–3; "The Planning of the Industrial City of Longview, Washington," *Proceedings of the American Society of Civil Engineers* 53 (August 1927): 1177–83; "Longview," *Tijdschrift voor Volkshuisvesting en Stedebouw*, no. 1 (January 1928): 1–11; and "American Small Towns: II. Longview, Washington," *Town Planning Review* 16 (December 1935): 279–86. Herbert submitted this final article, which followed Nolen's on Kingsport, in response to a March 1935 letter from Nolen suggesting he contribute to the Dutch publication.
76. Raymond Unwin wrote back thanking Herbert, noting his great interest in the "New Pacific City" and "very heartily" wishing him success with the venture. Unwin to Herbert Hare, August 25, 1924, folder 2, box 6, HHCR.
77. Herbert Hare, "Longview's Planning—In Retrospect," *American City*, August 1948, 137.

5. TEXAS AND A RETURN TO TULSA

1. Cheryl Caldwell Ferguson, *Highland Park and River Oaks: The Origins of Garden Suburban Community Planning in Texas* (Austin: University of Texas Press, 2014), 265.
2. Madeline Williams, "Master Planner of Parks and Cities Feels He's Citizen Here," *Fort Worth Star-Telegram*, June 18, 1950.
3. Kessler Plan Association to Hare & Hare, July 7, 1931, folder 25, box 8, HHCR.
4. Susan Allen Kline, *The History of Fort Worth's Public Parks* (Fort Worth Parks and Community Services Department, 2014). Also see Kline and Fort Worth Parks and Community Services Department, *Fort Worth Parks* (Charleston, SC: Arcadia Publishing, 2010).
5. Kline, *History of Fort Worth's Public Parks*, 66.
6. This was the assessment of park superintendent Harry Adams in "The Value of Advance Planning in Park Development," *Parks and Recreation* 18 (December 1934): 121, as cited in Kline, *History*, 74.
7. Obert stayed with Fort Worth parks through the postwar boom, leaving in 1954 to become the director of parks in Long Beach, CA.
8. See Susan Allen Kline, "Fort Worth Botanic Garden," National Register of Historic Places Nomination, Listed January 29, 2009.
9. Stephen Fox, *The Country Houses of John F. Staub* (College Station: Texas A & M University Press, 2007), 136–44.
10. Carter's will provided for the establishment of a public (nonprofit) museum, the Amon Carter Museum of American Art, to "aid in the promotion of cultural spirit in the city" and "stimulate the artistic imagination among young people residing there." Amon Carter Museum of American Art, Institutional Timeline, www.cartermuseum.org/about.
11. Hare & Hare–planned subdivisions in Fort Worth include Park Hill, Monticello, Meadowbrook Hills, Oakhurst, Colonial Hills, and Riverview Estates.
12. The park at White Rock Lake constituted 2,500 acres of the park land. Jay Firsching, "Historic Dallas Parks: Case Studies of Park/Neighborhood Relationships," *Legacies: A History Journal for Dallas and North Central Texas* 15 (Spring 2003): 4–15.
13. Dealey used his newspaper in the same way that William Rockhill Nelson had used his publication in Kansas City—as a vehicle to educate the public. He had served briefly on the national boards of the American City Planning Institute and the Na-

tional Municipal League and worked on a local level with the city's chapter of the American League for Civic Improvement and the chamber of commerce.

14. Ferguson, *Highland Park and River Oaks*, 111–21.
15. "Visitor Lauds Kessler Proposal as Ambitions [*sic*] City Development Plan," *Dallas Morning News*, August 30, 1924. As a gesture of respect, the Dallas group agreed to retain its original name, the Kessler Plan Association, after Kessler's death.
16. Kessler Plan Association to Cullen Thomas, September 29, 1934, folder 2, box 10, HHCR.
17. Ibid. The letter noted that the event could be "gaudy and tawdry" or "sublimely beautiful," depending on the "vision and genius" of the supervising landscape architect.
18. The letter to George Dahl, May 22, 1936, reads, "Mr. Foley says that you have been requested to change the title on the Master Plat Plan to include our name. I would greatly appreciate it if this could be done promptly and corrected copies sent to the publicity department for their use." The letter to William Webb, June 15, 1936, requests "fair recognition" of the firm's services. See folder 5, box 10, HHCR.
19. Herbert presented the firm's findings at several meetings including the Citizens Planning Conference, American Planning and Civic Association, April 22, 1946, in Dallas.
20. Their projection was close: in 1970, the Dallas population was slightly over 844,000.
21. Robert B. Fairbanks, "Harland Bartholomew and the Planning of Modern Dallas," *Legacies: A History Journal for Dallas and North Central Texas* 15 (Fall 2003): 34–49.
22. Only two reports, which addressed the character of the city and the scope of the proposed plan, were published in 1943 as *Your Dallas of Tomorrow, A Master Plan for Greater Dallas.*
23. Fairbanks, "Harland Bartholomew," 47.
24. Cydney Millstein, "Hare & Hare," *Legacies: A History Journal for Dallas and North Central Texas* 15 (Spring 2003): 45.
25. David G. McComb, *Houston: A History* (Austin: University of Texas, 1981), 9.
26. Dorothy K. H. Houghton, Barrie Scardino, Sadie Gwin Blackburn, and Katherine S. Howe, *Houston's Forgotten Heritage: Landscapes, Houses, Interiors, 1824–1914* (Houston: Rice University Press, 1991), 20.
27. In 1854–55, a young Frederick Law Olmsted rode near Houston and described the landscape as low and flat, covered with pines; near the bayous were magnolias "in full glory of bloom." *A Journey through Texas, Or, a Saddle-Trip on the Southwestern Frontier* (Austin: University of Texas Press, 1978; reprint of 1857 ed.).
28. McComb, *Houston*, 9–10.
29. Arthur Coleman Comey, *Houston: Tentative Plans for Its Development; Report to the Houston Park Commission* (Boston: Press of Geo. H. Ellis, 1913).
30. Stephen Fox, "Planning in Houston: A Historic Overview," in *Ephemeral City: "Cite" Looks at Houston*, ed. Barrie Scardino, William F. Stern, and Bruce C. Webb (Austin: University of Texas Press, 2003), 34–40.
31. For the complete history, see Barrie Scardino Bradley, *Houston's Hermann Park: A Century of Community* (College Station: Texas A & M University Press, 2014).
32. Fox, *Country Houses of John F. Staub*, 7.
33. Harvey T. D. Wilson to Sid Hare, January 4, 1910, folder 41, box 3, HMRC.
34. The neighborhood of Westmoreland is not to be confused with Westmoreland Farms near Bellaire (both were William Wright Baldwin projects). We thank Stephen Fox for pointing out the many social and commercial connections—often the result of ties in banking and railroads—between Houston and St. Louis.

35. Houghton et al., *Houston's Forgotten Heritage,* 36, 128.
36. Harvey T. D. Wilson to Sid J. Hare, March 3, 1910, folder 41, box 3, HMRC.
37. Vaundun Company to Sid J. Hare, March 8, 1910, ibid.
38. The blueprint and planting plan are in RG D 026, key 1772, Architectural Archive, HMRC.
39. Harvey T. D. Wilson to Sid J. Hare (telegram), April 27, 1910, and Harvey T. D. Wilson to Sid J. Hare, May 4, 1910, folder 41, box 3, HMRC. Ultimately the property became a part of Forest Park Cemetery.
40. Edward Teas to Sid J. Hare, July 7, 1912, ibid.
41. Ibid.
42. Stephen Fox, *Houston Architectural Guide* (Houston: American Institute of Architects, 1990), 175.
43. The exact nature of the business in Hollywood remains uncertain. A Western Union telegram from Herbert to his father, dated July 23, 1923, may provide a clue. It reads: "Told here large land subdivision at Hollywood to be designed by Kansas City firm presumably us stop have you any information stop Nichols may know stop" (folder 1, box 7, HHCR).
44. Herbert Hare to Clarence Brock, August 10, 1923, ibid.
45. Richard B. Fowler, "Herbert Hare's Turning Point Was a Spiral Curve," *Kansas City Star,* July 5, 1931.
46. In a May 13, 1924, letter to Clarence Brock, Herbert Godwin described Sutermeister as the individual responsible for "most of the inside work for Messrs. Hare and Hare" (folder 2, box 7, HHCR).
47. Herbert Hare to Herbert Godwin, April 4, 1924, ibid.
48. The drawing is located in General Collection (P1), Hare & Hare, Number 2, MVSC.
49. Fox, *Houston Architectural Guide,* 103.
50. Other Hare & Hare projects related to Hermann Park (proposed but not implemented) include a plan for an athletic area (1940) on land that was instead sold for the Texas Medical Center, a plan for a "Cultural Center" (across Main St.) which would have housed several museums, and a fountain to replace the original Sunken Garden at the park entrance (both 1948).
51. Herbert Godwin to Herbert Hare, June 2, 1924, box 7, folder 4, HHCR.
52. Kate Sayen Kirkland, *The Hogg Family and Houston: Philanthropy and the Civic Ideal* (Austin: University of Texas Press), 2009.
53. See Sara H. Emmott, *Memorial Park: A Priceless Legacy* (Houston: Herring Press, 1992).
54. These improvements began in the mid-1930s with the help of Works Progress Administration funding and labor.
55. "A Frontier Museum and Village for Memorial Park," *Houston Chronicle,* September 17, 1940.
56. Herbert Hare to Mayor Oscar F. Holcombe, September 13, 1940, folder 12, box 7, HHCR.
57. The plan is in RG A 018, key 726, Architectural Archive, HMRC.
58. Herbert Hare to Board of Park Commissioners, June 30, 1925, folder 4, box 7, HHCR.
59. Southwest Center for Urban Research and Rice University School of Architecture, *Houston Architectural Survey,* vol. 6 (City of Houston, 1981), 1284. For a contemporary mention of the firm's special emphasis on bayou shore preservation, see Theodora Kimball Hubbard and Henry Vincent Hubbard, *Our Cities To-day and To-morrow: A Survey of Planning and Zoning Progress in the United States* (Cambridge: Harvard University Press, 1929), 358–59.

60. Kirkland, *Hogg Family*, 54.
61. Hugh Potter, "Modern Residential Development—Its Relation to City Planning," River Oaks Corporation Scrapbook, vol. 3, HMRC. The author borrowed the words "make no little plans" from the architect and planner Daniel Burnham.
62. Will Hogg to Herbert Hare, March 4, 1925, box 8, HHCR.
63. Kirkland, *Hogg Family*, 74.
64. Aside from River Oaks, Huxtable considered Houston's "large and handsome parks and the landscaped corridor of the Buffalo Bayou" to be the only other "planned features" of the city. "Deep in the Heart of Nowhere," *New York Times*, February 15, 1976. See also Barry Kaplan and Charles Orson Cook, "Civic Elites and Urban Planning: Hogg and River Oaks," in *Houston: A Twentieth Century Urban Frontier*, ed. Francisco A. Rosales and Barry J. Kaplan (Port Washington, NY: Associated Faculty Press, 1983), 23.
65. William Clifford Hogg diaries, 1923–1930, as cited in Ferguson, *Highland Park and River Oaks*, 170–71, and River Oaks Corporation Scrapbook, vol. 1, HMRC.
66. Potter and Nichols worked together as members of the National Association of Real Estate Boards and the Urban Land Institute and were cofounders of the organization's Community Builders' Council. Hogg to Hare, March 4, 1925.
67. Cheryl Caldwell Ferguson, "River Oaks: 1920s Suburban Planning and Development in Houston," *Southwestern Historical Quarterly* 104 (October 2000): 201.
68. Kipp, who became vice president of the River Oaks Corporation in 1925, was responsible for drafting the subdivision plat plans for River Oaks as it grew incrementally in the decades that followed. Kipp and Hare & Hare worked together as late as 1951.
69. Due in part to the developers' formula, River Oaks quickly became out of reach for all but well-to-do homeowners.
70. Bayou Bend, now associated with the Museum of Fine Arts, Houston, was designed by the architects John F. Staub and Birdsall P. Briscoe. In the 1930s, the landscape architect Ruth London, and the firm of Fleming & Sheppard, designed Bayou Bend's gardens. Ideas proposed in Hare & Hare's 1928 plan for the grounds were incorporated. Kirkland, *Hogg Family*, 247.
71. *Report of the City Planning Commission, Houston, Texas* (1929), folder 104.26, box 104, HHCR.
72. Roscoe E. Wright, "Hare Tonic," *Houston Gargoyle*, December 18, 1928, 5.
73. When funding for the 1929 *Report* failed, Will Hogg's Forum of Civics, an organization formed to unite citizen groups and individuals in the act of building a better city, paid for its publication.
74. McComb, *Houston*, 157.
75. Ibid.
76. Ibid, 161.
77. Herbert was anxious for the city to be in competent hands but hesitant to lose Ellifrit to the new position. He insisted Ellifrit make the decision that was best for him. Herbert Hare to Ralph Ellifrit, January 25, 1940, box 7, folder 16, HHCR.
78. Fox, *Houston Architectural Guide*, 266. See also "Planning the City: An Interview with Ralph Ellifrit," *Houston Review* 3 (Winter 1981): 203–19.
79. "The Waite Phillips Dream Home Becomes Tulsa's Ideal Art Center," *Kansas City Star*, October 22, 1939.
80. James J. Yoch, *A Guide to Philbrook and Its Gardens* (Tulsa: Philbrook Museum of Art, 1991), 15.
81. Although the Phillipses attempted to rein in the costs of designing and constructing

the house, "in the garden [design] Waite permitted extravagances not tolerated elsewhere" (ibid., 59).

82. Thirty-seven documents, including drawings and plant lists, relating to Villa Philbrook are held in HHCR.
83. The scrolled volutes of Villa Lante's water chain are a play on the owner's last name, Gambara, similar to the Italian word for crayfish, *gambero.*
84. The 1928 "General Plan for the Development of 'Villa Philbrook'" was drafted by J. T. Roberts, an employee of the firm from 1927 to 1929 who then moved to the National Park Service.
85. Gardening was a favorite avocation of Waite's, and he likely oversaw the transplanting of these trees and shrubs. Yoch, *Guide to Philbrook*, 59.
86. Hare commented that "while it is not as large as others, it is one of the finer examples of garden development of the Renaissance." Herbert Hare to Bernard Frazier, Art Director, Philbrook Art Center, November 15, 1947, Archives, Philbrook Museum of Art. For Villa Lante, see David R. Coffin, *Magnificent Buildings, Splendid Gardens*, ed. Vanessa Bezemer Sellers (Princeton, NJ: Princeton University Press, 2008), and Claudia Lazzaro, *The Italian Renaissance Garden: From the Conventions of Planting, Design, and Ornament to the Grand Gardens of Sixteenth-Century Central Italy* (New Haven, CT: Yale University Press, 1990), 243.
87. On plans, Hare & Hare uses "rill" rather than "water chain" or the Italian term.
88. "Acceptance of Philbrook Gives City Rare Gardens," *Tulsa Daily World*, October 23, 1938.
89. These additions include a 2004 master plan by the landscape architecture firm of Howell & Vancuren.
90. "A. A. C. S. Kansas City," *Park and Cemetery and Landscape Gardening* 41 (November1931), 249.
91. S. R. DeBoer to Herbert Hare, October 31, 1938. HHCR. H. O. Whittemore was also a planning consultant for numerous Michigan cities. Thomas Desmond, who trained in agriculture at Cornell University, was a principal in the landscape architecture and planning practice of Desmond & Yarwood in Simsbury. Saco R. DeBoer served as the city of Denver's landscape architect from 1910 to 1921 and was involved in planning cities throughout Colorado, Utah, New Mexico, and Wyoming.
92. A. D. Taylor to Mr. and Mrs. Herbert Hare, October 26, 1938, folder 01.16 (1d), box 67, HHCR.
93. A. D. Taylor to Herbert Hare, October 27, 1938, ibid. Taylor wrote that "there have been two men in the landscape profession, in the so-called older group, whose friendship has meant much to me during a period of many years. One of these men was your father and the other was Warren H. Manning."

6. BALANCING RECREATION AND CONSERVATION

1. Herbert Hare, "A Year at War," *Landscape Architecture* 33 (April 1943): 79–81; "A Second Year at War," *Landscape Architecture* 34 (January 1944): 43–44; "A Third Year at War," *Landscape Architecture* 35 (January 1945): 43–44.
2. Hare, "A Second Year at War," 44.
3. Herbert Hare, "Planning for Postwar Parks," *Parks & Recreation* (Wheeling, WV: American Institute of Park Executives, September–October 1942), 6–8.
4. Hare, "A Year at War," 80.
5. Conrad L. Wirth, *Parks, Politics, and the People* (Norman: University of Oklahoma Press, 1980).

6. Lary M. Dilsaver, ed., *America's National Park System: The Critical Documents* (Lanham, MD: Rowman & Littlefield, 1994), 111.
7. According to Ethan Carr, "In many cases the CCC developed entire park systems on land rapidly acquired for the purpose." Carr, *Wilderness by Design: Landscape Architecture and the National Park Service* (Lincoln: University of Nebraska Press, 1998), 269. Dilsaver notes that "five-year plans were completed in a season" (ibid.).
8. Hare, "Planning for Postwar Parks," 6–8.
9. Herbert Hare is cited as a member of the landscape profession who "played a major role in the state park movement." Linda Flint McClelland, *Building the National Parks: Historic Landscape Design and Construction* (Baltimore: Johns Hopkins University Press, 1993), 58.
10. Herbert Hare, "Relation of Landscape Architect to State Park Movement," in *A State Park Anthology*, ed. Herbert Evison (Harrisburg, PA: Mount Pleasant Press, 1930), 176–82.
11. Herbert Hare's many articles and presentations include "Are Your Parks Planned, or Do They 'Jus[t]' Grow," *Landscape Architecture* 22 (October, 1931): 16–24; "Landscape Architecture in State and Provincial Parks," Convention of American Institute of Park Executives, Milwaukee, 1938; and "Elements of a Good Park Plan," National Conference on State Parks, Norris, TN, 1938.
12. Susan Flader, ed., *Missouri State Parks and Historic Sites: Exploring Missouri's Legacy*, 2nd ed. (Columbia: University of Missouri Press, 2016): 2–4. See also Ney C. Landrum, *The State Park Movement in America: A Critical Review* (Columbia: University of Missouri Press), 2004.
13. Their inclusion set an important precedent within the state park system, which continues to place cultural resources on a par with natural resources. Flader, *Missouri State Parks*, 4.
14. The project began in August 1929; construction continued through the early years of the Depression and was complete in February 1931.
15. Union Electric would not benefit from any Public Works Administration funding. The company was forced to divest its land holdings in the early 1940s by edict of the federal government.
16. Harland Bartholomew and Herbert Hare, "Suggested State Parks, Park Ways and Highways in the Lake of the Ozarks Region," unpublished report, Missouri Department of Natural Resources, Division of State Parks. An article outlining the plan, "State Parks on Lake of the Ozarks," was published in the October 1933 issue of *Missouri Magazine.*
17. The three park sites totaled just over 18,000 acres. The report stated that a portion of the Lake of the Ozarks in Miller and Camden Counties should be considered for national park status.
18. H. Dwight Weaver, *History and Geography of Lake of the Ozarks*, vol. 1 (Eldon, MO: Osage Valley Trader, 2006), 153.
19. The Niangua site was adjacent to Ha Ha Tonka, which had been earmarked early on as a potential state park. It would not be added to the system until 1978.
20. Bartholomew and Hare, "Suggested State Parks," 11.
21. FERA assisted in the purchase of land of "submarginal character" (unfit for agriculture or other types of production) for recreational purposes. Although RDAs were funded and developed by the federal government, they were eventually transferred to state ownership.
22. The Lake of the Ozarks RDA originally had six group camps with infrastructure and buildings constructed by the CCC. James Denny and Bonita Marie Wright,

"Emergency Conservation Work, Architecture in Missouri State Parks, 1933–1942," National Register of Historic Places Nomination, Listed November 7, 1984, 6. This was the first nomination of its type in the country.

23. Flader, *Missouri State Parks*, 91.
24. These responsibilities were illustrated by an organizational chart intended to educate the public about the planning process and its relationship to the state's economy, "A State Plan for Missouri: Facts, Findings and Recommendations" (1935), pl. 88, SHSMO-C.
25. This "picture" of Missourians failed to include African Americans with the exception of citing the "problem of illiteracy" and the influx of individuals settling in urban areas and the southeast corner of the state.
26. No park usage data specific to African Americans were among the information gathered for this report. Although segregation was not an official mandate in Missouri in the 1930s, African Americans were often denied use of "white" facilities. Designating separate areas within a state (or city) park for African Americans was customary. See Gary R. Kremer, *Race and Meaning: The African American Experience in Missouri* (Columbia: University of Missouri Press, 2014), and William O'Brien, *Landscapes of Exclusion: State Parks and Jim Crow in the American South* (Amherst: University of Massachusetts Press in association with Library of American Landscape History, 2016).
27. In 1935 and 1936, Hare and Bartholomew produced numerous separate reports on the state's waterways and river basins. That for the Current River Area, submitted to the NPS, requested its consideration for designation as a national park or national monument. Reports on the Grand and Chariton and the Lower Missouri River Basins (funded by the WPA) address flood protection, include an inventory of data relative to water resources, and propose a "coordinated water plan." HHCR.
28. Flader, *Missouri State Parks*, 15.
29. One section of this system, which ran from the Lake of the Ozarks to St. Louis, was proposed by the NPS Branch of Planning and the Missouri State Planning Board under the name "The Ozark Parkway (Unit One)." This would be overseen by a parkway commission of six members—three from Missouri and three from Illinois—and financed with federal funds.
30. "A State Plan for Missouri: Facts, Findings and Recommendations," 362.
31. Their plans reflected the objectives of the federal Park, Parkway, and Recreational-Area Study Act, passed in 1936, to assist states in undertaking comprehensive inventories of these facilities and aid in long-range planning. The first progress report by Herbert and Bartholomew, "What Is a Recreation Plan?" (1937), was presented to the Missouri State Planning Board. SHSMO-C.
32. "A State Plan for Missouri: Manual of Missouri State Parks Attendance and Use Data—1938," SHSMO-C. Visitor requests ranged from "eliminate snakes" and "add basketball courts" to "discourage Jews."
33. "A State Plan for Missouri: Summary Park Plan." The document, dated 1938, was published in early 1939 and acknowledged the assistance of the NPS, WPA, and the National Resources Committee, and numerous state departments and boards. SHSMO-C.
34. The parks are Mark Twain, Arrow Rock, Big Lake, Roaring River, Montauk, Pershing, Round Spring, Alley Spring, Bennett Spring, Wallace, Van Meter, and Meramec. Later the firm drafted plans for Table Rock (1956) and Pomme de Terre State Parks (1957–60).
35. Flader, *Missouri State Parks*, 11.

36. Booker Rucker, retired director of the Cultural and Natural Resource Management Program, Missouri Department of Natural Resources, to Carol Grove, May 15, 2015.
37. The family's primary residence, located at 240 Summit Avenue in St. Paul, was a Richardsonian Romanesque design by Peabody, Stearns & Furber (the Boston firm of Irving & Casson completed the project). Today it is a property of the Minnesota Historical Society.
38. Louis W. Hill Sr. graduated from Yale and began working his way up in the railroad business. As an adult he was appointed board chairman of the Great Northern Railroad.
39. Joan C. Brainard and Richard E. Leonard, *Three Bold Ventures: The History of North Oaks, Minnesota* (Edina, MN: Beaver's Pond Press), 51–52.
40. Louis Jr. served in the Minnesota House of Representatives from 1937 to 1951.
41. As cited in Brainard and Leonard, *Three Bold Ventures,* 47.
42. The reference is to the Victorian art critic John Ruskin and the Swiss-born naturalist Louis Agassiz.
43. A document titled "Space for Living" (likely drafted by a member of the Hill family) outlined the developers' goals and objectives and was probably used in conjunction with the Hare & Hare "Preview" when presenting the project to city officials and potential homeowners.
44. Brainard and Leonard, *Three Bold Ventures,* 70.
45. Bush described working with "Mr. Hill" and company presidents Frank Nichols and Kingsley Foster as a "great pleasure."
46. In 1999, the current owners of the North Oaks Company, Doug and Mari Harpur (granddaughter of Louis W. Hill Jr.), began collaborating with the conservation planner Randall Arendt to create The Pines of North Oaks. The neighborhood, adjacent to the land planned by Hare & Hare, added housing while preserving 944 acres of space protected by a conservation easement with the Minnesota Land Trust. The project is "a very special example of history and progress" in land planning from 1950 to the present. Mari Harpur to Carol Grove, October 26, 2017.
47. Hodges was a founder of the Louisiana Forestry Association, and his conservation efforts earned him the title "Father of Forestry in Northwest Louisiana."
48. *Hodges Gardens: A Charming Medley of Flowers, Trees and Wildlife,* with an essay by A. J. Hodges, unpaginated booklet, c. 1966, box 126, HHCR.
49. Donald Bush, "Brief Summary of Principal Professional Activities," n.d., folder 1.23, box 67, HHCR.
50. *Hodges Gardens.*
51. The Walker & Walker visitor center/gift shop dates to 1963. In 1959, Hare & Hare had executed a design for a "Souvenir House," also in a modernist idiom, sited right on the lake.
52. Nine hundred forty-eight acres of Hodges Gardens were donated to the Louisiana Office of State Parks in 2007. Due to the budgetary constraints, control of the site reverted to the A. J. & Nona Triggs Hodges Foundation on October 1, 2017; it is now closed to the public.
53. "S. Herbert Hare Dies," *Kansas City Star,* April 19, 1960; "S. Herbert Hare Rites," *Kansas City Times,* April 22, 1960. A short obituary appeared in the *New York Times,* April 20, 1960.
54. "Hare Fund to Sister," *Kansas City Star,* April 20, 1960.
55. Eldridge Lovelace, "Sidney Herbert Hare," *Landscape Architecture* 50 (Summer 1960): 242, 244.

LEGACY

1. As cited in Ethan Carr, *Wilderness by Design: Landscape Architecture and the National Park Service* (Lincoln: University of Nebraska, 1998), 249.
2. Although Hare & Hare is included in publications such as Norman Newton's *Design on the Land,* Mel Scott's *American City Planning since 1890,* and more recently, Philip Pregill and Nancy Volker's *Landscape in History,* the scope of the firm's work is not documented. See Newton, *Design on the Land: The Development of Landscape Architecture* (Cambridge, MA: Belknap Press of Harvard University Press, 1971), 471–74, 480–82; Scott, *American City Planning since 1890: A History Commemorating the Fiftieth Anniversary of the American Institute of Planners* (Berkeley: University of California Press, 1971): 234, 305; Pregill and Volker, eds., *Landscape in History: Design and Planning in the Eastern and Western Traditions,* 2nd ed. (New York: John Wiley, 1999): 602, 612, 634, 685, 697.
3. Sid J. Hare to R. J. Haight, November 15, 1907, box 1, HHCR.
4. Herbert Hare, "A Year at War," *Landscape Architecture* 33 (April 1943): 81.

Index

Page numbers in italics refer to illustrations.